McGRAW-HILL READING

Language Support

Teacher's Manual

Grade 1 Lessons/Practice/Blackline Masters

Trinity Christian College
6601 W. College Dr.
Palos Heights, IL 60463

Macmillan McGraw-Hill
New York Farmington

Table of Contents

Grade 1

Introduction .... **v-xviii**

Unit 1

Max, the Cat **1-9**
- Graphic Organizer: Blackline Master 1 5
- Build Skills: Blackline Masters 2-5 6-9

Quack **10-18**
- Graphic Organizer: Blackline Master 6 14
- Build Skills: Blackline Masters 7-10 15-18

What Does Pig Do? **19-27**
- Graphic Organizer: Blackline Master 11 23
- Build Skills: Blackline Masters 12-15 24-27

The Path on the Map **28-36**
- Graphic Organizer: Blackline Master 16 32
- Build Skills: Blackline Masters 17-20 33-36

Ships **37-45**
- Graphic Organizer: Blackline Master 21 41
- Build Skills: Blackline Masters 22-25 42-45

Unit 2

One Good Pup **46-54**
- Graphic Organizer: Blackline Master 26 50
- Build Skills: Blackline Masters 27-30 51-54

The Bug Bath **55-63**
- Graphic Organizer: Blackline Master 31 59
- Build Skills: Blackline Masters 32-35 60-63

Splash! **64-72**
- Graphic Organizer: Blackline Master 36 68
- Build Skills: Blackline Masters 37-40 69-72

What Bug Is It? **73-81**
- Graphic Organizer: Blackline Master 41 77
- Build Skills: Blackline Masters 42-45 78-81

A Vet **82-90**
- Graphic Organizer: Blackline Master 46 86
- Build Skills: Blackline Masters 47-50 87-90

Unit 3

Stan's Stunt **91-99**
Graphic Organizer: Blackline Master 51 95
Build Skills: Blackline Masters 52-55 96-99

Greg's Mask **100-108**
Graphic Organizer: Blackline Master 56 104
Build Skills: Blackline Masters 57-60 105-108

Sam's Song **109-117**
Graphic Organizer: Blackline Master 61 113
Build Skills: Blackline Masters 62-65 114-117

Snakes **118-126**
Graphic Organizer: Blackline Master 66 122
Build Skills: Blackline Masters 67-70 123-126

Let's Camp Out! **127-135**
Graphic Organizer: Blackline Master 71 131
Build Skills: Blackline Masters 72-75 132-135

Unit 4

The Shopping List **136-144**
Graphic Organizer: Blackline Master 76 140
Build Skills: Blackline Masters 77-80 141-144

Yasmin's Ducks **145-153**
Graphic Organizer: Blackline Master 81 149
Build Skills: Blackline Masters 82-85 150-153

The Knee-High Man **154-162**
Graphic Organizer: Blackline Master 86 158
Build Skills: Blackline Masters 87-90 159-162

Johnny Appleseed **163-171**
Graphic Organizer: Blackline Master 91 167
Build Skills: Blackline Masters 92-95 168-171

Ring! Ring! Ring! Put Out the Fire! **172-180**
Graphic Organizer: Blackline Master 96 176
Build Skills: Blackline Masters 97-100 177-180

Book 5 Unit 1

Seven Sillies **181-189**
Graphic Organizer: Blackline Master 101 185
Build Skills: Blackline Masters 102-105 186-189

Shrinking Mouse **190-198**
Graphic Organizer: Blackline Master 106 194
Build Skills: Blackline Masters 107-110 195-198

You Can't Smell a Flower With Your EAR! **199-207**
Graphic Organizer: Blackline Master 111 203
Build Skills: Blackline Masters 112-115 204-207

Owl and the Moon **208-216**
Graphic Organizer: Blackline Master 116 212
Build Skills: Blackline Masters 117-120 213-216

The Night Animals **217-225**
Graphic Organizer: Blackline Master 121 221
Build Skills: Blackline Masters 122-125 222-225

Book 5 Unit 2

A Friend for Little Bear **226-234**
Graphic Organizer: Blackline Master 126 230
Build Skills: Blackline Masters 127-130 231-234

New Shoes for Silvia **235-243**
Graphic Organizer: Blackline Master 131 239
Build Skills: Blackline Masters 132-135 240-243

The Story of a Blue Bird **244-252**
Graphic Organizer: Blackline Master 136 248
Build Skills: Blackline Masters 137-140 249-252

Young Amelia Earhart **253-261**
Graphic Organizer: Blackline Master 141 257
Build Skills: Blackline Masters 142-145 258-261

On the Go! **262-270**
Graphic Organizer: Blackline Master 146 266
Build Skills: Blackline Masters 147-150 267-270

INTRODUCTION

As a dynamic social process, learning calls for students and teachers to be partners. This Language Support Manual, which accompanies MCGRAW-HILL READING, was developed to help you achieve that partnership.

Students and teachers are partners in learning.

Sheltered Instruction

Throughout this Language Support Manual you will find strategies and activities designed to help ESL students become participants in classroom learning communities with their English-speaking peers. Based on current and proven methods for teaching ESL students, these strategies and activities reflect important ideas about the learner's role and about language and communication, which are at the heart of MCGRAW-HILL READING.

For ease of reference, this introduction is divided into two parts: the first part, **Teaching the ESL Student**, is designed to orient you to the unique needs of the ESL learner; and the second part, **Teaching the Reading Selection**, mirrors the corresponding lesson in the Teacher's Edition and offers suggestions on how to present the reading skills and concepts for classes with native speakers and second language students.

Teaching the ESL Student

This section of the introduction will help you adapt your skills to meet the needs of the ESL student. Differences between teaching native English speakers and ESL students are linguistic, social, and cultural. It is not enough for ESL students to know the appropriate language to use in a given context, although this is certainly critical. In addition, you, as teacher, must ensure that ESL students are active and equal participants in the classroom. Students must be made to feel that their contributions are valuable even though they may only approximate native English speaker accuracy. They must also feel that their culture and prior experience have a respected place in the classroom.

In the following chart, we provide you with the characteristics of language learners in each of the four stages of second language acquisition. You will find it useful in identifying language behavior and building a profile of your ESL students. In the remainder of this section, we will outline procedures and activities for accommodating ESL students, strategies for meeting their unique needs, group interaction patterns that foster effective learning, the classroom environment, assessment tools, and social factors and their relevance to learning.

© McGraw-Hill School Division

Stages of Second-Language Acquisition

Like their English-speaking classmates, ESL students will be at different levels of language and literacy proficiency in their native language. They will also be in various stages of English language acquisition. This Language Support Manual lists teaching prompts at four different levels which follow the chart below and summarizes the four stages of second language acquisition. As your ESL students move through the four stages, this chart may be helpful in making informal assessments of their language ability and in determining which prompts you should use.

nonverbal prompt for active participation

Preproduction

- Teachers ask students to communicate with gestures, actions, yes/no answers, and names.
- Lessons focus on listening comprehension.
- Lessons build receptive vocabulary.

(Reading and writing are incorporated.)

one- or two- word response prompt

Early Production

- Teachers ask students to respond to *either/or* questions.
- Students respond with one or two word phrases.
- Lessons expand receptive vocabulary.
- Activities encourage students to produce vocabulary they already understand.

(Reading and writing are incorporated.)

prompt for short answers to higher-level thinking skills

Speech Emergence

- Students respond in longer phrases or sentences.
- Teachers model correct language forms.
- Lessons continue to develop receptive vocabulary.

(Reading and writing are incorporated.)

prompt for detailed answers to higher-level thinking skills

Intermediate Fluency

- Students engage in conversation and produce connected narrative.
- Teachers model correct language forms.
- Reading and writing are incorporated.

© McGraw-Hill School Division

Procedures and Activities

Scaffolding Process

The teacher's role in the scaffolding process is to provide necessary and meaningful support toward each learning objective. The scaffolding process requires the student to take ownership for learning and the teacher to provide appropriate direction and support in teaching. It requires a form of collaboration between teachers and students in which both work together to ensure that students internalize rules and strategies for meaning-making. The following components of sheltered language instruction are methods which support the needs of second language learners and provide for optimal language arts learning.

- Reciprocal Teaching
- Cooperative Grouping
- Cross-age Tutoring

Reciprocal Teaching

Reciprocal teaching is one way to help ESL students successfully complete academic tasks. The process of reciprocal teaching involves structuring an interaction, assessing the student's comprehension from the response, and then restructuring the interaction to clarify or correct the student's response. As with other kinds of interactions in the classroom, *reciprocal teaching should be modeled and practiced as a whole class first, then it should be practiced in pairs.* The following are just some of the benefits which occur when this approach is implemented in the classroom.

- Teachers can show students not only what to learn but how to learn.
- Group interaction lends itself to varied learning styles.
- Students accept new responsibilities through a cooperative approach.
- Students' self-esteem is enhanced through shared responsibilities.
- Collaborative learning yields greater motivation, particularly for students at risk.

Cooperative Grouping

Through cooperative grouping, which is also very collaborative, students gradually assume responsibility for their learning. This approach is most effective when there is individual accountability. *Cooperative learning best provides the non-native speaker with opportunities similar to social experiences within which the native speakers have acquired the language.*

Cross-age Tutoring

The cross-age tutoring format provides yet another opportunity for students to study and learn together. *ESL students benefit from cross-age tutoring as they are engaged in focused conversation that will support their second language development.* Cross-age or peer tutoring has also been found to promote positive reading attitudes and habits.

Reciprocal teaching, cooperative grouping, and cross-age tutoring are approaches within the pedagogical framework of sheltered English instruction. The benefit of these varied grouping formats is that group members become interested in each other's opinions, feelings and interests. ESL students begin to feel more comfortable expressing themselves on the topic or in the presentation.

© McGraw-Hill School Division

Successful Group Interaction

How do I insure that ESL students participate?

nonverbal prompt for active participation

Being sensitive to the cultural backgrounds of ESL students is a critical function of the teacher. In many cultures, the teacher has absolute authority in the classroom and students play a relatively passive role. Students from such cultures may not participate as vigorously as their classmates.

Elicit experiences that relate to students' native cultures.

By creating a safe environment both in the classroom, and within the group structure, students will begin to participate more freely. You may facilitate this by eliciting experiences and including activities that relate to students' native cultures. For example, if you are discussing the weather, have students talk about the weather in their countries and ask them to bring in pictures that show the range of weather in their country. Ask such questions as: *Draw a picture of a rainy and cloudy day in your country.* This Language Support Manual offers many opportunities to incorporate individual cultural backgrounds. Every lesson includes activity suggestions and teaching prompts which introduce skills and strategies through a compare/contrast matrix in the **Evaluate Prior Knowledge** and **Develop Oral Language** sections.

How should I group my native English students and ESL students for maximum learning and cooperation?

ESL students benefit from social interactions with native speakers.

Social interaction plays an important role in language development. In group work, ESL students benefit from interactions with native speakers by having more chances to try out the language they are learning. But effective group work depends on careful organization, thoughtful selection of groups, and the active involvement of the teacher.

Additionally, the following chart details various strategies that can enhance both reading comprehension as well as the oral language proficiency of second language learners.

© McGraw-Hill School Division

A Pedagogical Overview of Strategic Sheltered Instruction

SCAFFOLD	APPROPRIATE TASKS	BENEFIT TO THE READER
Modeling	Teacher models task and provides examples. Individual/Group oral reading, repetitions. Direct experience through practice.	Clarifies concepts Provides understanding of objective
Connecting Content	Questions in: Think-Pair-Share Three-Step Interview Quick-Writes Anticipatory Charts Brainstorming	Addresses students' prior knowledge Provides a personal connection between learner and theme of the class
Creating a Context	Visualizations Focus questions and: Use of manipulatives Self-involvement Instructor provides an experiential environment. Students demonstrate knowledge for authentic audiences.	Enhances context and concept familiarity
Bridging Concepts	Compare/Contrast Matrix used as advanced organizer Story Graph used to skim through a text	Students gain heightened insight of the varied uses of the language. Students develop connections between concepts.
Perceptual Understanding	Reciprocal Teaching Self-monitoring Self-assessment Students discuss and model reading strategies	Self-autonomy is fostered Enhances students' knowledge of strategies through a conscious focus on the processes
Extension	Drama Journal writing Story Boards Collaborative posters with text Eye-witness accounts Post cards/letters	Students extend their understandings and personal relevance as they apply information to novel formats.

© McGraw-Hill School Division

Modeling

How do I adapt my teaching methods to accommodate the ESL learner?

Illustrate the Concept

In addition to traditional board work, ESL students need a significant amount more support and practice than native English speakers. Therefore it is essential that you give those students the necessary practice and it is vital that this support comes in the form of experiential and oral activities, before written work or reading. For example, writing the words *big* and *small* on the board and then asking students to name objects in either category, is not an adequate presentation for ESL learners. A more successful technique would be to illustrate the concepts through the use of physical objects in the room. For example, taking words that have already been associated with their objects, the teacher points to the larger of the two and says *This is big.* The students then repeat the phrase after the teacher's model. Next, the teacher points to the smaller object and says This is small. The students respond as in the previous example. The teacher can then point to two other objects (or pictures), one big and one small. Given the teacher's cue, the students point to and classify the two objects as either big or small.

By assisting the learner in producing utterances beyond his or her capacity, you are providing 'scaffolding'—that is, the necessary support and guidance needed for the learner's growth. Through this collaboration of teacher and student, the student should progress towards greater autonomy and ownership of his or her language, thereby fostering greater self-esteem and independence.

Total Physical Response

What activities should I use to supplement teaching?

ESL students need to cover concepts using a variety of sensory input. Total Physical Response (TPR) is a well-established and successful technique that links language to a physical response. The classic game of "Simon Says" is a vivid example. The teacher (or a student) can call out a series of commands (i.e., "Simon says, touch your toes,") and students respond with the appropriate physical gesture—in this case, by touching their toes. The advantage of this technique is it links language to the "here and now," giving learners, especially at the early stages, a concrete forum for language practice.

Because of linguistic, social, and cultural differences, ESL students will probably not cover concepts as quickly as native English speaking students. The teacher must be patient with these students and give them extra activities with varied sensory input. As with all learners, varying the pace and type of sensory input is essential—both for accommodating the various learning style preferences and maintaining interest in the lesson.

© McGraw-Hill School Division

Suggested TPR Commands

Stand up	Giggle	Turn your head to the *right*
Sit down	Make a face	Drum your fingers
Touch the *floor*	Flex your muscles	Wet your lips
Raise your *arm*	Wave to *me*	Blow a kiss
Put down your *arm*	Shrug your shoulders	Cough
Pat your *cheek*	Tickle your *side*	Sneeze
Wipe your *face*	Clap your hands	Shout *your name* ("help")
Scratch your *knee*	Point to the *ceiling*	Spell *your name*
Massage your *neck*	Cry	Laugh
Stretch	Yawn	Sing
Whisper *(a word)*	Hum	Hop on *one foot*
Step *forward*	Lean *backwards*	Make a fist
Shake your *hand*	(Name), walk to the door	(Name), turn on the *lights.*

Source: Richard-Amato, P. (1996) Making it happen: *Interaction in the second-language classroom,* 2nd ed. White Plains, N.Y.: Addison-Wesley Publishing Group/Longman.

© McGraw-Hill School Division

Connecting Content

How do I know my ESL students understand me?

Don't assume that ESL students don't know the answer.

When you question your students and get no answer don't automatically conclude that students don't know the answer. Adapt your questioning strategies to help ESL students understand what you say. Rephrase the question. Replace difficult vocabulary with words students know. Add context by using pictures, objects, graphic organizers to support meaning. Use gestures and facial expressions to cue feelings and moods. Draw analogies to past experiences.

Creating A Context

Use of Manipulatives

The Language Support Manual includes several blackline masters which coincide with the skills and strategies being taught within a reading selection. The blackline masters provide manipulatives to help students explore and practice skills. Use of manipulatives helps to enhance context while building concept familiarity.

How do I set up the classroom as a strategic learning environment?

The Classroom Environment

The environment of the classroom can have a great impact on students' ability to learn. The following are some ways to make the classroom environment more comfortable so that ESL students can get as much as possible out of their classroom experiences.

Special areas in the room provide chances for students to apply their English skills.

Create areas in the room designed to give ESL students opportunities to use the target language. For instance, if you are teaching the names of fruits, set up a "fruit market" and have students ask the "shopkeeper" for the fruits they want to buy. They can talk about how the fruits look and taste, how to prepare them, and how much they cost.

Set up a learner library with favorite books the students have chosen. Provide a "discussion" area where ESL students may sit with native language speakers to discuss their favorite books or to read to each other. Seating arrangements should always provide for flexible grouping.

© McGraw-Hill School Division

Bridging Concepts

How do I activate 'prior knowledge' for students from a different culture?

Allow ESL students to make connections for themselves.

With native English speaking students, the teacher has common ground on which to activate the students' prior knowledge. Although American culture is very diverse, there are certain associations and symbols that are familiar to all those who live here. However, for the ESL student the teacher faces a difficult challenge—being able to activate the students' prior knowledge often without knowledge of the students' cultures. With ESL students, as with all students, the teacher should be sure to allow students to make connections for themselves. Often the teacher has a pre-determined idea of the connection and by imposing that notion on the student, he or she does not serve the students' needs to the fullest. It is important for ESL students to develop autonomy and self-esteem.

Assessment

How do I assess ESL learners?

Use alternative ways to assess ESL students' learning.

When assessing ESL students' learning, you need to adapt your expectations of what constitutes an appropriate response. Assessment that relies heavily on a written test or questionnaire, on written answers or an essay, or on answering oral questions verbally, may present problems for ESL students. Some alternative strategies include the following:

- Allow students to draw, show, or point to an object, a procedure, or an illustration, rather than write or talk about it.

Invite students to draw, show, or point to objects.

- Use your own observations and interactions with the students as a basis for assessment.

Your observations may serve as a form of assessment.

- Ask students to perform an activity that will show the application of a concept. For instance, say: *Show me how a tired person acts.*

Students may perform activities to demonstrate their understanding.

© McGraw-Hill School Division

Teaching the Reading Selection to Students Needing Language Support

Each Language Support lesson in this Language Support Teacher's Guide mirrors the corresponding lesson in the Teacher's Edition of McGraw-Hill Reading. It either builds directly on that lesson, offering suggestions on how to adapt materials for students needing additional language support, or it offers alternative teaching and activities. The blackline masters following each lesson provide tools for students to use with alternative activities that develop skills and strategies taught in the lesson.

In this overview, the Language Support lesson described is from the grade one unit theme, Stories to Tell. The selection, *Sam's Song,* is the story of a young owl who learns to sing with her family. Variations on the lesson in Grades K, 2 and 3-6 are noted where appropriate.

Focus on Reading

Develop Phonological Awareness (Grades K-2)

Help develop children's awareness of sounds.

This part of the Language Support lesson is designed to help children develop their ability to hear the sounds in spoken language. These skills can be improved through systematic, explicit instruction involving auditory practice. Each selection in grades K-2 begins with a lesson designed to focus the children's attention on a particular phonological skill. In the grade one selection, for example, children are asked to listen for digraphs, *ch, wh,* and *nk.* As you read aloud the poem, "Lunch Munch," children are asked to clap their hands each time they hear a word that rhyme with *bunch.* The activity is repeated with the word *think.*

Children who may be having difficulty hearing these sounds are guided through an activity in which they make up a series of tongue twisters containing the digraphs. For example: *The child chomps on a chip.* Students listen for and identify the words in which they hear /ch/.

In these practical, learner-centered lessons from the Language Support Teacher's Guide, children are often asked to respond physically to the sounds they hear. For example, in this grade one lesson, they are asked to whistle, chomp, or blink when they hear words with *wh, ch,* or *nk.*

The Language Support Teacher's Manual identifies these activities as **TPR** (Total Physical Response).

© McGraw-Hill School Division

Total Physical Response

One of the most successful approaches to teaching English to language support children is Total Physical Response. At the heart of this approach is the belief that children should be active participants—as both fellow learners and experts—in learning communities where language and content are developed together.

TPR:

- is most appropriate for children just beginning to speak English. It recognizes that children will spend a period of time—the silent period—listening to English before they are able to speak it. Particularly focused TPR activities help ESL children learn vocabulary and concepts.
- recognizes that ESL children can understand physical prompts and can indicate their understanding through action before speech. TPR involves giving commands in which you model a physical action and to which learners respond with an action, one or two words, or short responses.
- allows children to involve their bodies and their brains in the TPR activity; they respond with the total body. The commands should be fun and should make the second language understandable.

As you work with children needing additional language support , you may find many other ways to use TPR prompts. As children continue to develop their phonological awareness, they will be asked to identify rhyming words, listen for separate syllables in a word, separate the first sound in a word from the rest of the word, and blend sounds together to make words. Recent research findings have strongly concluded that children with good phonological awareness skills are more likely to learn to read well. These lessons will help you work with children from diverse cultural and linguistic backgrounds as well as engage ESL children in productive activities to achieve literacy.

Develop Visual Literacy (Grades 3-6)

The Language Support Manual expands this lesson by suggesting physical activities which help clarify the Comprehension Strategy Objective stated in the Teacher's Edition. This section also presents an opportunity to involve the ESL student with discussion prompts which explore the individual students cultural background and uses their prior knowledge to do a compare and contrast activity which will assist in introducing the lesson content.

© McGraw-Hill School Division

Read the Literature

This section introduces the unit concepts and the vocabulary needed to understand them.

Vocabulary

Suggestions are given here for teaching the vocabulary strategies highlighted in the Teacher's Planning Guide. Notes may call attention to idioms, figurative language, or language special to the selection. The vocabulary words are included, together with questions and tips for helping children increase comprehension.

An example activity from the grade one lesson for *Sam's Song* follows:

> Invite children to play a game of "Find the Word." Organize the group into two teams. Write the vocabulary words on the board for both teams. Then invite one child from each team to the board and ask them to erase the word you call out. If a child erases the incorrect word, rewrite it. Play until one team erases all the words.

Evaluate Prior Knowledge

Building background is particularly important when children's cultural diversity interferes with comprehension. It is equally important to bring the reading topic to life—give it some immediate relevance—when it is unfamiliar to those children.

Recognize different prior knowledge bases; use familiar contexts to introduce unfamiliar topics.

This section of the lesson includes activities to help children get to know something about the cultural traditions and beliefs that move the story along and that may influence characters' actions. It is important to remember that ESL children's prior knowledge bases were not developed around the cultural traditions of English. They need help developing strategies to activate their own prior knowledge, so crucial to constructing meaning. Recognize that it takes time to learn concepts using a familiar language, let alone a new one.

Model the language and use props when possible.

The activities in this section help ESL children deal with culturally unfamiliar topics by giving it a familiar context. The concept is brought to life as children are encouraged to draw upon their personal experience and knowledge to get the big picture. Role-playing, objects, story props, pictures, gestures, stories with practicable patterns, and story maps are used in many of the activities to help set the topic in a meaningful context.

© McGraw-Hill School Division

The concept of learning something new is addressed in the grade one selection *Sam's Song.* An example from this section follows:

> Ask children to name things they have recently learned to do or would like to learn to do. Write their responses on the chalkboard. Ask one child to work with you as you model teaching how to do one of the activities. For instance, you might help a child learn to tie her or his shoe.
>
> Next invite children to work in pairs to learn something new from each other. They can learn something real, such as making a paper airplane, or pretend to learn something, such as how to drive a car.

Develop Oral Language

In the grade one selection, *Sam's Song,* children build background by focusing on the concept learning something new. It is important to help children become active participants in learning and confident language users. The activities in this section offer opportunities for children to respond orally to activities more suited to their abilities.

This part of the lesson also offers suggestions for TPR commands you can use when teaching story concepts. Like their English-speaking classmates, ESL children will be at different levels of language and literacy proficiency in their native language. They will also be in various stages of English language acquisition.

Guided Reading

Preview, Predict, Read In *Sam's Song,* children are guided through a picture walk of the book. As children are directed to look at the illustration, they are asked questions, such as: *What do Chuck, Mom, and Pop do under the moon? Who watches them sing? Why do you think Sam looks sad? What does Sam finally learn to do? How do you think he feels?* Based on the children's abilities, they are called on to give short answers.

Graphic Organizer A graphic organizer which follows each reading selection is designed to engage children in active learning. In the grade one selection, *Sam's Song,* a "Story Puppets" blackline master is available. Children are asked to color the pictures of Sam and his family and then cut them out. The pictures are glued to craft sticks and used as puppets. The children work in groups of four and use the puppets to act out the story as you reread *Sam's Song* aloud.

Engage children in active learning.

© McGraw-Hill School Division

Build Skills

Blackline Masters

This section contains directions for using the blackline masters as well as informal assessment suggestions.

Phonics and Decoding (Grades 1-2)

This section of the Language Support lesson provides suggestions and activities to help children acquire phonics and decoding skills. Like other sections of the lesson, it follows the Teacher's Planning Guide materials, modifying them and adapting them where possible or providing alternative approaches to the skill that are more appropriate for second-language learners. It covers:

Comprehension and Vocabulary Strategy

This section offers suggestions to help children develop comprehension and vocabulary skills throughout the selection. Lessons encourage you to ask simple questions that draw upon the children's own experiences, cultures, and ideas. The blackline masters give the students additional practice for each assessed skill introduced in the reading selection.

In the grade one selection, *Sam's Song,* the comprehension skill, Compare and Contract, is reviewed. Children are asked to use the story illustrations to help them find similarities and differences in the story. For example, children are directed to a page in the story, then asked: *Is Sam like the mouse? How is she different from the mouse?* Children then work in pairs to compare similarities and differences that they find.

Informal Assessment

After each skill or strategy has been practiced with the blackline master the Language Support Manual includes an informal assessment activity which requires the students to return to the reading selection and apply the skill.

© McGraw-Hill School Division

MAX, THE CAT pp. 8A–27R

Written by Ann Morris Illustrated by Kathi Ember

BUILD BACKGROUND FOR LANGUAGE SUPPORT

I. FOCUS ON READING

Focus on Skills

Develop Phonological Awareness

OBJECTIVE: Listen for short *a*

Read the poem "Nap, Cat" several times for children, emphasizing the short *a* sound in the words. Write the following words on the board and have children repeat them after you: *nap, bat, cat, mat, cap.* Invite children to suggest other short *a* words to add to the list.

TPR

Gather an assortment of items (some of which have the short *a* sound), such as a box, cap, pen, bat, dish, fan, map, place mat, jack, tack and toy boat. Ask children to select an item that has the short *a* sound and say the word. Have children take turns being the leader and select two items, one that has the short *a* sound and one that doesn't. Invite the other students to point out the item that has the short *a* sound. The student who picks correctly gets a turn as the leader.

II. READ THE LITERATURE

Vocabulary

VOCABULARY
one
this
likes
give

Print the vocabulary words on the chalkboard. Point to each word, as you demonstrate its meaning in the following way:

One: Point one finger into the air. Then go around the room, picking out one object from groups of many. Say, for example, *I have one book; I have one crayon.* Repeat the examples above but sometimes have more than one object. Ask: *Do I have one book?* Invite students to answer yes or no. Have the children choose one or more objects and take turns asking the class "Do I have one ________?"

This: Display all objects. Hold one at a time and say, for example, *This is an eraser.* Point at different objects and ask: *What is this?* Encourage children to respond with "This is a ________."

Likes: Hold an object close to you, and smile as you ask, *Who likes this book?* Then let each child select an object she or he likes. Have students complete the sentence "I like ________." Ask the class to repeat the sentence using the child's name for example: *Juan likes the (name the object Juan choose).*

Give: Using the same objects, present one to each child. Say: *I give you a pencil; I give you a marker.* Then ask for the object back, by saying: *What can you give me?* As children hand back the object encourage them to complete the sentence "I give you a ________."

Evaluate Prior Knowledge

CONCEPT
cats

To show children a cat, bring in a photo, book illustration, or stuffed animal. Talk about cats that children have or know about. Invite them to show you how a cat moves, what kinds of things it does, and what sounds it makes. Children may wish to pantomime alone or in pairs, but encourage them to get down on all fours and pretend to be cats. Have them meow, stretch, lick their paws, and so on.

© McGraw-Hill School Division

Develop Oral Language

nonverbal prompt for active participation	• Preproduction: *Show us* (point to class and self) *things cats do.*
one- or two-word response prompt	• Early production: *Do you like cats? Do you have a cat?*
prompt for short answers to higher-level thinking skills	• Speech emergence: *What do cats look like? What do cats like to do?*
prompt for detailed answers to higher-level thinking skills	• Intermediate fluency: *How do you feel about cats? What is your favorite thing that cats do?*

Guided Reading

Preview and Predict

Tell children that in this story, Max the cat likes to nap on Pam's mat and her cap. Explain that Pam does not want Max to nap on her mat and her cap. Tell children: *Max is mad at Pam because she won't let him nap on her mat or cap. So Pam gets an idea.* Have English-speaking children work in pairs with those needing more language support. Lead children on a picture walk, using the illustrations to reinforce the concept of cats. Have one child answer the questions, as the fluent speaker records one-word answers on paper. Ask questions such as: *What pet does Pam have? What does Pam sit on? What does Max want to do on the mat? What kind of cap does Pam have? What does Max do in Pam's cap? Why does Max want to nap? How does Pam feel about Max's naps? What do you think happens to Max?*

GRAPHIC ORGANIZER
Blackline Master 1

Objectives

- To reinforce story characters
- To encourage creative thinking
- To reinforce key story concepts

Materials

One copy of Blackline Master 1 per child; crayons; paste; scissors; craft sticks

Have children color the puppets and then cut them along the dotted lines. Next, have them paste each puppet to a craft stick. When children are done, invite them to get in groups of two and act out the story *Max the Cat*, using words they have learned. You may also encourage them to create new stories with the puppets. If children wish, they can take the puppets home to retell the story to their families.

© McGraw-Hill School Division

III. BUILD SKILLS

Phonics and Decoding

INTRODUCING SHORT *a*
Blackline Master 2

Objectives

- To develop print awareness
- To practice word identification
- To reinforce understanding of short *a* sounds

Materials

One copy of Blackline Master 2 per child; pencil; crayon

Have children point to each word on the page, as you read it aloud. Read the words again, encouraging children to repeat them after you. Identify the /a/ sound in each word, and guide children to trace over the letter that represents that sound. Finally, help them draw a line from each word on the left side of the page to its corresponding picture on the right.

INFORMAL ASSESSMENT

To assess recognition of the /a/ sound, ask pairs of children to review each page of the story and look for short *a* words. As they look at page 16, for example, they might identify *Pam, has,* or *cap*. Take turns calling on different pairs and asking them to name the /a/ words they have found.

Phonics and Decoding

REVIEW SHORT *a*
Blackline Master 3

Objectives

- To practice blending skills
- To reinforce understanding of the /a/ sound
- To practice following directions

Materials

One copy of Blackline Master 3 per child; scissors; pencil

Have children cut out each letter strip. Then help them cut the lines on each side of the short *a* shopping cart. Show them how to thread each strip through its corresponding cut line. Children can then work in pairs. One child can move the letter strips and say each new word. The other child can check off the words on the shopping list at the top of the page. Children can then take turns and repeat the activity.

INFORMAL ASSESSMENT

Invite children to return to the story text to see what the words on this page have in common with some words in the story. (They are three-letter words with an *a* in the middle.) Have children work in pairs to create new letter strips that will help them make short *a* words from the story.

© McGraw-Hill School Division

Comprehension

USE ILLUSTRATIONS
Blackline Master 4

Objectives

- To practice word identification
- To reinforce story concepts
- To use illustrations

Materials

One copy of Blackline Master 4 per child; crayons; pencil

Invite children to read the sentences and circle the picture that corresponds to each. Then ask children to make the faces at the bottom of the page show any feelings they choose. They might, for example, show a sad face, a mad face, a surprised face, a scared face, or a confused face.

INFORMAL ASSESSMENT

Refer children to the picture on page 20. Ask them to study the picture and decide how Max is feeling. Be sure children can identify specific picture clues that let them know Max is sad.

Vocabulary Strategy

INFLECTIONAL ENDING *-s*
Blackline Master 5

Objectives

- To recognize the inflectional ending *-s*
- To recognize subject-verb agreement

Materials

One copy of Blackline Master 5 per child; pencil; crayons

Ask children to look at each illustration and the incomplete sentences below it. Have them circle the word that correctly finishes each sentence and matches the illustration. When children are done, invite them to color the illustrations.

INFORMAL ASSESSMENT

Have children return to page 23 of the story and read the sentence *Max can nap and nap.* On the chalkboard, write the incomplete sentence, *Max and Pam can* ______________. Above it, provide the words *nap* and *naps.* Have each child say the word that correctly finishes the new sentence.

© McGraw-Hill School Division

Name________________________________ Date______________

Max and Pam

© McGraw-Hill School Division

Name______________________________ Date______________

Matching Words to Pictures

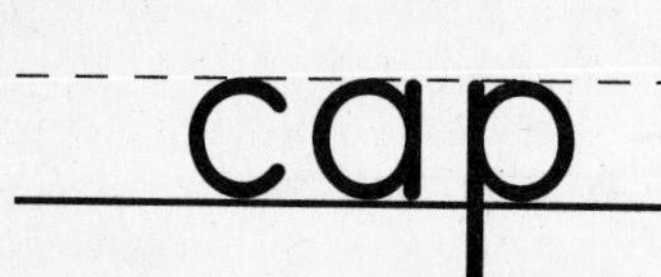

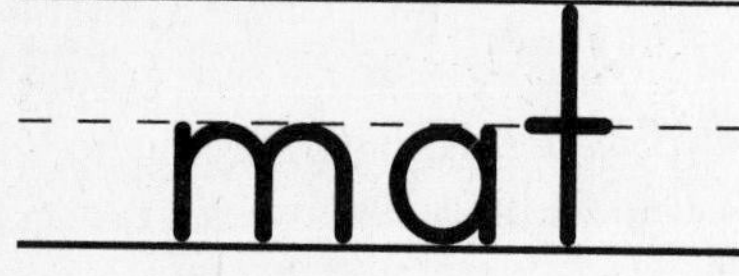

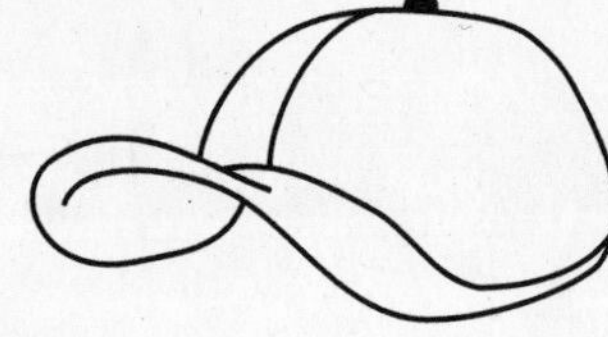

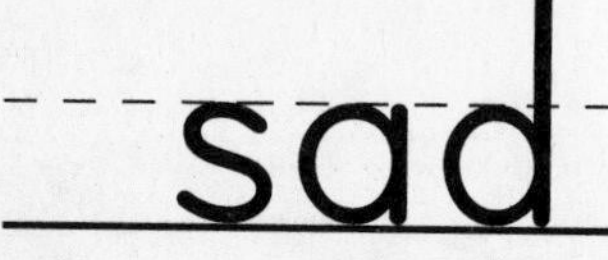

© McGraw-Hill School Division

Name________________________________ Date______________

Word Shopping

cab	pan	jam
bag	rat	nap
	bad	

c

b

p

r

b

j

n

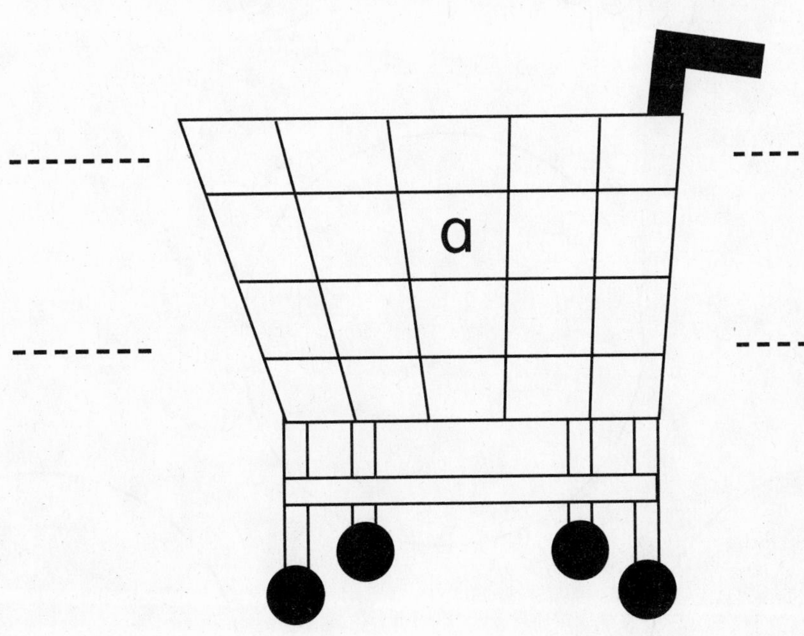

b

g

n

t

d

m

p

© McGraw-Hill School Division

Name______________________________ Date______________

Feelings

1. Pam is sad.

2. Pam is mad.

3. Max is mad.

4. Max is sad.

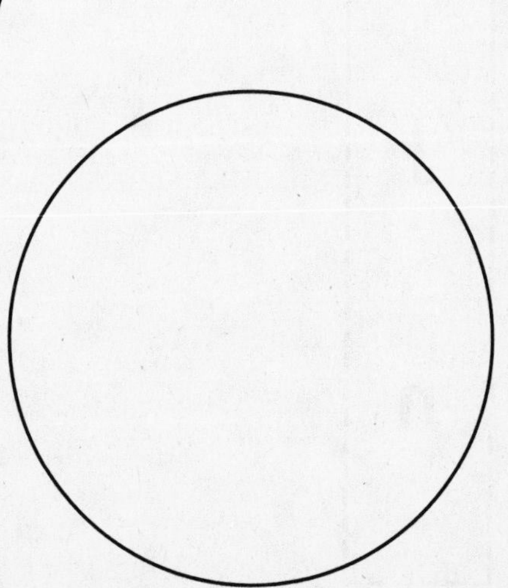

© McGraw-Hill School Division

Name________________________ Date____________

Things to Do

bat **bats**

This girl ________.

bat **bats**

These girls ________.

fan **fans**

She ________ her friend.

fan **fans**

They ________ their friend.

© McGraw-Hill School Division

QUACK pp. 28A–47R

Written by Judi Barrett, Illustrated by Luisa D'Augusta

BUILD BACKGROUND FOR LANGUAGE SUPPORT

I. FOCUS ON READING

Focus on Skills

OBJECTIVE: Listen for digraph *ck*

Develop Phonological Awareness

On the chalkboard write the letters *ck.* Say with children the sound the letters make. Then place several objects on a table, including a sock, a rock, a small clock, a plastic duck, a backpack, a picture of a boy (labeled *Jack*), and some other objects whose names do not contain the letters *ck*, such as a crayon, an eraser, a newspaper, and a toy.

TPR
Children raise their hands each time they say the name of an item that belongs in the sack.

Together, say the names of the objects once. Then hold up a large sack, and say *I'm going to pack my sack. I will only pack items with the letters ck.* Hold up one item at a time, prompting children to say its name aloud. Then, if the item belongs in the sack, invite them to say *PACK IT.*

II. READ THE LITERATURE

VOCABULARY
on
what
they
your

Vocabulary

Have children read the vocabulary from the chalkboard, helping them as needed. Play a game of "Simon Says" using the words, for example:

Simon says tell me your name.

Simon says tell me what is on my desk.

Simon says tell me who they are. (Point to a section of the class.)

Choose different students to be the leader. As they create "Simon Says" directions, write the sentences on the board. Have the leader underline the vocabulary word used in the sentence.

CONCEPT
moving

Evaluate Prior Knowledge

Demonstrate the act of moving your belongings from one place to another. For example, have a desk and chair, with materials laid out on the desk, such as pencils, books, scissors, and paste. Invite children to help pack the materials into a box. Move the box to another part of the room. Then move the desk and chair there as well. Unpack the materials from the box, and lay them out on the desk as they were before. Sit down at the chair, as if you have arrived in your new place.

© McGraw-Hill School Division

Develop Oral Language

Invite children to pantomime being movers. Have them work in pairs, moving light, unbreakable objects from one part of the room to another.

nonverbal prompt for active participation

- Preproduction: *Show us* (point to class and self) *what you are going to move. Show us where you are going to move it.*

one- or two-word response prompt

- Early production: *What are you moving? Where are you moving it?*

prompt for short answers to higher-level thinking skills

- Speech emergence: *What is the most important thing to pack? What is the first thing you need to unpack after you have moved?*

prompt for detailed answers to higher-level thinking skills

- Intermediate fluency: *How do you feel when you move? What do you like about moving?*

Guided Reading

Preview and Predict

Explain to children that in this story, Nan and her dad are moving out of their house. Jack and Mack are there to help them move. Nan is helping by packing her own things. Tell children: *Nan puts her box in the van. Then Jack hears a quack.* (Demonstrate the sound of quack, so children understand it is an animal sound.) *He wonders what the quack is.* Have children who need language support pair up with English-speaking children.

Take a picture walk through the story, stopping at illustrations that relate to the concept of *moving.* Encourage pairs to work together to find answers to questions. Invite children needing language support to represent their pair by answering each question aloud. Questions you may want to ask include the following: *What are Nan and her dad doing? Who is helping Nan and her dad? What goes into the van? What does Nan pack? What does Jack hear? Where do you think Nan and her dad and Quack will go?*

GRAPHIC ORGANIZER
Blackline Master 6

Objectives

- To reinforce story events
- To reinforce spatial relationships
- To practice following relationships
- To develop the concept *moving*

Materials

One copy of Blackline Master 6 per child; crayons; scissors

Have children color and then cut out the pictures at the top of the page. Then ask them to place the pictures in the back of the van in the same order they are placed in the van in the story. Encourage them to name each item as they place it in the van.

Reinforce the skill of sequence of events. Invite children to draw pictures of items they would put in the van if they were moving. Say: *You are moving. You pack. You do not want things to break. What do you pack first? What do you pack next? What do you pack last?* Prompt for detailed answers to higher-level thinking skills.

© McGraw-Hill School Division

III. BUILD SKILLS

Phonics and Decoding

INTRODUCE DIGRAPH *ck*
Blackline Master 7

Objectives

- To reinforce selection vocabulary
- To practice word identification
- To reinforce understanding of the digraph *ck*

Materials

One copy of Blackline Master 7 per child; scissors; paste

Have children read aloud the words at the top of the page. Help them recognize the letters *ck* in each word. Then have them trace these letters on each name tag. Instruct children to cut out each name tag and paste it to the proper character.

INFORMAL ASSESSMENT

Review page 36 with children. Select two words from the page, one that contains the letters *ck* and one that does not. Write the words on the chalkboard. Say each word aloud, and have children repeat it after you. Ask children to identify the word that contains the letters *ck*. Repeat this exercise on other pages with *ck* words.

Phonics and Decoding

REVIEW SHORT *a*; DIGRAPH *ck*
Blackline Master 8

Objectives

- To practice word identification
- To reinforce understanding of short *a* sounds; digraph *ck*
- To use illustrations
- To reinforce key story vocabulary and concepts

Materials

One copy of Blackline Master 8 per child; pencil; scissors; paste

Help children read aloud each word at the top of the page, calling attention to the short *a* sound. Have them trace the letter in each word that represents that sound. Then invite them to cut out the words and paste each word next to the illustration it represents.

INFORMAL ASSESSMENT

To assess children's knowledge of words containing the /a/ sound, have them work in pairs to identify words from the story text. Begin with page 32, and call on pairs to name the word on that page that contains the short *a* sound. Continue through the book, until all pairs have had an opportunity to identify a word.

© McGraw-Hill School Division

Comprehension

INTRODUCE SEQUENCE OF EVENTS
Blackline Master 9

Objectives

- To reinforce understanding of sequence of events
- To practice following directions
- To reinforce story concept

Materials

One copy of Blackline Master 9 per child; scissors; crayons

Explain to children that the pictures on the page tell the story, but not in order. Help children color and cut out each picture. Then ask them to place the pictures in order of the story. Invite children to retell the story in their own words, using the illustrations as a visual support.

INFORMAL ASSESSMENT

To assess children's understanding of sequence of events, reread the story, pausing at certain pages to ask what happens next. Begin by asking what happens first. After children respond, read on, stopping at certain pages. For instance, read aloud page 41 and say: *What happens next?* Continue reading in this way, asking children to share their understanding of what happens first, next, and last.

Vocabulary Strategies

REVIEW INFLECTIONAL ENDING *-s*
Blackline Master 10

Objectives

- To reinforce subject-verb agreement
- To review inflectional ending *-s*
- To recognize word meanings

Materials

One copy of Blackline Master 10 per child; pencil

Invite children to look at each picture. Help them read aloud the incomplete sentences. Then help children read the two words above each sentence. Let them try each word in the sentence and then decide which one is correct. They should circle the word that completes the sentence correctly.

INFORMAL ASSESSMENT

To assess children's understanding of the inflectional ending *-s*, turn to the illustration on page 38. Write on the chalkboard the words *pack* and *packs*, and read them aloud with children. Then say the incomplete sentence, *Nan __________ the map,* and point to the two options. Have children work in pairs to decide and write down which word correctly completes the sentence. Prompt for detailed answers to higher-level thinking skills.

© McGraw-Hill School Division

Name________________________________ Date______________

Pack the Van

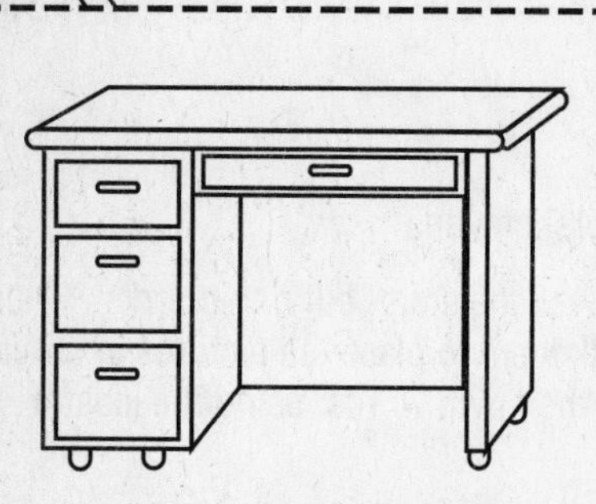

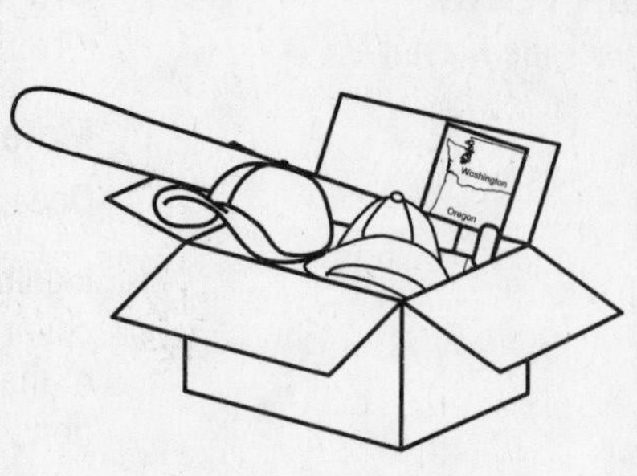

© McGraw-Hill School Division

Name ______________________________ Date ______________

What's My Name?

Jack	Mack	Quack

© McGraw-Hill School Division

Name______________________________ Date______________

Pack the Short a Words

bat	cap	backpack
cat	map	Quack

© McGraw-Hill School Division

Name________________________________ Date______________

Then What Happened?

© McGraw-Hill School Division

Name______________________________ Date____________

-s Endings

 **wag** **wags** One dog ________ its tail.	 **wag** **wags** Many dogs ______ their tails.
 **tap** **taps** He ________ on a drum.	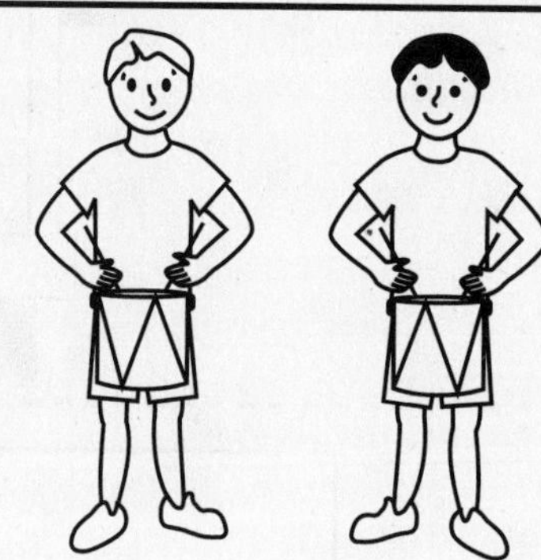 **tap** **taps** They ______ on their drums.
 **nap** **naps** He ________ in the sun.	 **nap** **naps** They ________ in the sun.

© McGraw-Hill School Division

WHAT DOES PIG DO? pp. 50A–67R

Written by Angela Shelf Medearis Illustrated by Barbara Reid

BUILD BACKGROUND FOR LANGUAGE SUPPORT

I. FOCUS ON READING

Focus on Skills

OBJECTIVE: Listen for short *i*

Develop Phonological Awareness

On the chalkboard, write the words *pig, jig,* and *wig*. Say the words aloud. Ask children how the words are alike. Help them understand that all three words contain the /i/ sound. Invite children to use the alphabet to discover and say aloud other rhyming words, such as *big, dig,* and *fig*. Write all the words on the board, and use them to create funny sentences that children can say with you. (Example: The big pig danced a jig. That pig will dig to find a twig.)

TPR
Children can pantomime the silly sentences as they say them.

II. READ THE LITERATURE

VOCABULARY
does
her
look
there

Vocabulary

Write each of the vocabulary words on large index cards. Use the following activities to increase children's vocabulary.

does: Have two children stand together, one holding up the card, while the other holds a box of colors, a box of cookies, or a carton of juice. Have the card holder point to the other child and ask: *Does she like to color?* or *Does she like cookies?* Encourage verbal responses such as *She does like to color.* or *She does not like cookies.*

look: Have one partner hold up the card while the other points to an object, and says, for example: *Look at the book.*

her: Ask a girl to hold the card as her partner points to an item of the girl's clothing and says, for example: *This is her shoe.*

there: Have one partner stand next to an object while the other stands in another part of the room. Encourage the speaker to say, for instance: *There is the fish tank.*

CONCEPT
calendar/time

Evaluate Prior Knowledge

Dramatize the concept of time by drawing on the chalkboard three pictures: a picture of the rising sun; the sun at noon; and the sun setting with a moon in the sky. Point to each picture and ask the students to pantomime an activity for each part of the day—getting up, eating lunch, and going to bed. Identify this sequence of events as one day. Then write the days of the week on the chalkboard. As you say each day, pantomime something you do. Say, for example: *On Monday, I shop for food. On Tuesday, I swim at the gym.*

© McGraw-Hill School Division

Develop Oral Language

Invite children to act out and say activities they do on certain days of the week. You may wish to have them stand in a circle and have each child act out one day of the week.

nonverbal prompt for active participation

- Preproduction: *Show us* (point to class and self) *what you do on Saturday.*

one- or two-word response prompt

- Early production: *Do you like Sundays? Do you spend Sundays with your friends?*

prompt for short answers to higher-level thinking skills

- Speech emergence: *What is your favorite day of the week? What do you do that day?*

prompt for detailed answers to higher-level thinking skills

- Intermediate fluency: *How do you feel when you wake up in the morning? How do you feel at the end of the day?*

Guided Reading

Preview and Predict

Explain to children that in this story Pig does something different each day of the week. *On one day, she does not do anything special.* Then, organize children into groups of seven. Lead them on a picture walk using the story illustrations to reinforce the concept of time. Have one child in each group responsible for predicting what Pig does on a given day.

As you flip through the pages, point out the days of the week and ask questions such as: *What do you think Pig will do on Monday? What do you think Pig will do on Tuesday? What day comes next? What day comes after Sunday? What do you think Pig will do that day?*

GRAPHIC ORGANIZER
Blackline Master 11

Objectives

- To practice sequence of events
- To practice word identification
- To reinforce key concepts

Materials

One copy of Blackline Master 11 per child; crayons; pencil

Have children color and label the activity that Pig does each day of the week. In the Sunday section, encourage them to recall what Pig did, and to draw and label that picture. Have children work in pairs to take turns asking each other what the pig did first, second, third, and so on, until the last day is reached.

© McGraw-Hill School Division

III. BUILD SKILLS

Phonics and Decoding

REVIEW SHORT *i*
Blackline Master 12

Objectives

- To review short *i*
- To reinforce story vocabulary
- To practice blending sounds

Materials

One copy of Blackline Master 12; crayons; scissors; paste

Read over the words at top of page with children. Help them connect the meanings of these words to the illustrations below. Then help children cut out each word and paste it in the correct box.

INFORMAL ASSESSMENT

To assess children's recognition of words containing the short *i* sound, have pairs return to the text on page 60, for instance, and identify words that contain the /i/ sound. Encourage children to look at other pages as well, so that each pair has a turn pointing out the appropriate words.

Phonics and Decoding

REVIEW /i/ SOUND AND -ck BLEND
Blackline Master 13

Objectives

- To reinforce word identification
- To reinforce consonant blend *-ck*
- To reinforce short *i* sound

Materials

One copy Blackline Master 13 per child; scissors; paste

Have children read aloud the name of the animals behind the two baskets and identify the vowel sound in each animal's name. Then help them cut out the picture-word cards at the top of the page. Next, ask children to decide what vowel sound they hear in each picture-word card. They can paste the card on the cat's basket if they hear a short *a* and on the pig's basket if they hear short *i*.

INFORMAL ASSESSMENT

To assess children's recognition of words containing the short *i* sound, turn to the illustration on page 52 and ask children to identify two things whose names contain the /i/ sound. (pig, wig) To assess children's understanding of the digraph *-ck*, turn to the illustration on page 54 and ask children to read what the pig does here. (kicks)

© McGraw-Hill School Division

Comprehension

REVIEW SEQUENCE OF EVENTS
Blackline Master 14

Objectives

- To reinforce sequence of events
- To follow directions
- To use illustrations

Materials

One copy of Blackline Master 14 per child; crayons; scissors

Invite children to color and then cut out each picture. Next, have them place the pictures in an order that shows what would happen to a birthday cake. If children wish, they can create their own stories to tell using the illustrations.

INFORMAL ASSESSMENT

To ensure children have a strengthened sense of sequence of events, turn to pages 52 and 53 of the story. Ask children which day comes first. Then ask if they know which day comes next. Finally, ask them to name what the Pig does on the last day of the week.

Vocabulary Strategy

INTRODUCE UNFAMILIAR WORDS
Blackline Master 15

Objectives

- To reinforce sequence of events
- To reinforce concepts *calendar/time*
- To practice word identification

Materials

One copy of Blackline Master 15 per child; crayons; scissors

Help children see that the pictures on the cards represent scenes from the story. Help children cut the pictures out. Next, have children shuffle the cards. Challenge them to then replace the cards in the correct order. Help them see that the pictures, when in correct order, make a whole week. Finally, invite children to draw on the back of each picture something that they do on that day of the week.

INFORMAL ASSESSMENT

Assign a day of the week to each child and revisit the book. As you read the book, pause to let each child say aloud her or his day of the week when it appears. Repeat the exercise until everyone has been given a day of the week to say aloud.

© McGraw-Hill School Division

Name_______________________________ Date_______________

What Does Pig Do?

Monday 
Tuesday 
Wednesday 
Thursday 
Friday 
Saturday 
Sunday

© McGraw-Hill School Division

Name________________________ Date____________

Jim Does It!

dig	kick	jig
lick	win	sit

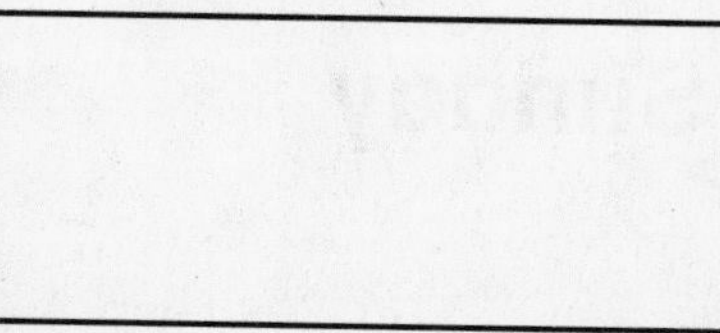

© McGraw-Hill School Division

Name_______________________________ Date_______________

Match the Sounds

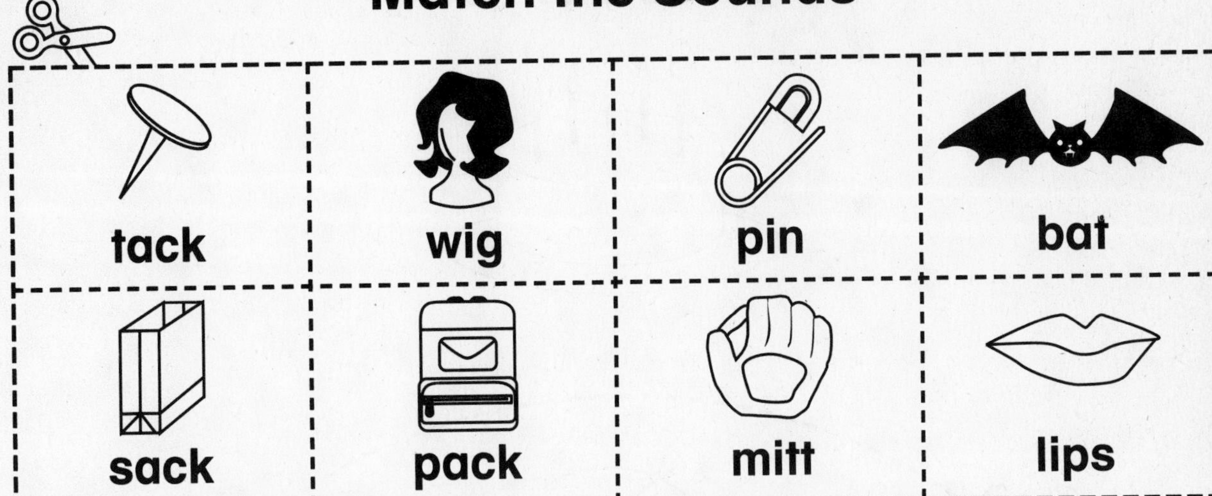

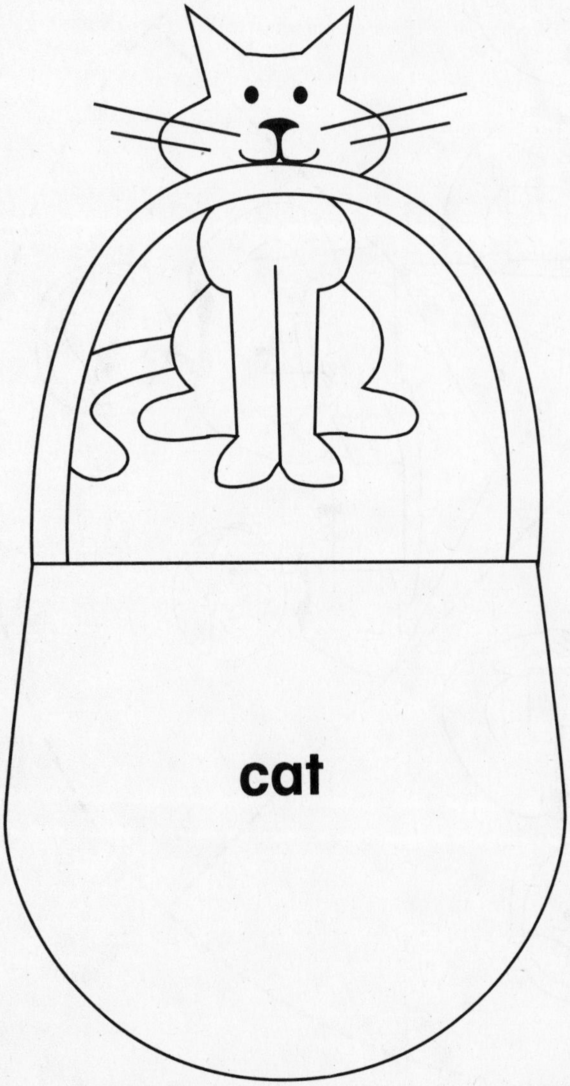

cat

pig

© McGraw-Hill School Division

Name________________________________ Date________________

Snack Time

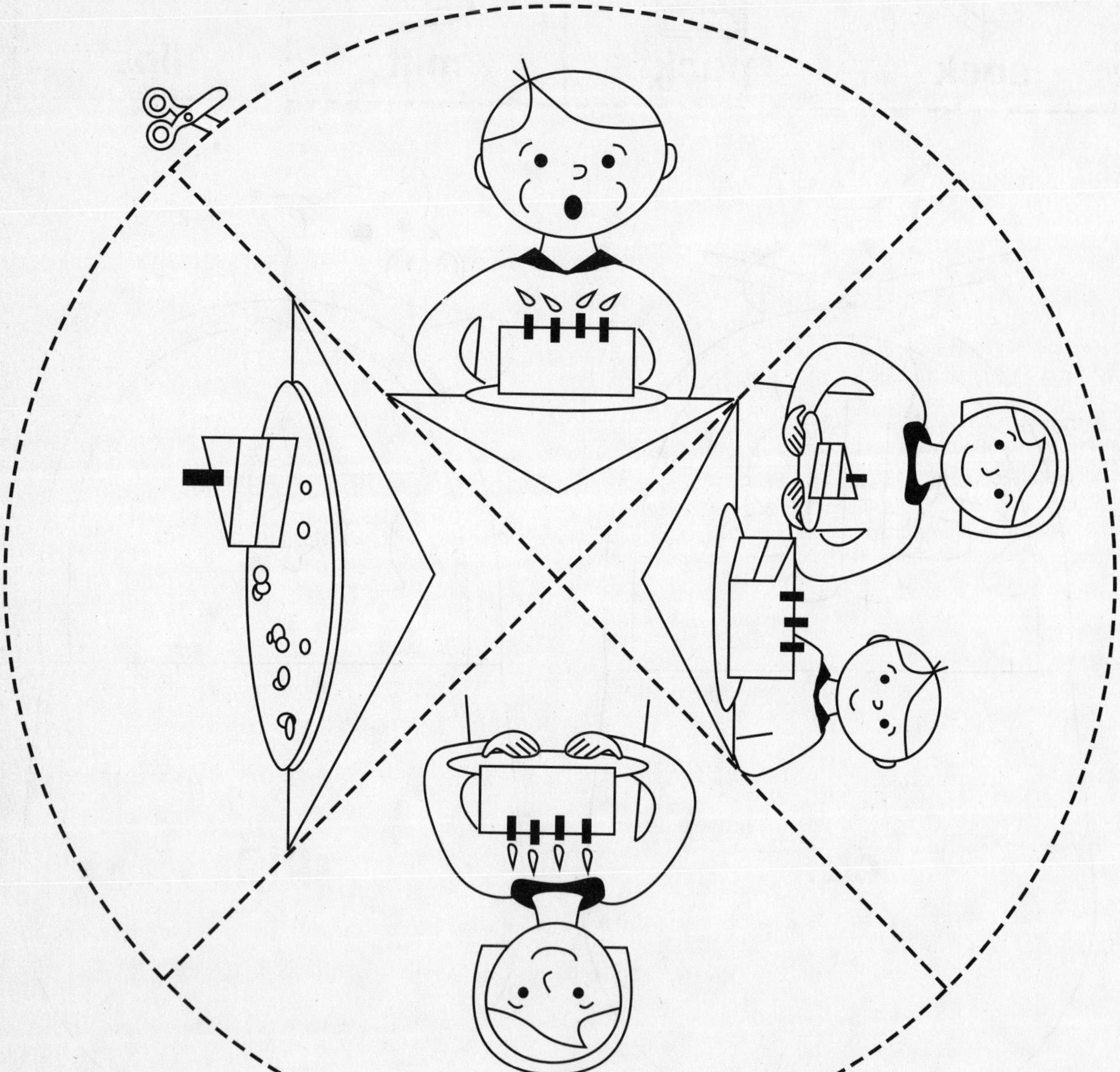

© McGraw-Hill School Division

Name ____________________ Date ____________

A Piggy Week

Monday

Tuesday

Wednesday

Thursday

Friday

Saturday

Sunday

© McGraw-Hill School Division

THE PATH ON THE MAP pp. 70A–87R

Written by Jean Marzollo Illustrated by Peggy Tagel

BUILD BACKGROUND FOR LANGUAGE SUPPORT

I. FOCUS ON READING

Focus on Skills

OBJECTIVE: Listen for Digraphs *sh* and *th*

Develop Phonological Awareness

Bring in objects such as the following: a plastic fish, a dish, a toy ship, a toy shark, a shirt, a map that shows a path, bath soap. Give children time to look over and identify the objects. Help them recognize the /sh/ and /th/ sounds in the names of these objects. Hold up each object and repeat its name, emphasizing the /sh/ or /th/ sound. Then guide children to separate the objects into two groups, those that contain the /sh/ sound and those that contain the /th/ sound.

TPR

Have children use body language and physical responses to identify /sh/ and /th/ sounds.

II. READ THE LITERATURE

VOCABULARY

down
see
could
be

Vocabulary

Write the following sentences on the board and underline the vocabulary words:

What is <u>down</u> here?

What <u>could</u> it <u>be</u>?

Let's go <u>see</u>!

Just you and me!

Have children pantomime the rhyme as a volunteer tracks and reads each sentence from the board. Encourage them to pretend to be looking down a long road. Talk about what might really be "down there."

CONCEPT

animals

Evaluate Prior Knowledge

Dramatize the actions and sounds of various farm animals with the children. For example, pretend to crow like a rooster. Also, pretend to graze and moo like a cow. Ask children to guess what you are pretending to be. Ask: *Where do these animals live?* Continue examples until children arrive at the correct answer: you are pretending to be farm animals.

© McGraw-Hill School Division

Develop Oral Language

TPR
Encourage children to describe what they are doing as they pantomime.

In small groups invite children to pantomime different animals they might see on a farm. Have one child choose an animal to act out and have the other children guess the animal.

nonverbal prompt for active participation

- Preproduction: *Show us* (point to class and self) *what* (name of farm animal) *do.*

one- or two- word response prompt

- Early production: *Do* (name of farm animal) *like to eat grass? Do they sleep in a barn?*

prompt for short answers to higher-level thinking skills

- Speech emergence: *What is your animal called? What do* (name of animal) *eat? Where do* (name of animal) *sleep?*

prompt for detailed answers to higher-level thinking skills

- Intermediate fluency: *Tell us* (point to class and self) *what you know about* (name of animal). *How do you feel about* (name of animal)?

Guided Reading

Preview and Predict

Tell children that in this story, a group of people follow a path on a map to see different kinds of animals. Explain that in some of the pictures, the people are looking at the map, and in other pictures they are actually on the path they see on the map. Tell children: *The map shows a path that is on a farm. The people who walk along the path see a pig, a cow, and other farm animals.*

Then look at the illustrations in the book with children, stopping to ask the following questions: *What are the people doing at the beginning of the story? Where are they? What is the first animal they see on the path? What animal comes next? Where does the duck live? Where does the fish live? What animal do the people see sitting right on the path? What do you think is at the end of the path? What other animals might these people see?*

GRAPHIC ORGANIZER
Blackline Master 16

Objectives

- To reinforce sequence of events
- To reinforce directionality
- To use illustrations

Materials

One copy of Blackline Master 16 per child; pencils; crayons

Have children look over the page as you remind them of the places they visited in the story. Then reread the story and invite children to trace the path according to the sequence of events in the story. Invite children to draw cats in the appropriate places.

To reinforce sequence, have children write numbers next to each place that was visited on the path, in the proper sequence.

© McGraw-Hill School Division

III. BUILD SKILLS

Phonics and Decoding

INTRODUCE DIGRAPHS *sh* AND *th*
Blackline Master 17

Objectives

- To support vocabulary development
- To practice word identification
- To reinforce *sh* and *th* digraphs

Materials

One copy of Blackline Master 17 per child; scissors; paste or glue

Have children look over the words at the top of the page and their corresponding pictures. Then help them cut out each word and illustration along the dotted lines. Have children say the words aloud and paste them in the proper column, on the appropriate shelf.

INFORMAL ASSESSMENT

To assess children's understanding of the digraphs *sh* and *th,* have them work in pairs. Turn their attention to page 72. Ask children to name the word that contains the sound /th/. (path) Then turn to page 80, and ask them to name the word that contains the sound /sh/. (fish) Call on pairs to share the words aloud.

Phonics and Decoding

REVIEW DIGRAPHS *sh* AND *th*
Blackline Master 18

Objectives

- To support hands-on learning
- To reinforce the digraphs *sh* and *th*
- To encourage creative thinking

Materials

One copy of Blackline Master 18 per child; pencils

Have children look over each incomplete sentence and the illustration beside it. Discuss each picture with children. Then have them work in pairs. Ask them to circle each word that will correctly complete each sentence. When children are finished, ask them to read each completed sentence aloud.

INFORMAL ASSESSMENT

Turn children's attention to the illustration on page 73, which shows two children standing on a path. Do not show the text. Ask volunteers to point to and name something in the picture that has the /th/ sound. (path) Repeat the exercise with the illustration on page 81, this time asking them to identify something in the picture that has the /sh/ sound. (fish)

© McGraw-Hill School Division

Comprehension

INTRODUCE USE OF ILLUSTRATIONS
Blackline Master 19

Objectives

- To use illustrations
- To encourage creative thinking

Materials

One copy of Blackline Master 19 per child; pencils

Invite children to look over the pictures on the page. Explain to them that the pictures on the right side show how the pictures on the left side would look if they were on a map. Then ask children to draw a line between each picture on the left side and its matching symbol on the right.

INFORMAL ASSESSMENT

To assess children's understanding of maps and illustrations, turn to page 72 for example, and ask: *What do you see on the map?* Then turn to page 74 and repeat the question.

Vocabulary Strategy

INTRODUCE UNFAMILIAR WORDS
Blackline Master 20

Objectives

- To practice word identification
- To reinforce story vocabulary
- To use illustrations
- To reinforce story characters

Materials

One copy of Blackline Master 20 per child; scissors; crayons; pencils

Help children cut out each of the six cards along the dotted lines and fold them on the solid lines. Invite them to work in pairs to review their knowledge of the words. Have one child hold up a word for the other to read. Instruct children to check each other's answers by looking at the pictures. Encourage them to create an additional card by illustrating and labeling the blank card.

INFORMAL ASSESSMENT

To assess children's knowledge of farm animal vocabulary, turn to illustrations in the story and ask partners to name the animal they see. For instance, turn to page 76, and ask children to identify the cow.

© McGraw-Hill School Division

Name_____________________________________ Date_______________

A Story Map

© McGraw-Hill School Division

Name________________________________ Date________________

Frame Game

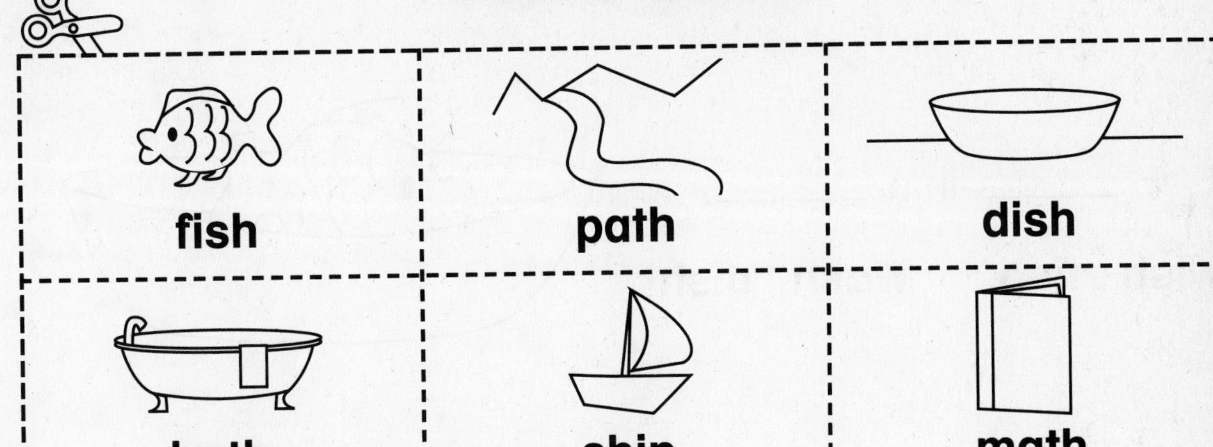

th

sh

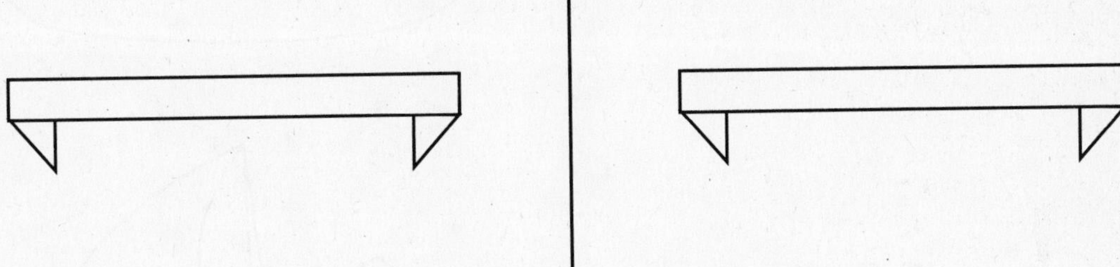

© McGraw-Hill School Division

Name________________________ Date______________

Fish in a Dish

1. A ______ in a ______.

wish fish **wash dish**

2. A ______ in a ______.

fish ship **dish wish**

3. A ______ in a ______.

fish dish **ship wash**

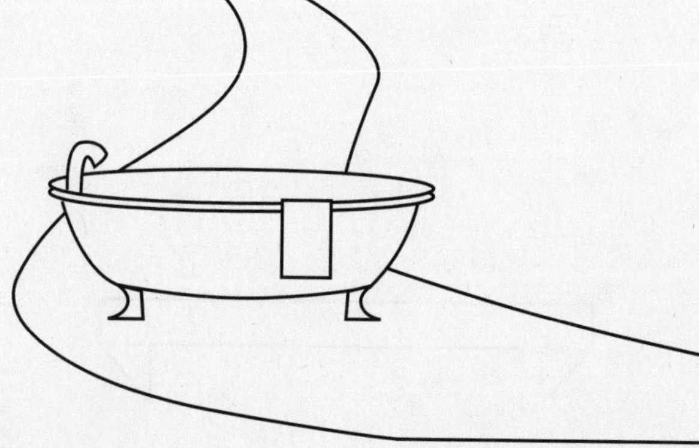

4. A ______ on a ______.

with bath **path wish**

© McGraw-Hill School Division

Name________________________________ Date____________

On the Map

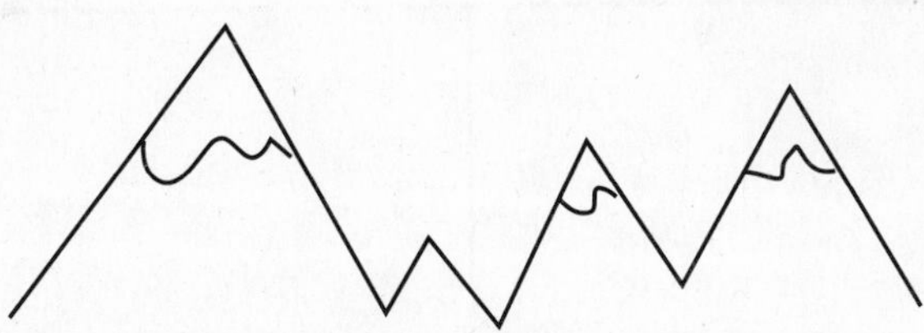

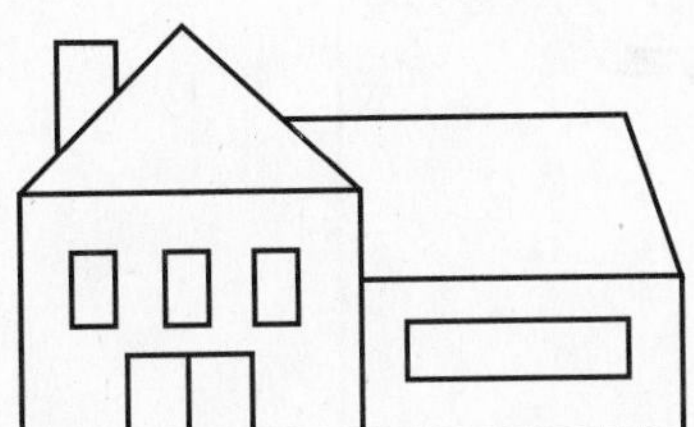

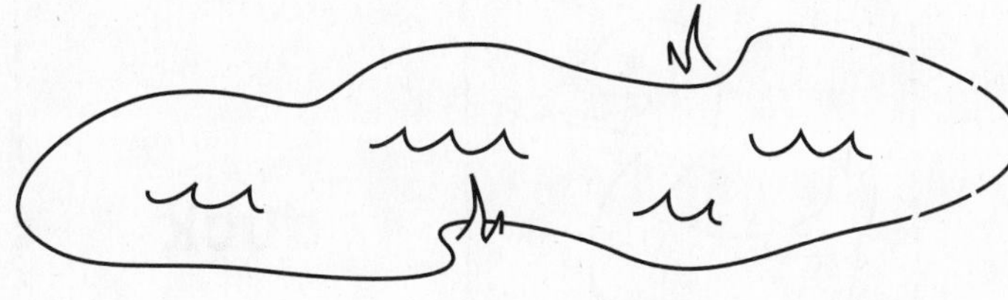

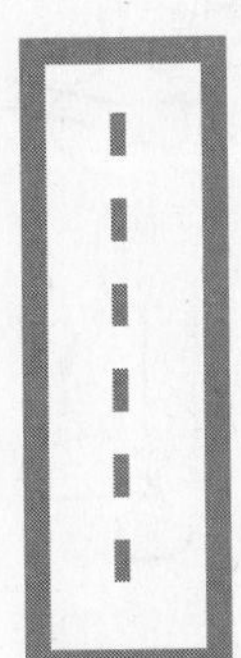

© McGraw-Hill School Division

Name________________________________ Date______________

Animal Picture Cards

	cow		fish
	cat		duck
	pig		

© McGraw-Hill School Division

SHIPS! pp. 90A–101R

Time For Kids

BUILD BACKGROUND FOR LANGUAGE SUPPORT

I. FOCUS ON READING

Focus on Skills

OBJECTIVES: Listen for Short *a* and *i;* Listen for Digraphs *ck, sh,* and *th*

Develop Phonological Awareness

Make up a series of sentences with words that have short *i* and the digraphs *ck, sh,* and *th.* For example: *Six ships missed the dock on Thursday.* Say the sentences aloud, and ask children to identify the words they hear which contain the short *i* sound, and/or the *ck, sh,* and *th* sounds.

Repeat the exercise with short *a* words and the digraphs *ck, sh,* and *th.* (Example: *That black cat was on Shawn's back.*) Write words from the sentences on the board, and encourage children to practice saying them and using them in sentences of their own.

TPR
Use body language and physical response to demonstrate recognition of short *a* and *i* sounds, as well as the *ck, sh,* and *th* sounds.

II. READ THE LITERATURE

VOCABULARY
look
this
one
what

Vocabulary

Sit in a circle with children and read the following sentences. Use intonation and body language to emphasize the meaning of each word. For example:

Look at my face. (Use both hands to point to your face.)

This is a nose. (Point to your nose.)

What are these? They are my teeth. (Point to your teeth.)

These are my eyes. This one is closed. (Point to your eyes. Then wink and point to the closed eye.)

After each sentence, go around the circle, inviting children to create their own vocabulary word sentences modeled after yours.

CONCEPT
ships and boats

Evaluate Prior Knowledge

Bring in pictures of boats and ships as well as small toy boats. Pass the pictures and toys around, identifying them as *boats* and *ships.* Then draw a picture of the main body of a ship on the chalkboard. Invite volunteers to come to the board and complete the drawing. As they draw, ask them to explain what they are drawing. Then ask children if they can think of any other kinds of ships or boats, other than what has been drawn on the chalkboard. Talk about where ships/boats are found and why.

© McGraw-Hill School Division

TPR
Use physical and visual prompts.

Develop Oral Language

On sheets of paper, invite children to draw as many different kinds of ships and boats as they can think of, such as sail boats, motor boats, steam boats, canoes, row boats, rafts, and so on.

nonverbal prompt for active participation

- Preproduction: *Show us* (point to class and self) *the kind of ship or boat you have drawn.*

one- or two- word response prompt

- Early production: *Have you ever ridden on a* (kind of ship or boat)? *Is it something you would like to do?*

prompt for short answers to higher-level thinking skills

- Speech emergence: *What kind of ship or boat have you drawn? Who uses these kinds of ships/boats?*

prompt for detailed answers to higher-level thinking skills

- Intermediate fluency: *Why do you like* (kind of ship or boat)*? Where did you learn about them?*

Guided Reading

Preview and Predict

Tell children that this is a story about ships. Explain that there are many kinds of ships, as shown in the photographs. Tell children: *Some of the ships in this story are very big. Some have sails. Others do not. Some people work on ships. Other people play with ships.*

Have children answer the following questions as you take them on a picture walk through the story: *What is special about the ship on the first page? How is the second kind of ship different from the first kind? Who do you think uses the ship with the airplanes on it? What do you think the boy might like to do when he grows up?*

GRAPHIC ORGANIZER
Blackline Master 21

Objectives

- To practice organizing skills
- To encourage creative thinking

Materials

One copy of Blackline Master 21 per child; crayons; scissors; glue or paste; manila folder

Help children cut out the picture along the dotted lines. Then invite them to color in each ship. Next, have them paste their picture to a manila envelope. Explain to children that they can use this folder as a place to store pictures they draw for each ship they see in the story.

Invite children to use their folder to store pictures of additional ships they draw or find in magazines.

© McGraw-Hill School Division

III. BUILD SKILLS

Comprehension

REVIEW USE OF ILLUSTRATIONS
Blackline Master 22

Objectives

- To reinforce story comprehension
- To practice following directions
- To use illustrations

Materials

One copy of Blackline Master 22 per child; scissors; stapler; crayons

Invite children to look over the pictures on the page and choose the ones that are connected to this story. Help them cut out each picture. Explain that they are going to make a book about ships, so they should only include those pictures that have to do with ships. Help them assemble their pages with the book cover at the front. Staple the books together on the left edge of the pages. Invite each child to tell a story using their completed book.

INFORMAL ASSESSMENT

To assess children's comprehension of use of illustrations, turn to pages 93 and 94 and ask them to describe how the two ships are different. Repeat the exercise, using page 114.

Comprehension

REVIEW SEQUENCE OF EVENTS
Blackline Master 23

Objectives

- To reinforce sequence of events
- To use illustrations
- To encourage creative thinking

Materials

One copy of Blackline Master 23 per child; scissors; crayons

Have children look over the pictures and describe what is happening in each. Then explain that pictures can tell a story. Invite children to color in each picture and cut it out on the dotted lines. Ask them to place the pictures in order so they show how the girl makes her boat.

INFORMAL ASSESSMENT

To assess children's comprehension of sequence of events, return to pages 92, 93, and 94 with children. After reviewing the names of the ships, ask: *Which ship did we see first? Which ship did we see next? Which ship did we see last?* Allow different children to share their answers. Repeat the exercise using different combinations of pages and ships.

© McGraw-Hill School Division

Vocabulary Strategy

REVIEW INFLECTIONAL ENDING *-s*
Blackline Master 24

Objectives

- To reinforce subject-verb agreement
- To review inflectional ending *-s*
- To encourage hands-on learning

Materials

One copy of Blackline Master 24 per child; pencils

Have children look over each picture and its corresponding incomplete sentence. Ask them to finish the sentences by circling the correct word.

INFORMAL ASSESSMENT

Ask children to examine the photograph on page 97. Write the incomplete sentence, *The boy* __________ *the ship.* Above it, write the words *hold* and *holds.* Have children work in pairs to choose the correct answer.

Vocabulary Strategy

REVIEW UNFAMILIAR WORDS
Blackline Master 25

Objectives

- To practice word identification
- To reinforce story vocabulary
- To use illustrations
- To support hands-on learning

Materials

One copy of Blackline Master 25 per child; scissors

Have children cut out the cards along the dotted lines. Then have them work in pairs to play a game where they take turns matching the words to their corresponding pictures.

INFORMAL ASSESSMENT

To assess children's knowledge of story vocabulary, return to the book and look at different photographs, asking: *What kind of a ship is this?* Have children work in pairs to come up with correct answers.

© McGraw-Hill School Division

Name________________________________ Date______________

Picture File

© McGraw-Hill School Division

Name________________________ Date____________

Ship Story

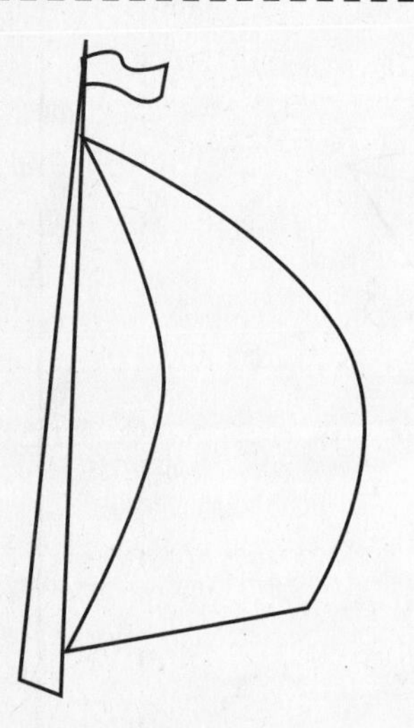

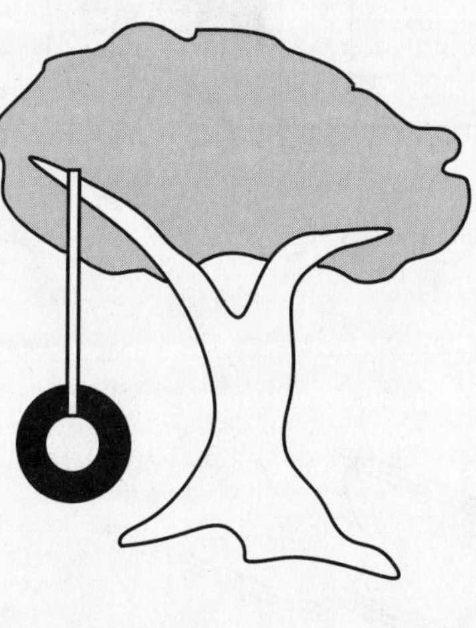

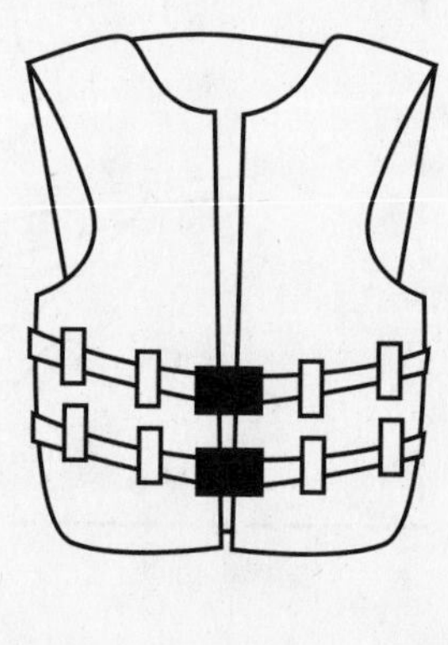

© McGraw-Hill School Division

Name________________________________ Date______________

Building a Ship

© McGraw-Hill School Division

Name______________________________ Date______________

On a Ship

She | pack packs |.

They | nap naps |.

She | pat pats | the dog.

They | dip dips |.

© McGraw-Hill School Division

Name________________________ Date____________

Ships Match-up

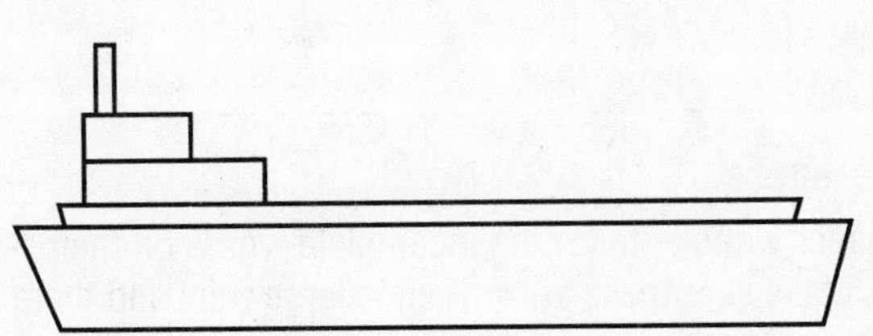	Steam Ship
	Toy Ship
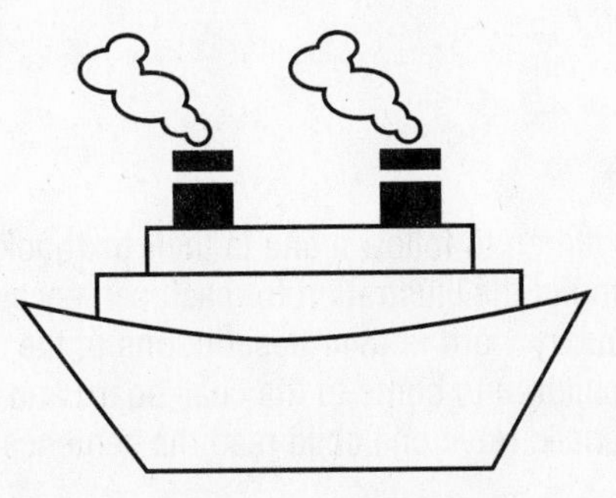	Ship with Sail
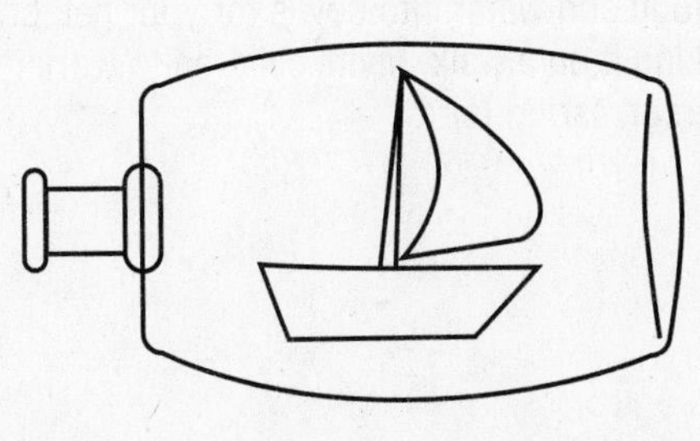	Navy Ship

© McGraw-Hill School Division

ONE GOOD PUP pp. 8A–35R

Written and Illustrated by Frank Asch

BUILD BACKGROUND FOR LANGUAGE SUPPORT

I. FOCUS ON READING

Focus on Skills

OBJECTIVE: Listen for short *u*

Develop Phonological Awareness

Offer children slips of white paper with the following incomplete words on them: *m_d; t_b; f_n; r_b; h_m; s_n.* Make sure these are written in large print and there is enough space to fill in the blanks. On red pieces of paper, have children write the letter *u*. Then invite them to complete each word by placing the *u* in the blank spaces. Have them segment each sound and then say the word aloud.

TPR
When children call out each word, they can pantomime the meaning of the word in an appropriate way.

II. READ THE LITERATURE

VOCABULARY
no
ride
small
out

Vocabulary

Write the following sentences on the chalkboard. Point to each word as you read them aloud:

But it is wet out. (p. 13)

Sit in this small ship with me. (p. 18)

Take a little ride, Pup. (p. 28)

It is no fun for Pup. (p. 29)

Read the sentences again, inviting children to follow along in their textbooks. Ask children to describe what is happening in the illustration for each sentence. Encourage children to use the vocabulary word in their descriptions of the illustrations. Then, on a third reading, ask children to come to the chalkboard and underline each vocabulary word with colored chalk. Have one child read the sentence as two other children act out the meaning.

CONCEPT
pet care

Evaluate Prior Knowledge

Invite children to demonstrate the many ways a person can take care of a pet. For example, pantomime pouring some food and water into bowls for your pet; brushing your pet; making a nice bed for it; taking it on a walk. Invite children to work in pairs, taking turns being the pet and the person caring for it.

© McGraw-Hill School Division

Develop Oral Language

Encourage students to express their experiences with pets. For students who do not have pets, invite them to answer the following questions about a pet they would like to own.

nonverbal prompt for active participation

- Preproduction: *Show us* (pointing to class and self) *how you take care of your pet.*

one- to two-word response prompt

- Early production: *Do you give your pet good food? Do you walk your pet?*

prompt for short answers to higher-level thinking skills

- Speech emergence: *What do you do to take care of your pet? What kind of food do you give your pet?*

prompt for detailed answers to higher-level thinking skills

- Intermediate fluency: *How do you feel about taking care of your pet? Who helped you learn to take care of your pet?*

Guided Reading

Preview and Predict

Share with children that in this story a boy has a problem because it is raining and his puppy wants to go outside. The boy tries to find a solution to his problem by finding things for the puppy to do inside. Tell children: *The boy asks the pup if he wants to do things with the boy inside. The boy asks the pup to take a nap, sit in a play ship, and play tug.*

Ask children to pair up, making sure that a child needing language support is working with an English-speaking child. With children, go through the book, noting how the pictures demonstrate how the boy cares for his puppy. Have one child record the answers to the following questions: *What does the pup want to do? Why does the boy want the pup to stay inside? What do the boy and the pup do in the small ship? Where do the boy and the pup fish? Do you think it is fun for the pup to ride in the wagon? What do you think the boy and the pup will do next?*

GRAPHIC ORGANIZER
Blackline Master 26

Objectives

- To use illustrations
- To reinforce story comprehension
- To reinforce sequence of events

Materials

One copy of Blackline Master 26 per child; crayons; scissors; hole punch; yarn

Have children cut out the cards on the dotted lines. Then help them assemble the pages by punching holes in the appropriate spaces and tying the cards together with yarn. Tell children the cover of the book should come first, and that they should number each page that follows. Then have them draw a picture and label it each time the boy and his pup do something new.

© McGraw-Hill School Division

III. BUILD SKILLS

Phonics and Decoding

REVIEW SHORT *u*
Blackline Master 27

Objectives

- To reinforce understanding of short *u* sound
- To develop word identification
- To encourage critical thinking

Materials

One copy of Blackline Master 27 per child; scissors; paste

Direct children's attention to the pictures on the left side of the page. Say the name for each picture, and have students repeat it after you. Then have children cut out the pictures along the dotted lines. Ask them to select the pictures for words that have the short *u* sound they hear in *up*. Tell them to paste the pictures on the stairs of the *up* escalator.

INFORMAL ASSESSMENT

To assess recognition of words with the /u/ sound, have children work in pairs. Lead them to page 29 of the story text, for example, and ask them to name words they see that contain the short *u* sound. (fun, pup) Call on different sets of partners to identify the words with the short *u* sound.

Phonics and Decoding

REVIEW SHORT *u, i, a; sh, th*
Blackline Master 28

Objectives

- To review short *u, i, a; sh, th*
- To use illustrations
- To practice following directions

Materials

One copy of Blackline Master 28 per child; pencil

Explain to children that the puppy in the picture is wishing for other things whose names contain the short *u* sound. Help children read the word below each picture. Tell them that if the word has a short *u* sound, they should draw a line connecting it to the puppy.

INFORMAL ASSESSMENT

Have children look at the illustration on page 20 and look for actions or objects whose names contain the short *u* sound. Children should point out the *pup*, and that the pup and the boy are playing *tug*. Repeat the exercise on page 12 with the sound *sh*.

© McGraw-Hill School Division

Comprehension

REVIEW STORY ELEMENTS
Blackline Master 29

Objectives

- To reinforce character and plot
- To support critical thinking
- To reinforce story comprehension

Materials

One copy of Blackline Master 29 per child; pencil; crayons

Ask children to recall how one character in the story, the boy, has a problem, because it is raining and the other character, the pup, wants to go out. The boy tries to solve the problem by giving the pup other things to do. Now ask children to look at each picture on this page and circle the problem in each square. When they are done, invite children to tell how they might solve each problem.

INFORMAL ASSESSMENT

To assess children's recognition of character and plot, have them work in small groups. Invite them to look at the illustrations on pages 11–12. Let each group explain who the characters are and what problem they are facing. Expand the exercise by turning to various pages and asking children to identify solutions the boy is trying to provide.

Vocabulary Strategy

INTRODUCE INFLECTIONAL ENDING *-ed*
Blackline Master 30

Alternate Teaching Strategy
Teacher's Edition p. T67

Objectives

- To reinforce recognition of inflectional ending *-ed*
- To follow directions

Materials

One copy of Blackline Master 30 per child; scissors; paste

Have children cut out the *-ed* cards along the dotted lines. Ask them to paste the cards beside each word. Invite children to say the words aloud and then use them in sentences.

INFORMAL ASSESSMENT

To assess children's understanding of the inflectional ending *-ed*, have them work in pairs. Turn to the illustration on page 26 and ask children to imagine this story happened yesterday. Have pairs create a sentence that describes the picture. For instance, a team might say: *The boy and the pup mixed the cake.* If children do not use the inflectional ending *-ed*, remind them the story took place in the past.

© McGraw-Hill School Division

Name_______________________________ Date_______________

A Pup's Log

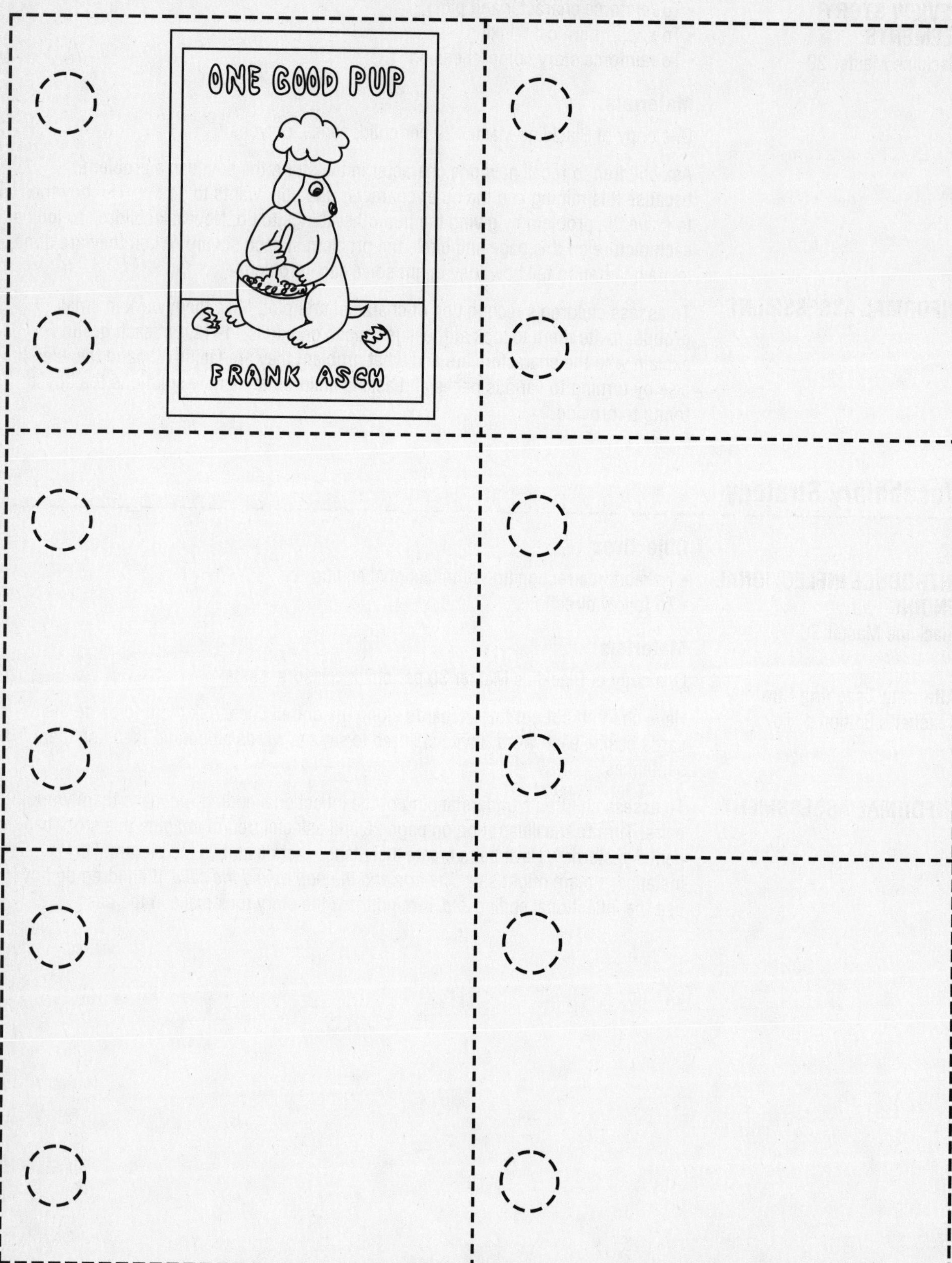

© McGraw-Hill School Division

Name_________________________________ Date_______________

Up and Up

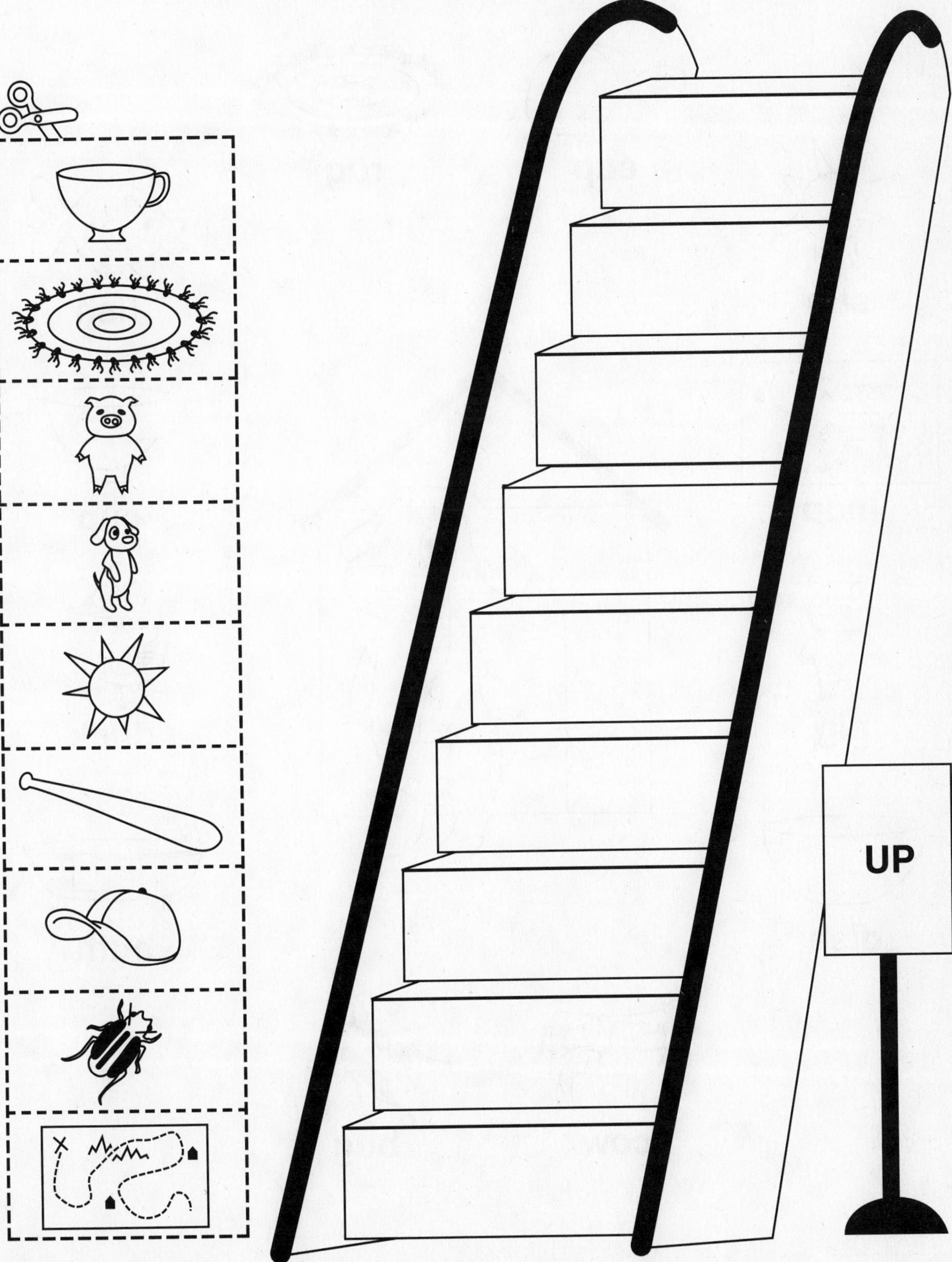

© McGraw-Hill School Division

Name______________________________ Date______________

Puppy Wishes

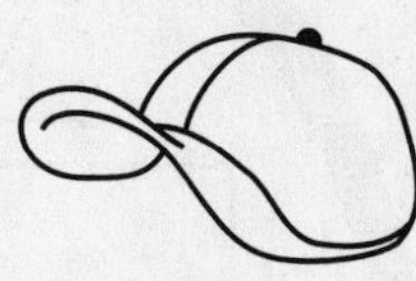

cap

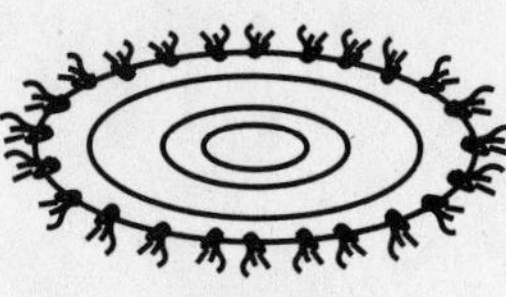

rug

sun

fish

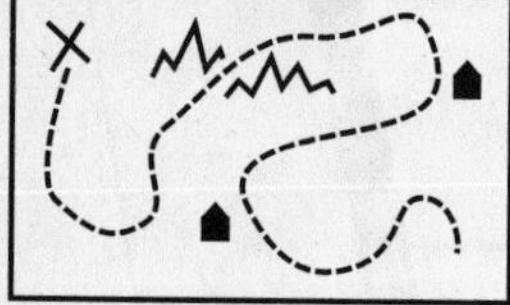

map

cup

pig

duck

dish

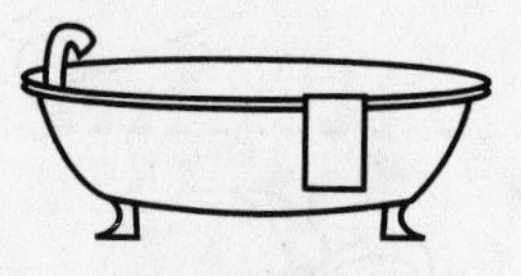

bath

cow

bug

© McGraw-Hill School Division

Name________________________________ Date____________

What's the Problem?

1.

2.

3.

4.

© McGraw-Hill School Division

Name_______________________________ Date_______________

Add -ed Endings

ed	ed	ed	ed

kick ☐ pack ☐

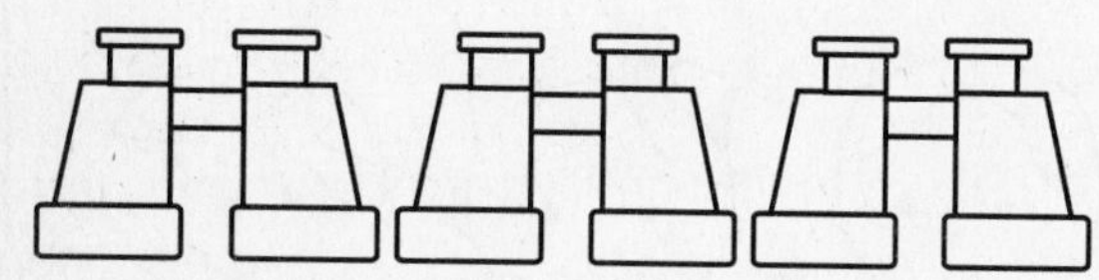

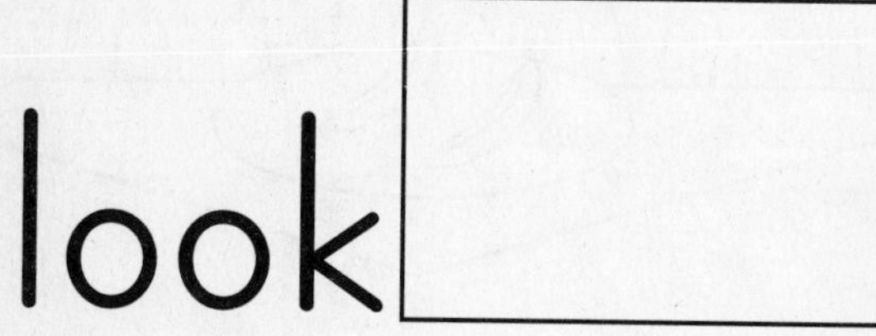

look ☐ wish ☐

© McGraw-Hill School Division

THE BUG BATH pp. 36A–65R

Written by Anne Miranda Illustrated by Bernard Adnet

BUILD BACKGROUND FOR LANGUAGE SUPPORT

I. FOCUS ON READING

Focus on Skills

OBJECTIVE: Listen for short *o*

Develop Phonological Awareness

Copy the poem onto the chalkboard, and read it aloud once, clapping your hands on the words with short *o* sounds. On the second and third readings, have children join you in chorus and clapping. On the fourth reading, let children say the short *o* words alone. Support them by reading the other parts of the poem and continuing to clap at the right times.

TPR
Invite children to hop each time they hear a short *o* word.

II. READ THE LITERATURE

VOCABULARY
saw
want
very
two

Vocabulary

Write each of the vocabulary words on word cards. Have volunteers match the cards for *saw, want, very,* and *two* to the corresponding words in the story. Then pass the cards around, one at a time, and have each child who receives one make up a short sentence that begins with the starters below:

I saw ____________.

I want ____________.

My friend is very ____________.

I have two ____________.

CONCEPT
perspective

Evaluate Prior Knowledge

Model how things appear from different perspectives. For instance, place an apple on a table, and pretend to be a bird flying above it. Say: *The apple is small.* Now use your fingers to pretend to be an ant crawling on the table. Say: *The apple is big.* Next, stand across the room. Exaggerate straining to see the apple. Say: *The apple is small.* Finally, stand right next to the apple, and say: *The apple is big.*

Develop Oral Language

Invite children to work in pairs to look at and describe each other from several different perspectives. Have children hold a yard stick and measure how many inches tall their partner is when standing across the room and halfway across the room.

nonverbal prompt for active participation
- Preproduction: *Show us* (point to class and self) *how the person you are looking at looks.* (Model how to show small and big with your hands.)

one- or two-word response prompt
- Early production: *Is the person you see small? Is the person you see far away?*

prompt for short answers to higher-level thinking skills
- Speech emergence: *What is the name of the person you see? What does she or he look like?*

prompt for detailed answers to higher-level thinking skills
- Intermediate fluency: *How does the person you see change when you stand in different places?*

© McGraw-Hill School Division

Guided Reading

Preview and Predict

Tell children that in this story, two ladybugs named Al and Bob fly into a window and discover a bathtub. Explain that when they get into the tub, they soon find that other things are getting into the tub also. Tell children: *Bob and Al meet a fish, a duck, and a boy in the tub. To Bob and Al, these other things look very big. They do not like being in the bath with the fish, the duck, and the boy, so they leave.*

To reinforce the concept of perspective, have English-speaking children and children needing language support work together as you lead them on a picture walk. Pause at illustrations, as you ask questions such as: *What do Al and Bob do in the bathtub? What gets Al and Bob wet? What lands on Al and Bob? Who seems very big to Al and Bob? Why do you think they leave? Do you think they are happy in their new bath? Why? Do you think they will ever go back to the first tub?*

GRAPHIC ORGANIZER
Blackline Master 31

Objectives

- To encourage creative thinking
- To develop understanding of character
- To reinforce spelling skills

Materials

One copy of Blackline Master 31 per child; pencil

Help children read the headings at the top of each column and the names of the characters that are listed. Ask children to write one word in each box to describe what each character looks like and what the character does.

To reinforce various aspects of characters, invite children to work in pairs to compare their written descriptions of each character and its actions.

III. BUILD SKILLS

Phonics and Decoding

REVIEW SHORT *o*
Blackline Master 32

Objectives

- To review short *o*
- To reinforce sound/symbol correspondence

Materials

One copy of Blackline Master 32 per child; crayons; scissors; paste; cardboard backings for each set of cards

Have children color each picture. Then have them cut out the pictures and the word cards, and paste them each to a cardboard backing. Create one for yourself, as well. Hold up a picture card, and say its name. Then hold up its matching name card. Ask children to do the same. Now pick a random card, and ask children to pick the card from their own set that matches yours. Children also can play matching games, in which one child displays a picture card and the other matches it with a word card.

© McGraw-Hill School Division

INFORMAL ASSESSMENT

Show children page 42. Choose two words from the text, one that contains the short *o* sound and one that does not—for example, *hot* and *bath.* Write the two words on the chalkboard, and say the words. Ask children to say the word that contains the /o/ sound. Repeat the exercise with words from other pages, such as *top, fish; got, up* from page 55.

Phonics and Decoding

CUMULATIVE REVIEW: SHORT VOWELS *o, u, a, i*
Blackline Master 33

Objectives

- To reinforce short vowels *o, i, a, u*
- To encourage creative thinking
- To practice word identification
- To develop print awareness

Materials

One copy of Blackline Master 33 per child; scissors

Help children cut out the pictures and the word cards. Have them work in pairs to play a matching game. Ask them to place the picture cards in a line and the word cards in a pile. Identify each story character, and help children decide what short vowel sound they hear in the character's name. Then invite players to take turns selecting a word card and matching it to the story character whose name has the same short vowel sound.

INFORMAL ASSESSMENT

To assess children's knowledge of words containing short vowel sounds, bring their attention to the illustrations on pages 46–47. Have children work in pairs to find as many objects as possible containing either the short *a* sound, the short *i* sound, the short *o* sound, or the short *u* sound. Words in these pictures include *Al, Bob, fish, tub, bugs, swim,* and *bath.*

Comprehension

REVIEW STORY ELEMENTS
Blackline Master 34

Objectives

- To reinforce word identification
- To reinforce story concepts
- To practice following directions

Materials

One copy of Blackline Master 34 per child; pencil; crayons

Have children read aloud the names of the story characters at the top of the page. Ask them to color the pictures that show events in the story and draw an X through the pictures that are not from this story.

INFORMAL ASSESSMENT

Turn to page 52 of the story, and remind children that this story has characters and a plot, or the action in a story. Ask children to name the characters that appear in this illustration. Then ask children to explain what the problem in the picture is. Repeat the exercise on page 57, where there is another character and a new problem within the plot.

© McGraw-Hill School Division

Vocabulary Strategy

REVIEW INFLECTIONAL ENDING *-ed*
Blackline Master 35

Objectives

- To reinforce inflectional ending *-ed*
- To practice word identification

Materials

One copy of Blackline Master 35 per child; scissors

Have children cut out the center picture and place the *-ed* figure in the seat at the end of each word, to create a new word. Invite children to say the new word aloud and use it in a sentence of their own.

INFORMAL ASSESSMENT

To assess children's understanding of the inflectional ending *-ed*, turn to page 47, and ask children to work in pairs to identify the sentence with an *-ed* word. (The first sentence does not; the second one contains the word *landed.*) Repeat the exercise on pages 50 and 55.

© McGraw-Hill School Division

Name ____________________ Date ____________

Character Chart

Characters	What They Look Like	What They Do
Al		
Bob		
Fish		
Duck		
Boy		

© McGraw-Hill School Division

Name______________________ Date__________

Dot-Pot-Cot Cards

dot	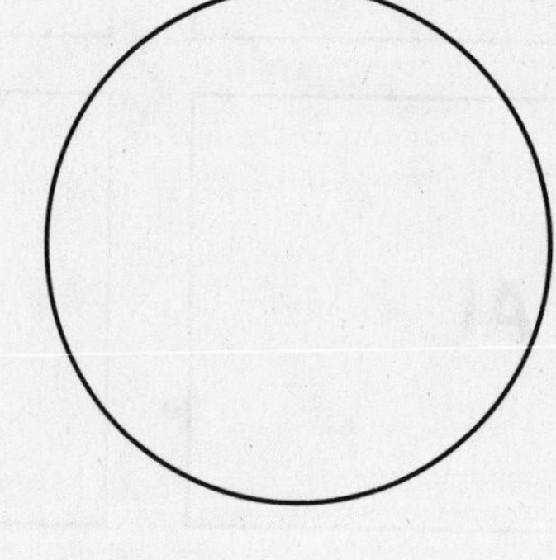
pot	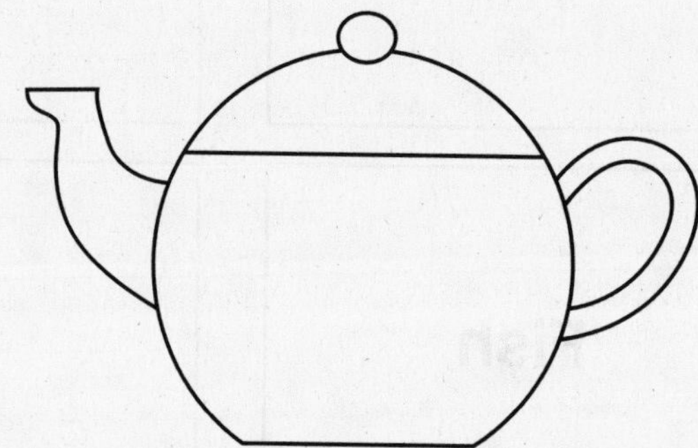
cot	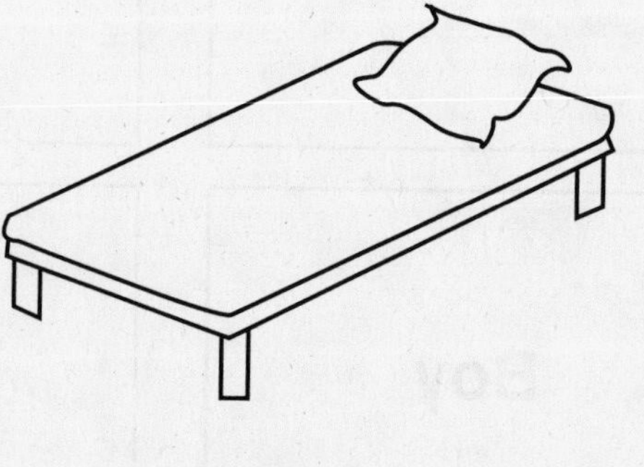

© McGraw-Hill School Division

Name________________________________ Date________________

A Matching Game

rock	fan	kick	hug
sock	cat	dig	cup
top	tab	pick	tug
mop	hat	wig	duck

© McGraw-Hill School Division

Name________________________________ Date________________

Who and What?

Al	Bob	boy

© McGraw-Hill School Division

Name________________________________ Date______________

Have a Seat, Ed

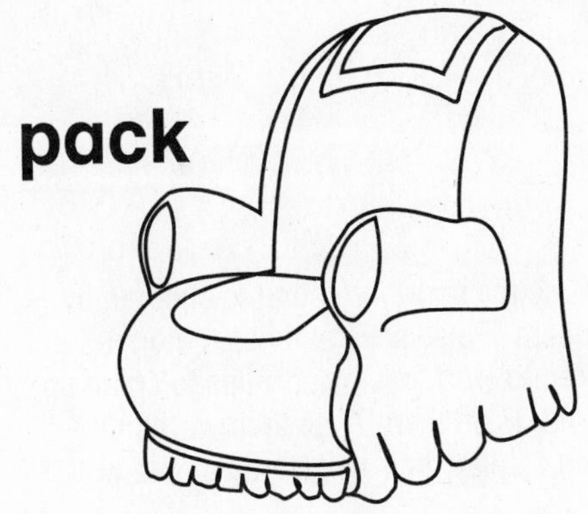

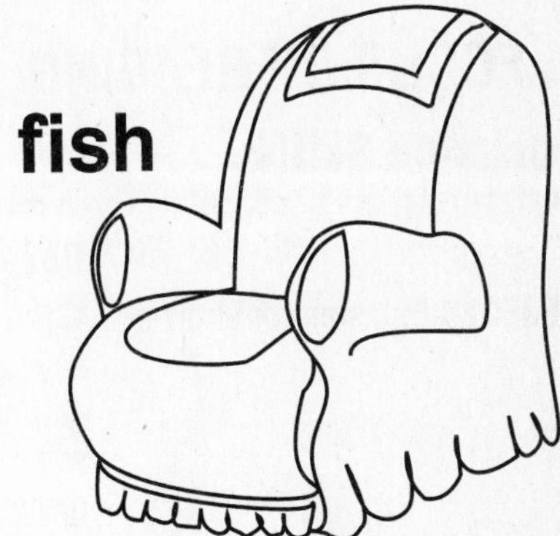

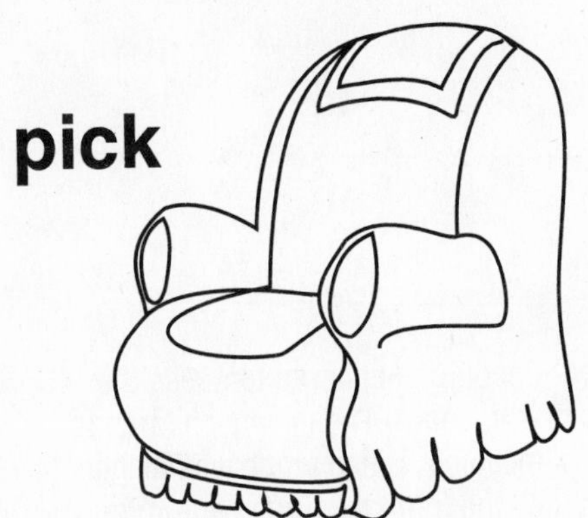

ed

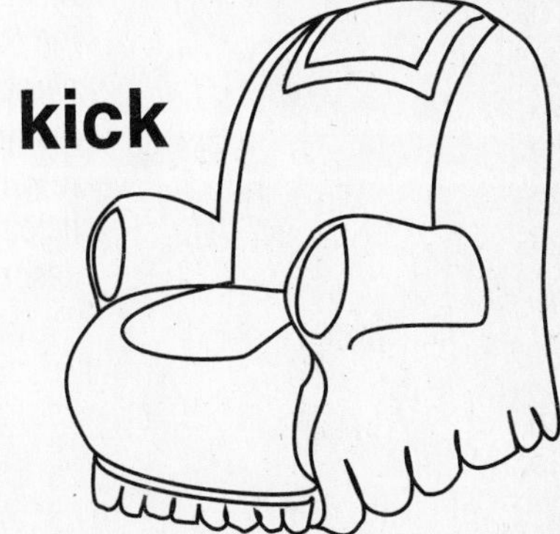

© McGraw-Hill School Division

SPLASH! pp. 66A–95R

Written by Jessica Clerk Illustrated by Ken Spengler

BUILD BACKGROUND FOR LANGUAGE SUPPORT

I. FOCUS ON READING

Focus on Skills

OBJECTIVE: Listen for short *e*

Develop Phonological Awareness

Write the word *wet* on the chalkboard. Introduce the short /e/ sound to children by saying the word aloud. Then read aloud the poem "Pets" several times, putting emphasis on each short /e/ words. Ask children to work in small groups to come up with other words containing the short /e/ sound. Have them write their words on pieces of blue paper shaped like raindrops and display their *wet* words on the wall.

TPR
Children can make the gesture of rain coming down as they call aloud each word.

II. READ THE LITERATURE

VOCABULARY
good
put
into
away

Vocabulary

Write the vocabulary words on the chalkboard. Encourage children to guess the meaning of each word. Record their guesses on the board. Then invite children to call out the correct word as you pantomime its meaning. When you have finished with the last word, review children's guesses. Let children take turns pantomiming the words for the other children.

Good: Pretend to bite into an apple and say: *This tastes good!*

Put: Demonstrate putting objects into different places. Say, for example: *I put the book on the shelf.*

Into: Act out walking into the room and looking into your desk drawer. Say: *I walk into the room and look into my drawer.*

Away: Demonstrate walking away from several objects. Say, for example: *I am walking away from the desk.*

CONCEPT
helping out

Evaluate Prior Knowledge

Model different ways of helping others through pantomime. For example, pretend to meet someone who is carrying more items than she or he can handle. Act out offering to carry some of her or his things. In another instance, pretend to help an elderly person get out of a car and walk into a house. As children watch and listen, point out that you are demonstrating ways of helping others. Ask children for examples of how they have helped others. Then show various magazine photographs of one person helping another. Pass the photos around, giving volunteers an opportunity to describe who is helping and how.

© McGraw-Hill School Division

Develop Oral Language

Invite children to work in pairs to create their own examples of how one person might help another. Have partners act out helping each other with simple tasks, such as: setting the table, carrying heavy packages, and looking for lost objects. Have the other children guess the activity and discuss the benefits of helping others and working together.

nonverbal prompt for active participation

- Preproduction: *Show us* (point to class and self) *how you are helping your friend.*

one- or two-word response prompt

- Early production: *Are you helping your friend to* (name activity)*? Have you ever really helped a friend in this way? Do you like helping others?*

prompt for short answers to higher-level thinking skills

- Speech emergence: *How are you helping your friend? Is it easy or difficult to help in this way? Why?*

prompt for detailed answers to higher-level thinking skills

- Intermediate fluency: *How do you feel when you help your friend* (name activity)*? How did you learn to* (name activity)*? Why would you choose to help someone in this way?*

TPR

Invite volunteers to help act out various scenes. Other children can clap when they see a scene where one person helps another.

Guided Reading

Preview and Predict

Share with children that in this story, a young girl named Meg gets caught in the rain while waiting for a bus. Meg, who does not like getting wet, soon finds that her pets come to help her stay dry. Tell children: *Meg is standing in the rain. Her head, neck and legs are wet. Meg feels that being wet is no fun at all. Her cat, her hen, and her dog bring her things to keep her dry.* Then take children on a picture walk through the story to preview and predict exactly how each pet helps Meg. Reinforce the concept of helping others. Ask questions such as: *Where is Meg standing at the beginning of the story? What is the weather like? Do you think Meg is staying dry? Who is the first pet to help her? Who is next? last? What does each pet bring Meg? Why do you think the pets are helping Meg?*

GRAPHIC ORGANIZER
Blackline Master 36

Objectives

- To reinforce key story concepts
- To support hands-on learning
- To encourage creative thinking
- To practice following directions

Materials

One copy of Blackline Master 36 per child; crayons; scissors; paste; craft sticks

Have children color in the full picture of the girl and the accompanying rain accessories. Then help them cut out these pictures, along with the two pictures showing the girl with a happy face and the girl with a sad face. Ask children to paste the two faces to craft sticks. Then have them work in groups of three to retell the story. One child can add clothes to the girl as the story proceeds. The other two can take turns holding up the appropriate face for each scene in the story.

To review analyzing characters and plot, have children work in pairs. One child can be the reporter, asking the girl how her pets helped her on a rainy day and how this made her feel. The other child can respond appropriately as they role-play the girl.

© McGraw-Hill School Division

III. BUILD SKILLS

Phonics and Decoding

SHORT *e*
Blackline Master 37

Objectives

- To recognize the short /e/ sound
- To practice word identification
- To develop print awareness

Materials

One copy of Blackline Master 37 per child; scissors

Help children cut out the word cards at the top of the page. Have them read each word aloud and help them discover that some words contain the short /e/ sound. Tell them to put these words in the rainy picture where it is wet and to put the words without the short /e/ sound under the umbrella where they will stay dry.

INFORMAL ASSESSMENT

To assess children's recognition of words containing the short /e/ sound, have them work in pairs. Ask each partner to find a word containing the /e/ sound on page 70. (One child can call out the word *shed* and the other can call out the word *red*.) Have teams take turns calling out words. Repeat the exercise on page 79 (hen/then) and page 81 (wet/Meg).

Phonics and Decoding

SHORT *e, o, u, i, a;* DIGRAPH *th*
Blackline Master 38

Objectives

- To reinforce understanding of short *e, o, u, i, a*; digraph *th*
- To practice word identification
- To support hands-on learning
- To develop print awareness

Materials

One copy of Blackline Master 38 per child; crayons

Give children the following instructions to help them discover what made Meg *wet*.

1. Color the pieces yellow that have the short vowel sound you hear in *cat*.
2. Color the pieces green that have the short vowel sound you hear in *Meg*.
3. Color the pieces red that have the short vowel sound you hear in *big*.
4. Color the pieces brown that have the short vowel sound you hear in *box*.
5. Color the pieces orange that have the short vowel sound you hear in *up*.
6. Color the pieces blue that have the ending sound you hear in *teeth*.

INFORMAL ASSESSMENT

To assess children's understanding of short vowel words, have them work in pairs. Take turns calling on different teams as you ask them to identify the short /i/ words on page 70 (big, it), the short /e/ words on page 71 (wet, Meg), the short /u/ word on page 73 (fun), the short /a/ words on page 75 (cat, hat), and the short /o/ word on page 82 (dog). Repeat the exercise with the digraph *th* on page 74. (path, with)

© McGraw-Hill School Division

Comprehension

MAIN IDEA AND SUPPORTING DETAILS
Blackline Master 39

Objectives

- To develop understanding of main idea and supporting details
- To use illustrations
- To reinforce creative thinking

Materials

One copy of Blackline Master 39 per child; crayons; pencils

Help children see that in one picture at the top of the page, Meg is wet and in the other she is dry and wearing her rain gear. Invite children to color in the picture where they think Meg is happier. Then have them circle the pictures below that show how Meg was able to get dry. Encourage children to tell how each picture is related to Meg being dry and happy

INFORMAL ASSESSMENT

Turn to the illustration on page 90 and ask children this question: *What is the main idea of this picture?* (Meg and her pets are dry under her umbrella.) Ask children to explain how they know this. (Meg is wearing all her rain gear.) Repeat the exercise on other pages, inviting children to share the details of how each pet brought Meg something to help her stay dry.

Vocabulary Strategy

UNFAMILIAR WORDS
Blackline Master 40

Objectives

- To practice finding the meanings of unfamiliar words
- To encourage critical thinking
- To develop word identification

Materials

One copy of Blackline Master 40 per child; scissors

Assist children in cutting out the puzzle pieces. Then have them mix up the pieces and match corresponding words and pictures. You may also invite children to play a game of Concentration with the cards, taking turns flipping the cards face up, two at a time to make a match.

INFORMAL ASSESSMENT

To assess children's understanding of new vocabulary words, write the words on the chalkboard. Read the story aloud and when you come to one of the words, pause to have children call out the word. Then ask them to draw or explain the meaning of the word.

© McGraw-Hill School Division

© McGraw-Hill School Division

Name____________________________ Date______________

Dress Meg!

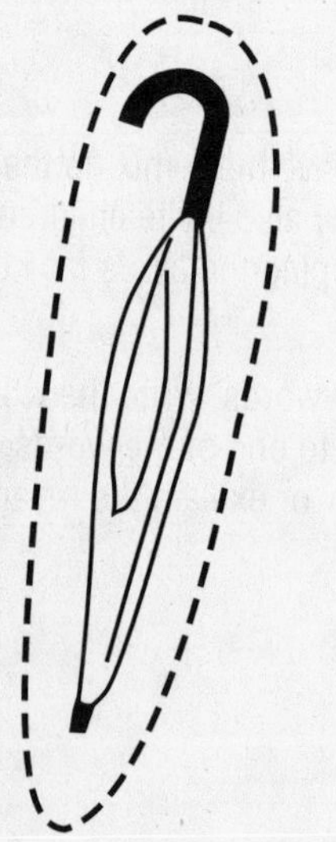

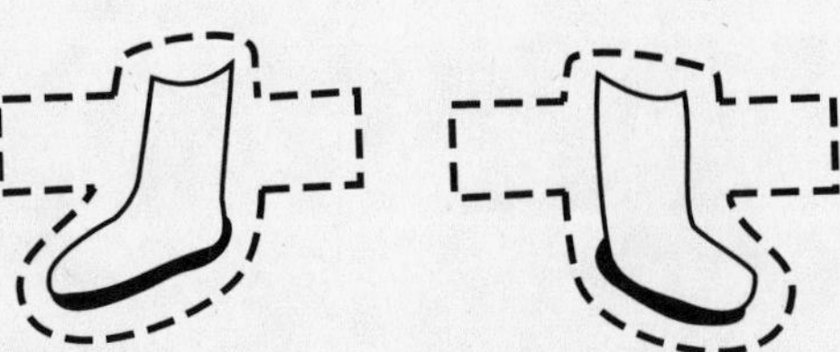

© McGraw-Hill School Division

Name________________________________ Date______________

Get Wet

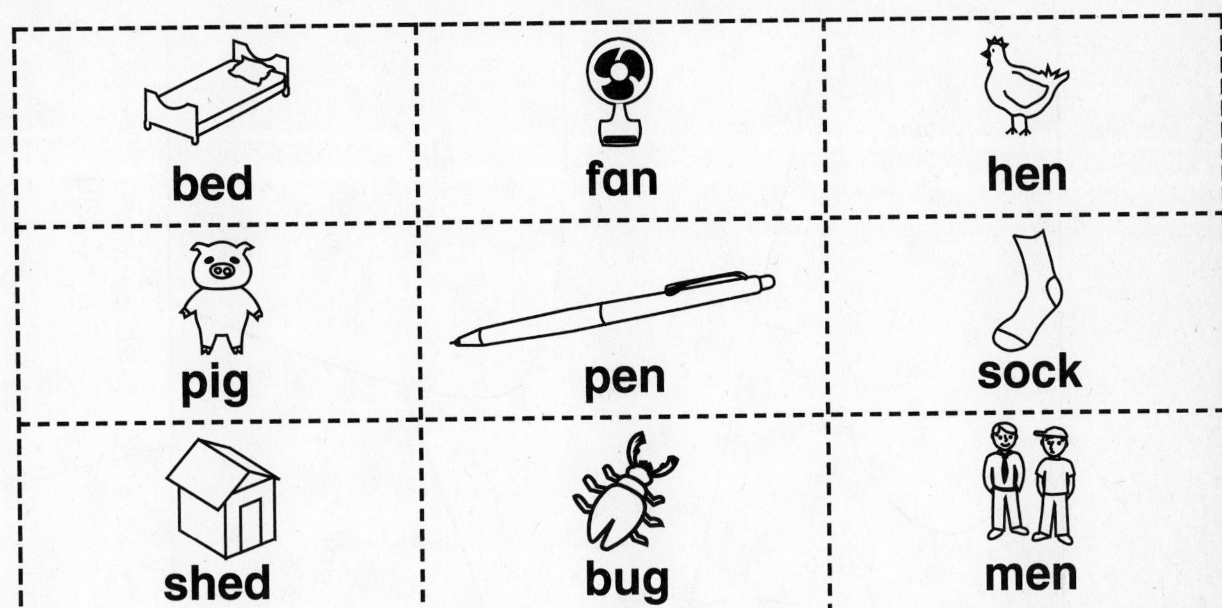

© McGraw-Hill School Division

Name________________________________ Date________________

Meg Gets Wet

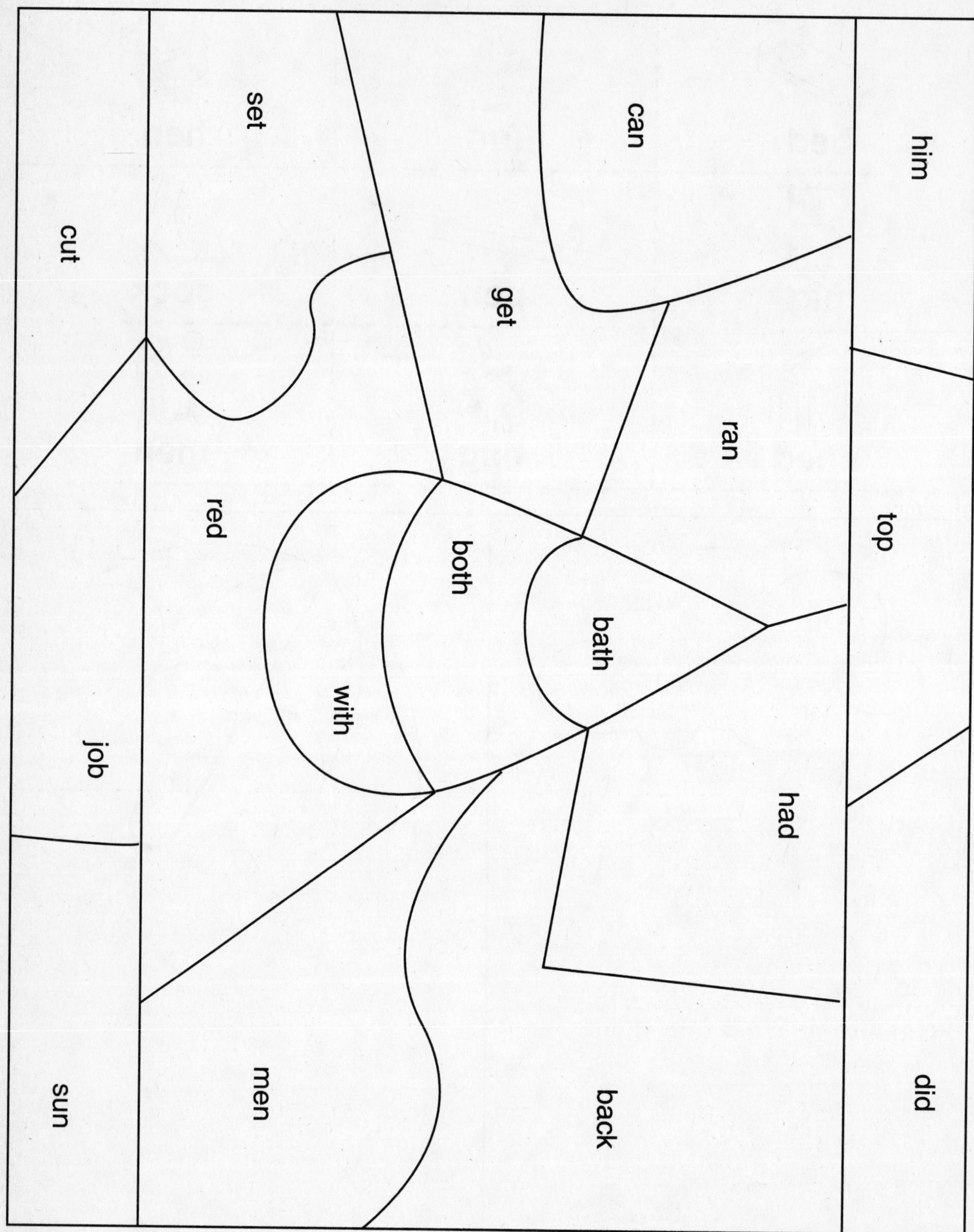

© McGraw-Hill School Division

Name______________________________ Date______________

Who Helps Meg?

© McGraw-Hill School Division

Name____________________ Date____________

Puzzles Match Game

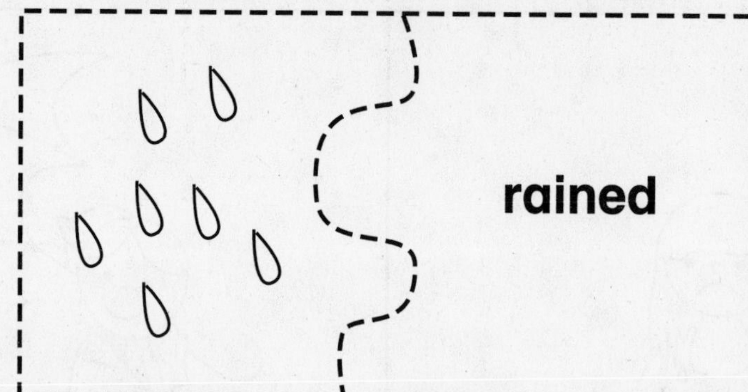

© McGraw-Hill School Division

WHAT BUG IS IT? pp. 96A–123R

Written and Illustrated by Pat Cummings

BUILD BACKGROUND FOR LANGUAGE SUPPORT

I. FOCUS ON READING

Focus on Skills

OBJECTIVE: Listen for blends *sn, sl, ff, ss,* and *ll*

Develop Phonological Awareness

After reading the poem aloud, write the blends *sn__, sl__, __ff, __ll,* and *__ss* across the chalkboard, and model each sound. Invite children to call out words that contain these blends.

You may wish to help them by dramatizing words such as *sniff, pass,* and *snack.* As they suggest words, write each one under the corresponding blend. When the lists are complete, have children work in small groups to illustrate one word for each blend. Label and display each group of words.

TPR
Children can underline the letters that represent the blend in each word written on the chalkboard.

II. READ THE LITERATURE

VOCABULARY
about
use
around
again

Vocabulary

Write the vocabulary words on the board, and point to each word as you say it. Use each word in a sentence, and talk about its meaning. Then have children write the words on index cards. As you say the following sentences, ask children to hold up the correct card.

1. *Mary is sad ____________ her missing pet bug.*
2. *Will she ever see her bug ____________?*
3. *Mary sees tiny foot prints ____________ the bottom of a hill.*
4. *She will ____________ a net to catch her bug.*

CONCEPT
bugs

Evaluate Prior Knowledge

To help children understand the concept of bugs, bring in illustrations or photos (available in many science magazines) of various bugs. Point out how they differ in color, shape, number of legs, and so on. Have children look for examples of different kinds of bugs in magazines and books.

© McGraw-Hill School Division

Develop Oral Language

Using props, dramatize what it would be like to be different kinds of bugs. For instance, pretend to be a spider by making a web with string; pretend to be an ant digging an anthill; pretend to be a bee by buzzing and sniffing flowers.

Invite children to pretend to be various bugs and have other children guess what bug it is. Stand in a circle, and encourage each child to take a turn.

nonverbal prompt for active participation

- Preproduction: *Show us* (point to class and self) *what kind of bug you are.*

one- to two-word response prompt

- Early production: *Do you like to fly? Can you make webs?*

prompt for short answers to higher-level thinking skills

- Speech emergence: *What kind of bug are you? What do you look like?*

prompt for detailed answers to higher-level thinking skills

- Intermediate fluency: *Can you tell us something about the kind of bug you are? Where do you live? What kinds of things do you do?*

Guided Reading

Preview and Predict

Explain to children that in this story a teacher and her class go outside to learn about different kinds of bugs. Each time one of Miss Lin's students sees a bug, she or he describes what it is like and then someone identifies it. For instance, Miss Lin and Jill see a bug that is red with black spots, and has wings that open and close. Another child realizes it's a ladybug. Tell children: *The class looks at five different kinds of bugs. Rick sees an ant. Nell and Yan see a spider. Others see other kinds of bugs.*

Then have children work in groups of five. As you lead them on a picture walk through the story, have children from each group take turns identifying the bugs and describing them in as much detail as they can. Along the way ask questions such as: *What are Miss Lin and her class looking at? What is the first bug that the class sees? What does it look like? What bug do they see next? What does the class learn about spiders? What bug does the class see last? Why do you think the children are laughing?*

GRAPHIC ORGANIZER
Blackline Master 41

Objectives

- To reinforce main idea and details
- To support hands-on learning
- To reinforce key concept

Materials

One copy of Blackline Master 41 per child; crayons; pencil

Invite children to color in each bug on the chart as it is introduced in the story. When the story is finished, help children review the text and pictures and list a detail or draw a picture of one thing they have learned about each bug. At the bottom of the chart, ask children to dictate the main idea of this story to a child fluent in English.

To further reinforce main idea and details, have children work in pairs. Invite them to add their partners' details to their charts. Let them compare the main ideas they have written and change or rewrite as necessary.

© McGraw-Hill School Division

III. BUILD SKILLS

Phonics and Decoding

REVIEW BLENDS
Blackline Master 42

Objectives

- To practice continuant blends
- To follow directions
- To use illustrations

Materials

One copy of Blackline Master 42 per child; pencil; crayons

Ask children to identify each picture at the top of the page and then circle the word below it that begins with the same sound. Next, have them name each picture at the bottom and circle the word that ends with the same sound. Children may wish to color the pictures.

INFORMAL ASSESSMENT

To assess children's recognition of continuant blends, have them work in pairs. Turn to page 104, and select two words from the text—one that contains a blend *(spots)* and one that does not contain a blend *(bug)*. Have teams work to come up with the correct answer. Repeat the exercise on page 105. *(snap/web)*

Phonics and Decoding

CUMULATIVE REVIEW OF BLENDS
Blackline Master 43

Objectives

- To reinforce continuant blends
- To develop print awareness

Materials

One copy of Blackline Master 43 per child; pencil

Have children read aloud each pair of words. Then ask them to underline the parts that sound the same. Invite children to use each word in a sentence of their own.

INFORMAL ASSESSMENT

Turn children's attention to page 113, and read the sentences aloud. Tell children there are two words on this page that start with the same sound. *(flies/ flower)* Have children work in pairs to find the two words. Then turn to page 110, and ask the same pairs to find one of the words they found previously. *(flies)* You may wish to explain that on this page, this word actually has a meaning different from its meaning on page 113.

© McGraw-Hill School Division

Comprehension

REVIEW MAIN IDEA AND SUPPORTING DETAILS
Blackline Master 44

Objectives

- To reinforce main idea and details
- To practice organizing skills
- To practice critical thinking
- To reinforce word identification

Materials

One copy of Blackline Master 44 per child; scissors; paste

Help children cut out the cards at the top of the page. Then have them complete the chart below, by pasting each card to the right of the bug it best describes.

INFORMAL ASSESSMENT

To assess children's knowledge of main ideas and details, return to the text, and read about the ant on pages 101–103. Ask children to tell you everything they learned about ants from reading these pages.

Vocabulary Strategy

REVIEW UNFAMILIAR WORDS
Blackline Master 45

Objectives

- To encourage critical thinking
- To develop word identification
- To recognize word meanings

Materials

One copy of Blackline Master 45 per child; scissors

Have children point to each bug and then point to its name. Then tell them to cut out the puzzle pieces. Have them mix up the pieces and match each word with its corresponding picture.

INFORMAL ASSESSMENT

Have children locate the word *spider* on page 111 and then frame the word with their hands. Invite them to look at the illustration to help them identify the word. You may also wish to help children read aloud pages 108–111. Have them search for details that help them recall this bug's name. Repeat the exercise with the other bugs.

© McGraw-Hill School Division

Name________________________________ Date_______________

What Bug Is It?

	Details	
	Details	
	Details	
	Details	
	Details	

Main Idea: ______________________________

© McGraw-Hill School Division

Name______________________________ Date_____________

Beginnings and Endings

 sit snag	 fat flat
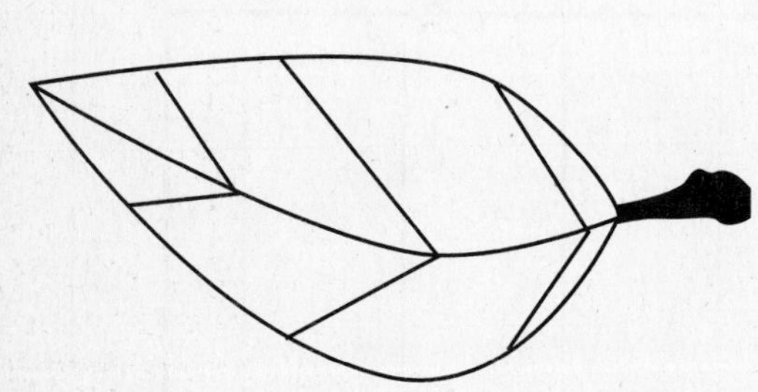 for off	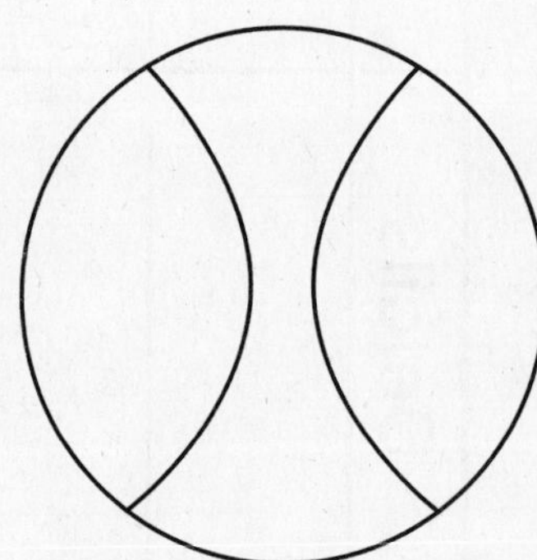 smack small

© McGraw-Hill School Division

Name________________________________ Date________________

Same Sounds

shut	shop	snow	snug
bath	with	flower	flag
duck	quack	hall	pill
slap	slot	pass	less
smog	smell	off	buff

© McGraw-Hill School Division

Name____________________________ Date______________

Bug Facts

digs a hill	is red with black spots
makes a web	has big, beautiful wings

makes a buzz

	has 6 legs	
	has 6 legs	
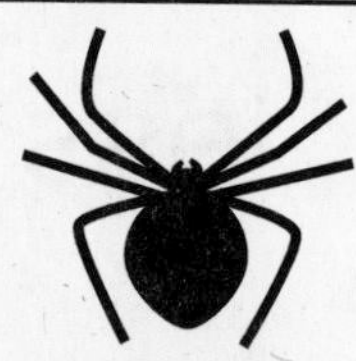	has 6 legs	
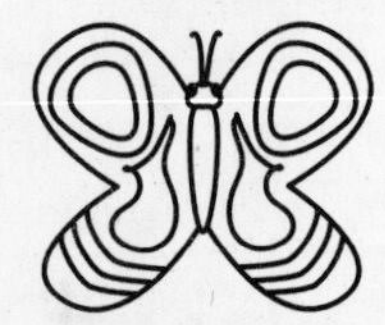	has 6 legs	
	has 6 legs	

© McGraw-Hill School Division

Name________________________________ Date______________

Bug Mix Up

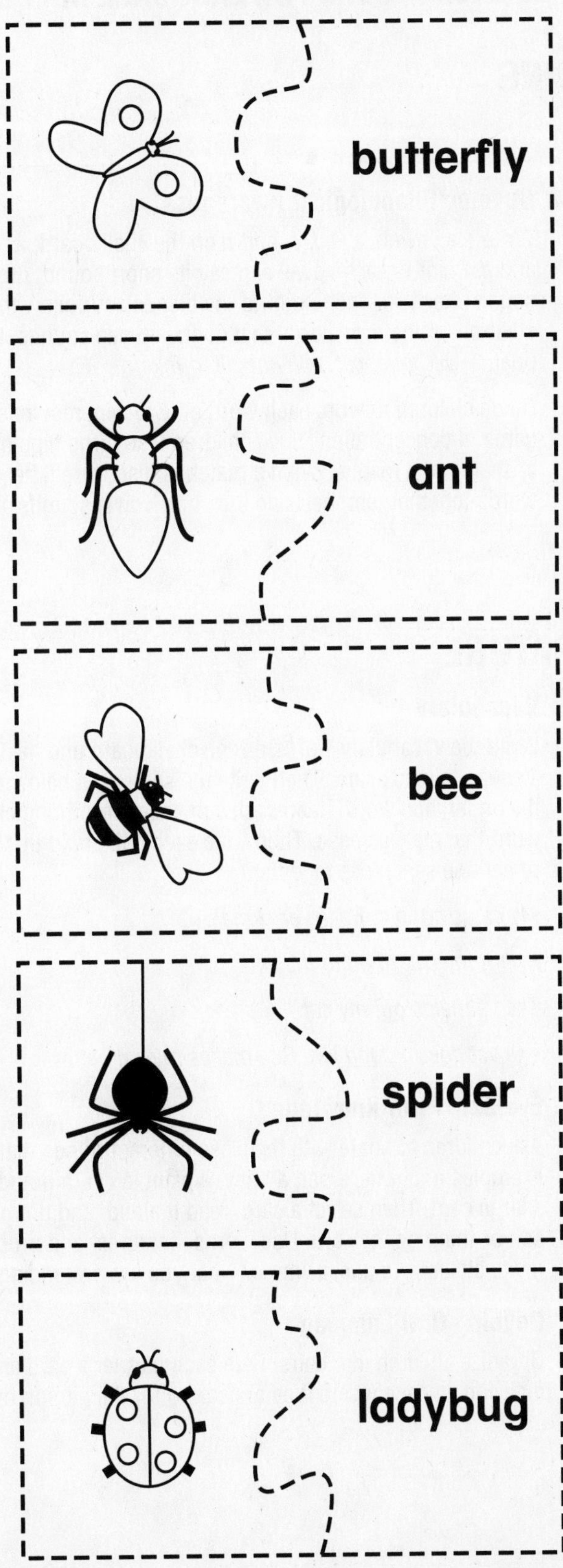

© McGraw-Hill School Division

A VET pp. 124A–137R

Time For Kids

BUILD BACKGROUND FOR LANGUAGE SUPPORT

I. FOCUS ON READING

Focus on Skills

OBJECTIVES: Listen for Short *a, e, i, o, u;* Listen for Blends

TPR
Children can hold up matching cards and call out, "Match!"

Develop Phonological Awareness

Write the vowels *a, e, i, o,* and *u* on the chalkboard, as well as the sound blends *nk* and *ll*. Point to each vowel and say its short sound, prompting children to say the sound after you. Then point to the blends and follow the same procedure. Help children brainstorm words that contain these sounds, including words from the poem—*vet, pup, cat, pill, hog, ill, drinks.*

Guide children to write each word on two separate index cards, and then play a class game of concentration. Have children take turns flipping two cards at a time face up in search of a match. When a match is discovered, help children read and say the words together, emphasizing the short vowel sounds and the blended sounds.

II. READ THE LITERATURE

VOCABULARY
small
out
good
want

Vocabulary

Write the vocabulary words on the chalkboard and have children copy each one onto a separate index card. Then write the sentences below on the chalkboard, omitting the underlined word. Read each sentence, prompting children to help you select the word that makes sense. Then have each child hold up the matching word card as you reread the sentences together.

My cat is not big. He is very small.

I want my cat to go to the vet.

The vet helps out my cat.

The vet does a good job. She makes my cat better.

CONCEPT
caring for something or someone

Evaluate Prior Knowledge

Ask children to share with the class different things that need to be cared for. Some examples might be: a pet, a baby, a plant, a car, a grandparent. Write each answer on a large card. Then select a card, read it aloud, and dramatize taking care of the person or thing on the card. Use words, gestures, and props in your dramatizations. Invite children to guess who or what you are pretending to care for.

Develop Oral Language

Organize children into pairs. Give each partner a card and have them take turns dramatizing a scene where they are caring for the person or thing on the card.

© McGraw-Hill School Division

nonverbal prompt for active participation	• Preproduction: *Show us* (point to class and self) *how you take care of* (item or person on card).
one- or two- word response prompt	• Early production: *Have you ever taking care of* (item or person)*? Do you think you could do this alone, or would you need help?*
prompt for short answers to higher-level thinking skills	• Speech emergence: *What is the* (item or person) *you are taking care of called? Who taught you how to take care of* (the item or person)*?*
prompt for detailed answers to higher-level thinking skills	• Intermediate fluency: *How do you feel about taking care of* (item or person)*? What (or who) else do you take care of?*

Guided Reading

Preview and Predict

Tell children that in this story, a woman works as a doctor, or vet, taking care of many different kinds of animals. People who live in the country and who have pets come to this vet, or they ask her to come to the place where their pet is sick or hurt. Say to children: *This vet helps a dog in her office. She goes to a farm to see a sick hog. She also takes care of other animals.*

Have children in need of language support pair up with English-speaking children. Go through the pictures in the book, stopping to ask questions along the way. Ask questions such as: *Who is the first animal we see the vet take care of? How does the vet take care of the cat? How does the vet take care of the duck? Does the vet only take care of small pets? What kind of animal do you think the vet will take care of next?*

GRAPHIC ORGANIZER
Blackline Master 46

Objectives

- To reinforce main idea and details
- To encourage critical thinking
- To reinforce key concepts

Materials

One copy Blackline Master 46 per child; pencils; crayons

Help children recall and then write or draw a detail from the story in each of the top three boxes. Then have them use these details to identify the main idea of the story. Help them write the main idea of *A Vet* in the bottom box.

Have children work in groups of four. Children can take turns asking other group members for details from the story that tell more about the main idea.

© McGraw-Hill School Division

III. BUILD SKILLS

Comprehension

REVIEW STORY ELEMENTS
Blackline Master 47

Objectives

- To reinforce characters and plot
- To reinforce word identification
- To use illustrations
- To reinforce story comprehension

Materials

One copy Blackline Master 47 per child; scissors; paste or glue

Have children look over the letter that the vet has written to a friend. Explain that in the letter, the vet tells her friend about the work she does. Read aloud the letter with children. Help them cut out the picture cards at the top of the page. Then guide them to paste each picture in the proper place in the letter.

INFORMAL ASSESSMENT

Direct children to the photographs on page 129 to assess their understanding of story elements including characters and plot. Ask them who appears in these photographs. (the vet, a cat, and a duck) Then ask them to describe what the characters are doing. (The vet is helping the cat and duck. The cat and the duck are hurt.) Repeat the exercise on page 130.

Comprehension

MAIN IDEA AND SUPPORTING DETAILS
Blackline Master 48

Objectives

- To encourage critical thinking
- To reinforce main idea and supporting details
- To reinforce story concepts

Materials

One copy Blackline Master 48 per child; pencils

Help children read the two sentences at the top of the page and ask them to underline the sentence that best explains the main idea of the story. Then have children circle only the pictures that support, or tell more about, that idea.

INFORMAL ASSESSMENT

Direct children's attention to the photographs on pages 128 and 131. Ask children to explain the main idea in these photographs. (They both share how a vet helps animals.) Ask them what things in the photographs help show the main idea. Encourage children to share other examples from different pages.

© McGraw-Hill School Division

Vocabulary Strategy

REVIEW INFLECTIONAL ENDING *-ed*
Blackline Master 49

Objectives

- To review inflectional ending *-ed*
- To develop print awareness
- To develop spelling skills

Materials

One copy Blackline Master 49 per child; scissors

Read aloud the words on the word strip with children. Help them cut out the word strip and the two slits before the *-ed*. Then guide them to fit the word strip through the slits. Have them move the strip up and down and call out the words that are created with the ending *-ed*.

INFORMAL ASSESSMENT

To assess children's understanding of the inflectional ending *-ed*, have them work with a partner. Turn to page 130. Tell children to imagine this scene happened yesterday. Have teams volunteer to tell what happened in the past tense. For instance, a child might say: *The vet helped the hog.* Repeat the exercise on other pages, encouraging children to use words with the *-ed* ending.

Vocabulary Strategy

REVIEW UNFAMILIAR WORDS
Blackline Master 50

Objectives

- To recognize story vocabulary
- To use illustrations

Materials

One copy Blackline Master 50 per child; pencils

Have children read the words and look at the pictures. Then ask them to draw a line between each word and its corresponding picture.

INFORMAL ASSESSMENT

To assess children's understanding of the new vocabulary, turn to page 128. Have children locate the word *vet*. Help children read the text aloud and invite them to look at the accompanying picture. Have pairs take turns explaining the meaning of the word using clues from the text and the picture. Repeat the exercise on other pages, with words such as *horse, hog,* and *help*.

© McGraw-Hill School Division

Name________________________________ Date________________

What's The Main Idea?

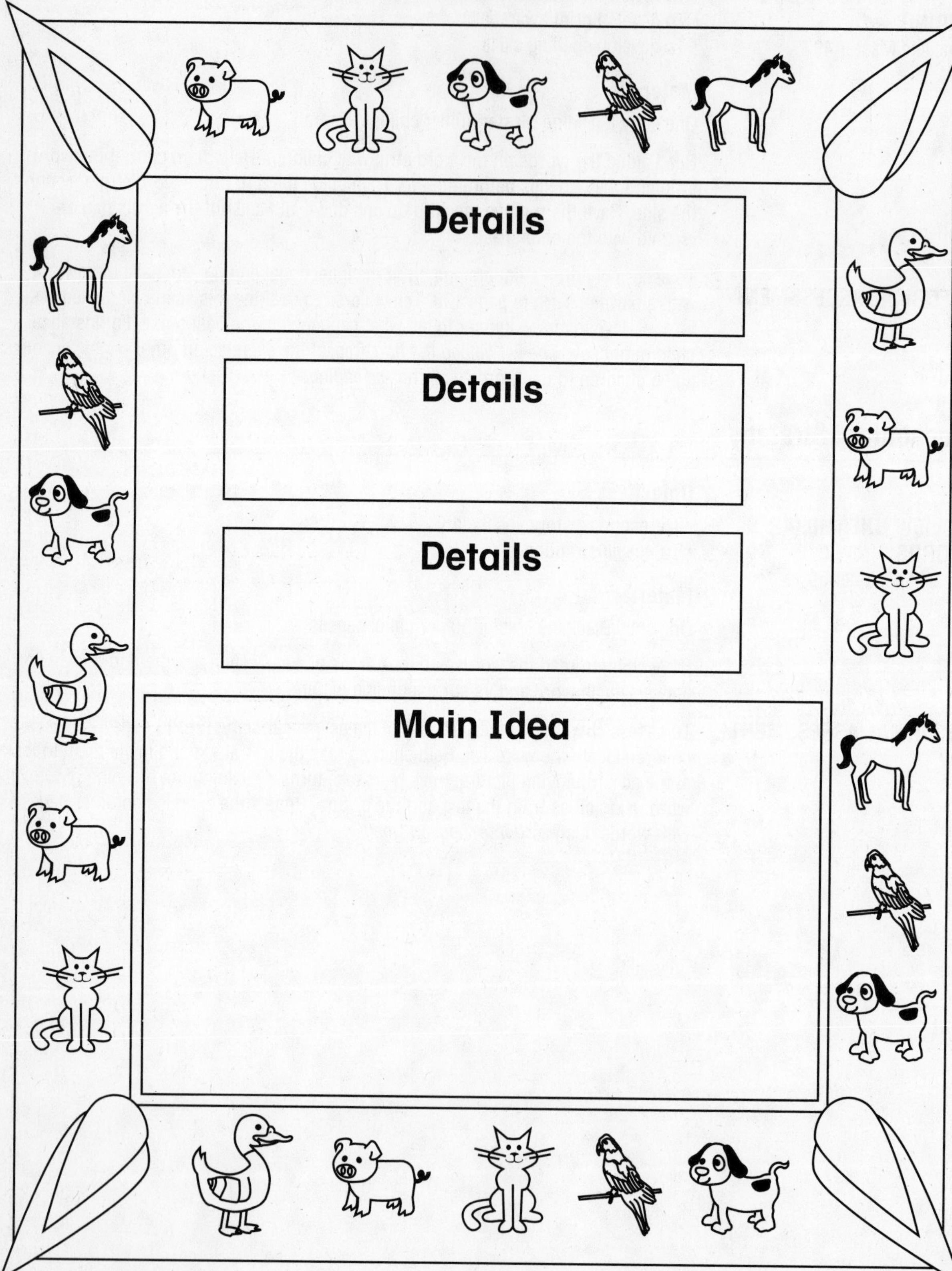

© McGraw-Hill School Division

Name________________________________ Date______________

Letter from a Vet

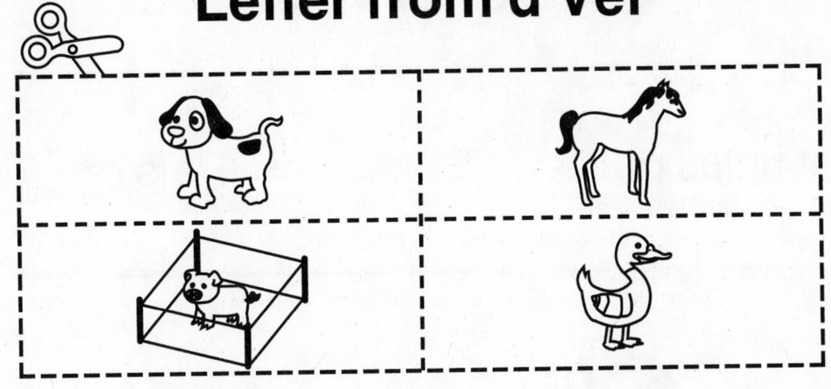

Dear Dan,

My job is fun.

This pet had a checkup. [ ]

This pet got help on a foot. [ ]

This sick pet got a visit in its pen. [ ]

This pet got help on a wing. [ ]

All the pets got well.

Love,

Pat, the Pet Vet

© McGraw-Hill School Division

Name________________________________ Date_______________

A Vet at Work

A vet helps pets.	Pets are fun.

© McGraw-Hill School Division

Name________________________________ Date_______________

Word Strip

look

help

walk

buzz

pass

---------------------------- ed

© McGraw-Hill School Division

Name_____________________________ Date______________

Vet Words

vet

hog

horse

© McGraw-Hill School Division

STAN'S STUNT pp. 8A–37R

Written by Lynn Plourde Illustrated by Pam Levy

BUILD BACKGROUND FOR LANGUAGE SUPPORT

I. FOCUS ON READING

Focus on Skills

OBJECTIVE: Listen for Blends *nt, st, ng, mp, fl,* and *sk*

TPR

Develop Phonological Awareness

Write the following blends on the chalkboard: *nt, st, ng, mp, fl, sk.* Say the sound each blend represents, and then have children say the sounds with you. Help children brainstorm words that contain the blends, write them on the chalkboard, and invite children to circle or underline blends.

Then read the poem "Circus Stunts," asking children to stand and stomp when they hear a word that contains the blends *nt* and *st.* Repeat with the remaining blends.

II. READ THE LITERATURE

VOCABULARY
their
would
try
fall

Vocabulary

Write the following sentences on the board:

Stan's pals held their noses so they would not smell the skunk.

"I would like to do my stunt," said Stan. Stan will try Bat's stunt. Stan went upside down like Bat. "Do not fall!" yelled Stan's pals.

Encourage children to read these sentences aloud, helping them as necessary. As you say each vocabulary word, have children go to the board and underline the word with colored chalk. Then prompt volunteers to act out the scene as you reread it, asking them to hold their noses, raise their hands to try a stunt, and say, "Do not fall!"

CONCEPT
woodland animals

Evaluate Prior Knowledge

Bring in a poster or a large photograph of a forest. Tell children that this is a picture of a forest, where all kinds of animals live. Invite children to talk about some of the animals that live in the woods.

Then staple or tape large sheets of butcher paper to the wall. Encourage small groups to use crayons, markers, or paints to create woodland scenes. Let each child add a woodland animal to her or his scene.

© McGraw-Hill School Division

Develop Oral Language

Invite children to describe the animals they added to the woodland scenes.

nonverbal prompt for active participants

- Preproduction: *Show us* (point to class and self) *what your woodland animal is like.*

one-or two-word response prompt

- Early production: *Does your woodland animal live in (*name a woodland habitat, such as a tree, a cave, or a stream)*? Does it eat* (name foods)*?*

prompt for short answers to higher-level thinking skills

- Speech emergence: *What is your woodland animal called? Where does it live? What does it eat?*

prompt for detailed answers to higher-level thinking skills

- Intermediate fluency: *What can you tell us about* (name of animal)*? Why did you choose this animal?*

Guided Reading

Preview and Predict

Tell children that in this story a skunk named Stan wants to show his friends a stunt, or a good trick. Explain that every time he starts to do his stunt, his friends ask him not to. Tell children: *Whenever Stan starts to do his stunt, his friends stop him and show him a stunt they know instead. Stan then copies each of his friends' stunts.*

Then lead children on a picture walk through the story illustrations to reinforce the concept of woodland animals. Ask questions such as: *What stunt do you think Stan the skunk wants to show his friends? What animals do you see in this picture? What stunt do you think an owl might do? What stunt do you think the frog is doing? What stunt do you think the bat can do? What other stunts might the animals do?*

GRAPHIC ORGANIZER
Blackline Master 51

Objectives

- To reinforce story comprehension
- To practice following directions

Materials

One copy of Blackline Master 51 per child; crayons; scissors; paste or glue; craft sticks

Ask children to color in each picture and then cut them out. Next, have them paste the back of each picture to a craft stick. Invite children to work in groups of four to retell the story with the puppets they have made.

© McGraw-Hill School Division

III. BUILD SKILLS

Phonics and Decoding

REVIEW BLENDS
Blackline Master 52

Objectives

- To develop print awareness
- To practice word identification
- To reinforce sound/symbol correspondence
- To review blends

Materials

One copy of Blackline Master 52 per child; pencils

Help children read the tongue twister aloud, using the illustrations as aids. When they have finished reading, have them circle the words containing the same beginning sound as the word *skill*, then underline the words with the same beginning sound as *stop*. Invite children to read the tongue twister a few more times, as quickly as they can.

INFORMAL ASSESSMENT

To assess children's recognition of the continuant blends *sk* and *st*, write these blends on the chalkboard and turn to page 12. Have pairs of children take turns identifying the words containing *sk* and *st* (stunt, Stan, skunk) and saying them aloud.

Phonics and Decoding

REVIEW STOP BLENDS
Blackline Master 53

Objectives

- To practice following directions
- To reinforce word identification
- To develop print awareness
- To review blends

Materials

One copy of Blackline Master 53 per child; pencils

Have children read along in silence as you read each sentence aloud. Ask them to then underline the two words in each sentence that have the same ending sound.

INFORMAL ASSESSMENT

Explain to children that in this story some words end with the letters *nk, nt,* and *mp.* Write these blends on the chalkboard and say them aloud with children. Then turn to page 20 and read the text aloud. Ask children to identify words containing any of these sounds. (stunt, jump, bump) Repeat the exercise on page 15, with the words *stunt, blink, wink,* and *Stan.*

© McGraw-Hill School Division

Comprehension

INTRODUCE SETTING
Blackline Master 54

Objectives

- To practice recognition of setting
- To encourage creative thinking
- To use illustrations
- To follow directions

Materials

One copy of Blackline Master 54 per two children; scissors

Help children understand that all stories happen in a certain place or places. Provide some examples of the many places where a story could occur, explaining that each place is called the story's *setting.* Then help children cut out the story character and each setting. Invite pairs to place the girl in each setting and create a story in their own words. Encourage children to share their stories with the class.

INFORMAL ASSESSMENT

To assess children's understanding of settings, have them look at the illustrations on pages 22 and 23. Ask them to describe the story's setting. (the woods) Ask children why they think this story takes place in this setting. (Animals like skunks, frogs, owls, and bats live in the woods.)

Vocabulary Strategy

INTRODUCE POSSESSIVES
Blackline Master 55

Objectives

- To reinforce print awareness
- To use illustrations
- To encourage critical thinking
- To support hands-on learning
- To introduce possessives

Materials

One copy of Blackline Master 55 per child; pencils

Tell children that when an apostrophe and *s* are added to the end of a character's name, it means that something belongs to that character. Explain that each picture on the right side of the page belongs to a character on the left side of the page. Help children read each line of text aloud, then have them draw a line between each character and its corresponding possession. When children are finished, invite them to write their own names with an apostrophe and *s* at the end, then draw a picture of something that belongs to them.

INFORMAL ASSESSMENT

Turn children's attention to the text on page 13. Point out the words *Stan's* and *pals.* Have children work in pairs to decide which word means that something belongs to a character. (Stan's) You may also wish to ask them who has something (Stan) and what that character has. (pals) Repeat the exercise on page 15 with the words *Owl's* and *lids.*

© McGraw-Hill School Division

Name______________________________ Date______________

Story Puppets

© McGraw-Hill School Division

Name______________________________ Date______________

Tongue Twister

The  sat on the 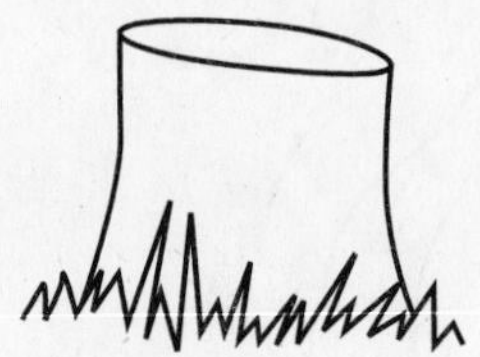.

The  thought the 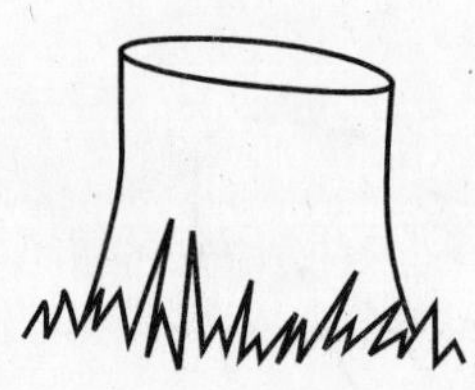.

The  thought the  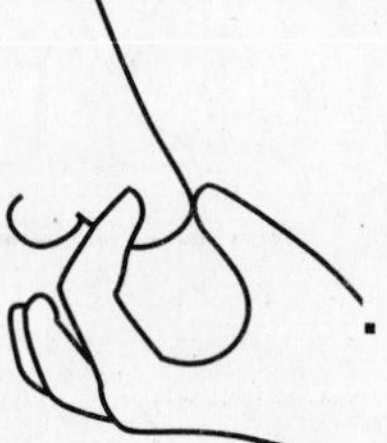.

© McGraw-Hill School Division

Name______________________________ Date______________

Ending Sounds

We can sing a song.

There is sand by the pond.

Sift the sand to make it soft.

The small hill is green

© McGraw-Hill School Division

Name______________________________ Date______________

Settings

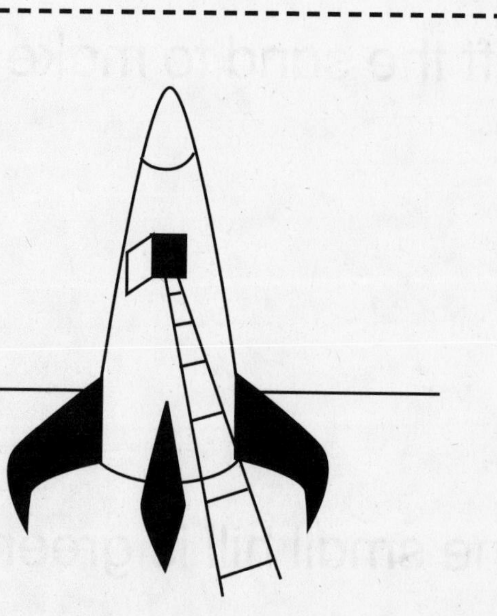

© McGraw-Hill School Division

Name________________________________ Date______________

Who Does It Belong To?

Owl's lids

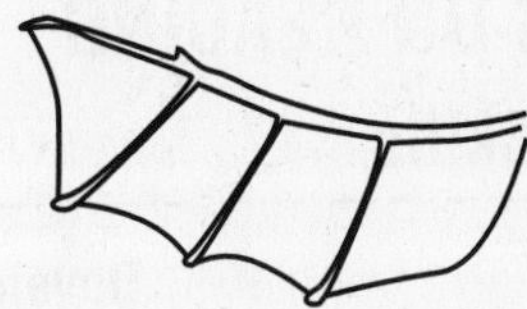

Frog's legs

Bat's wing

Stan's tail

Stan's pals

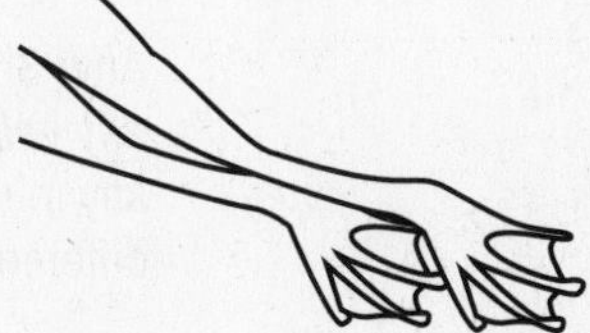

____

- -

____

© McGraw-Hill School Division

GREG'S MASK pp. 38A–67R

Written by Ann McGovern Illustrated by Winky Adam

BUILD BACKGROUND FOR LANGUAGE SUPPORT

I. FOCUS ON READING

Focus on Skills

OBJECTIVE: Listen for Blends *pl, dr, sl,* and *cl*

TPR
Have children act out each sentence as they say it. Encourage them to emphasize *loud* in the first example.

Develop Phonological Awareness

After reading the poem, "Drips! Drops!" write the following lines on the chalkboard:

The drops are big and loud.

Brett and Glen slip and slop

As they play and dig.

For the first line, underline and say the word drops, emphasizing the /dr/ sound. Then say other words (drink, dress, black) and have students clap when they hear the same beginning sound as in *drag.*

Follow the same procedure with *slip* (slide, slam, bed), and *play* (plant, rock, plot).

II. READ THE LITERATURE

VOCABULARY
old
grow
any
new

Vocabulary

Act out the following sentences for the class:

Old: Hold up an old, used crayon. Say: *I have an old crayon.*

New: Hold up a new, unused crayon. Say: *I have a new crayon.*

Invite students to make up other sentences describing objects as *old* or *new*.

Grow: Draw a small tree. Then say: *This tree will grow bigger.* Invite a child to draw a tree that demonstrates this concept. Continue asking children to draw pictures and use the word grow to show the progression of a tree or other living thing that grows as it develops.

Any: Show children a set of crayons, 3 yellow, 3 brown, and 3 green. Ask: *Do I have any yellow crayons?* Say: *No, I don't have any yellow crayons.* Invite children to use any in other question-and-answer sentences about the crayons, as well as with different groups of similar objects.

CONCEPT
sibling relations

Evaluate Prior Knowledge

Bring in photographs and pictures showing siblings relating to each other in different ways. Point to the people in each picture and identify them as sisters or brothers. Ask children to describe what the sisters and brothers are doing and how they seem to be getting along. Write children's responses on the chalkboard. For example, they might say, *They are having fun; They are mad at each other; They are making something.* Then have pairs act out a sibling scene, using sentences from the board.

© McGraw-Hill School Division

Develop Oral Language

nonverbal prompt for active participation

- Preproduction: *Show us* (point to class and self) *how sisters and brothers might get along.*

one- or two-word response prompt

- Early production: *Do you have a sister or brother? Do you play together? If you don't have a brother or sister, do you wish you did?*

prompt for short answers to higher-level thinking skills

- Speech emergence: *What do you like to do with your brother(s) and/or sister(s) ? Do you ever get mad at your brother(s) and/or sister(s)?* For students who don't have siblings, ask: *If you had brothers or sisters, what would you like to do with them?*

prompt for detailed answers to higher-level thinking skills

- Intermediate fluency: *How do you feel when your sister or brother is nice to you? How do you feel when she or he is not very nice? How do you treat your sister or brother?* For students who do not have siblings, ask questions such as: *If you had a brother or sister, how would you treat him or her? How would you help your brother or sister? How might your brother or sister help you?*

Guided Reading

Preview and Predict

Tell children that in this story a young boy named Greg needs to make a mask for his class skit. (You may want to review the meaning of the word *skit* at this time.) He has a lot of fun making it. But when he shows it to his sister, Tam, his feelings are hurt. Tell children: *Tam does not show her brother Greg that she likes the mask. Greg is so sad that he throws the mask away.* Have children sit in a circle as you lead them on a picture walk through the story. As you stop to ask the following questions, have children take turns briefly acting out their answers. Ask questions such as: *What does Greg do at the start of the story? What does Greg do as he works? How do you think Greg feels about his mask? What does Greg do when he is done making the mask? How does Tam feel about Greg's mask?Why do you think she feels this way? How does that make Greg feel? How does Tam make Greg feel better? What does Greg do for Tam? How do the two children seem to feel at the end of the story? How do you know this?*

GRAPHIC ORGANIZER
Blackline Master 56

Objectives

- To reinforce understanding of settings
- To encourage creative thinking

Materials

One copy of Blackline Master per child; crayons; scissors; paste

Have children look over the two pictures. Help them discover that one picture shows a kitchen in a home and the other picture shows a school classroom. Tell children to color in the pictures, cut them out, and then paste them to separate sheets of construction paper. Invite them to listen as you read, "Greg's Mask." As they listen, they can hold up the appropriate card for each scene.

Ask partners to take turns asking each other questions about where certain scenes in the story take place. Each child can answer by holding up the appropriate card.

© McGraw-Hill School Division

III. BUILD SKILLS

Phonics and Decoding

REVIEW BLENDS
Blackline Master 57

Objectives

- To practice following directions
- To reinforce blending and spelling
- To practice word identification
- To develop print awareness

Materials

One copy of Blackline Master 57 per child; scissors; paste

Have children cut out the letter cards at the top of the page. Then have them paste each card in the blank space that has the same background as the card. Have children read aloud each word that is created. Finally, invite children to act out each word.

INFORMAL ASSESSMENT

To assess recognition of blends, have children work in pairs. Point to the text on page 42 and tell them there are two words that contain the sound *sk*. Call on teams to share the words they find. (skit, mask) Turn to page 46 and repeat the exercise with the blend *tw* (twist), and to page 50 to repeat the exercise with the blend *tr* (trash).

Phonics and Decoding

REVIEW BLENDS
Blackline Master 58

Objectives

- To review blends
- To use illustrations
- To practice word identification

Materials

One copy of Blackline Master 58 per child; pencil

Have children look over each illustrated book cover. Then tell them to circle the appropriate letters in order to complete the book's title. Invite children to choose one of the books and tell a story based on the title and the cover.

INFORMAL ASSESSMENT

Direct children to page 52 and read aloud the sentence, "It was time for the skit." Ask children to identify the word that contains the blend *sk*. Repeat the exercise on page 59 with *sn* and the sentence, "Snip it here." (snip)

© McGraw-Hill School Division

Comprehension

INTRODUCE COMPARE AND CONTRAST
Blackline Master 59

Objectives

- To develop compare-and-contrast comprehension
- To reinforce print awareness
- To practice following directions

Materials

One copy of Blackline Master 59 per child; scissors; paste

Invite children to look at the two masks from the story and note how they are similar to and different from each other. Help them read and cut out the words at the top of the page. Then guide them as they paste each phrase in the appropriate column of the chart. When children are finished, invite them to take turns reading their charts aloud.

INFORMAL ASSESSMENT

Have children turn to the illustrations on pages 56 and 57. Ask them how the masks the children are wearing are alike. Then ask them to describe how the masks are different. Ask children whether they agree with Tam's choice of a favorite mask. Ask children: *Which is your favorite mask? Why?*

Vocabulary Strategies

REVIEW POSSESSIVES
Blackline Master 60

Objectives

- To develop print awareness
- To reinforce possessives
- To practice critical thinking

Materials

One copy of Blackline Master 60 per child; pencil

Have children look at each illustration on the left and right sides of the page. Explain that each item on the right belongs to someone on the left. Then have children write in the appropriate space the name of the child to whom the item belongs. Help them read the completed phrase aloud.

INFORMAL ASSESSMENT

To assess children's understanding of possessives, turn to the illustration on page 44 and ask: *Who is watching?* (Greg's cat is watching.) Write the sentence on the board and point out how the apostrophe *–s* indicates *belonging.* Invite students to find examples of objects in the story that belong to specific characters, and create questions that require a possessive answer. As an example, ask: *On pages 46–47, whose room are the children in?* A response might be *They are in Tam's room.* Discuss how the possessive is used in each response you transcribe on the chalkboard.

© McGraw-Hill School Division

Name______________________________ Date____________

Settings

© McGraw-Hill School Division

Name________________________________ Date_______________

New Words

tw
cl
sk
pl
tr
pr

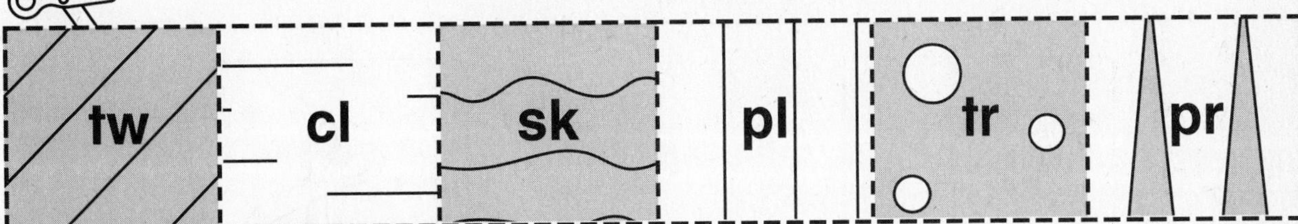

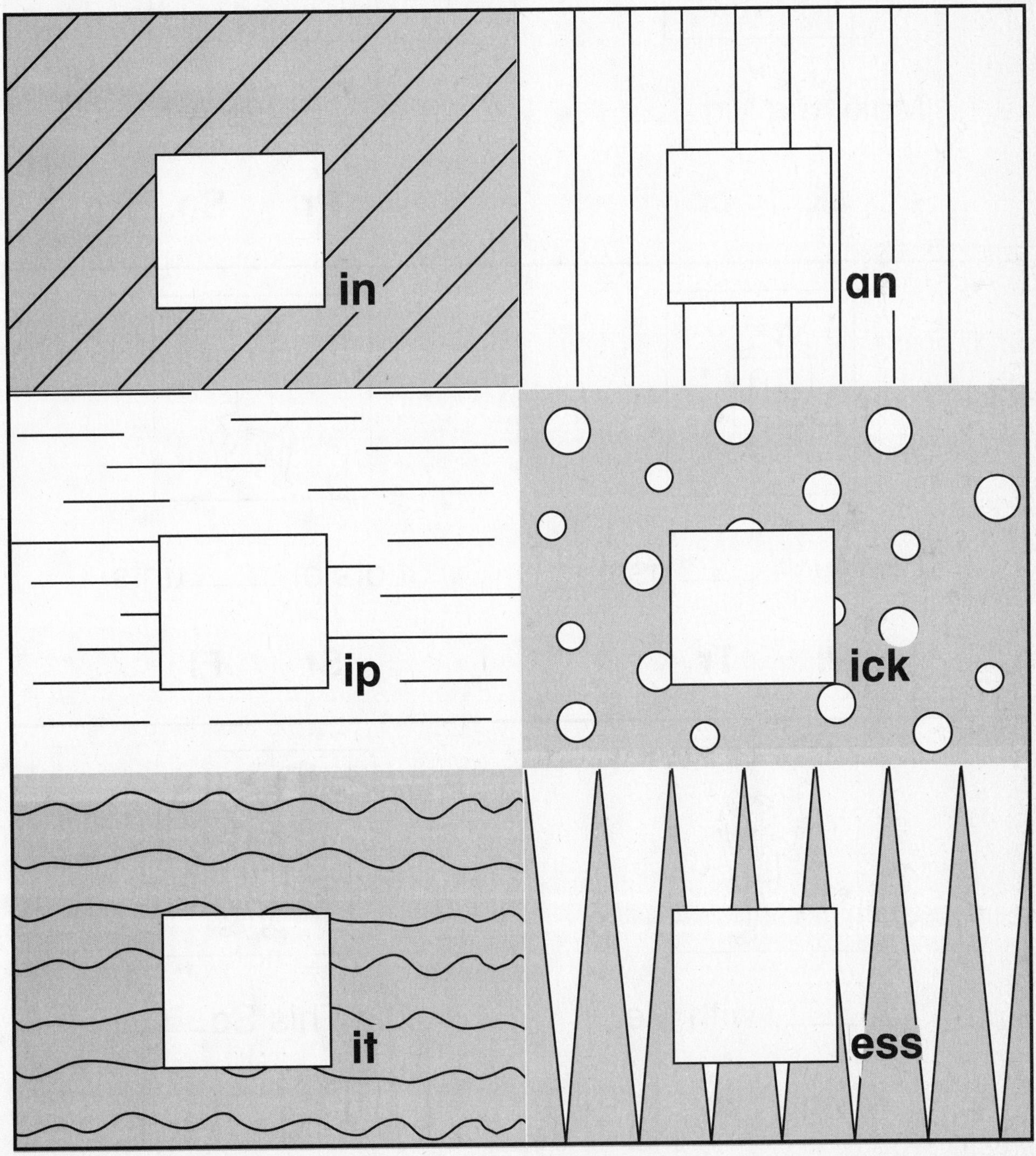
in
an
ip
ick
it
ess

© McGraw-Hill School Division

Name______________________________ Date______________

Look at Books

 Making a Ma_____ **sk** **cr**	 _____ip Art **Pr** **Sn**
 Too Much _____ash! **Pl** **Tr**	 Lots of _____unts **St** **Fl**
 Ju_____ with Me **ng** **mp**	 Dig This Sa_____ **nd** **ng**

© McGraw-Hill School Division

Name ______________________ Date ____________

Same and Different

made of paper	for class skit	painted
size	color	owner

looks like an animal

© McGraw-Hill School Division

Name______________________________ Date______________

Whose Is It?

Ken

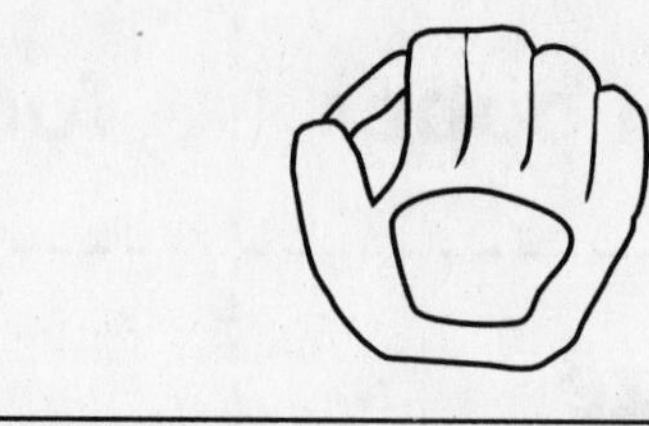

_______________'s glove

Mary

_______________'s shoe

Pat

_______________'s mitten

Rick

_______________'s jam

© McGraw-Hill School Division

SAM'S SONG pp. 92–93

Written by Alyssa Satin Capucilli Illustrated by Melissa Iwai

BUILD BACKGROUND FOR LANGUAGE SUPPORT

I. FOCUS ON READING

Focus on Skills

OBJECTIVE: Listen for Digraphs *ch, wh,* and *nk*

Develop Phonological Awareness

As a class, make up a series of tongue twisters containing the digraph *ch.* For example: *The child chomps on a chip.* Ask children to say the sentences aloud, identifying words in which they hear /ch/. As they identify each word, write it on the chalkboard. Repeat the exercise with the digraphs *wh* and *nk. (Why does that whale have whiskers? Hank has a stuffed pink skunk.)*

TPR
Children can whistle, chomp, or blink when they hear words with *wh, ch,* or *nk.*

II. READ THE LITERATURE

VOCABULARY
together
eat
too
now

Vocabulary

Invite children to play a game of "Find the Word." Organize the group into two teams. Write the vocabulary words on the board for both teams. Then invite one child from each team to the board and ask them to erase the word you call out. If a child erases the incorrect word, rewrite it. Play until one team erases all the words.

CONCEPT
learning something new

Evaluate Prior Knowledge

Ask children to name things they have recently learned to do or would like to learn to do. Write their responses on the chalkboard. Ask one child to work with you as you model teaching how to do one of the activities. For instance, you might help a child learn how to tie her or his shoe.

Next, invite children to then work in pairs to learn something new from each other. They can learn something real, such as making a paper airplane, or pretend to learn something, such as how to drive a car.

Develop Oral Language

nonverbal prompt for active participation

- Preproduction: *Show us* (point to class and self) *what you are learning to do.*

one- or two-word response prompt

- Early production: *Are you learning how to* (name activity)*? Have you wanted to learn to* (name activity) *for a long time?*

prompt for short answers to higher-level thinking skills

- Speech emergence: *What are you learning to do? Where do you* (do the activity)*?*

prompt for detailed answers to higher-level thinking skills

- Intermediate fluency: *What is hard about learning to do* (name activity)*? What is easy about it? Why do you want to learn to* (name activity)*?*

© McGraw-Hill School Division

Guided Reading

Preview and Predict

Tell children that in this story a new baby owl named Sam is sad because she cannot sing like her brother Chuck or like her mom and pop. Explain that Sam tries to learn to sing, but nothing comes out. Tell children: *Sam wishes on a star one night, and soon she learns to sing. But she still thinks her song is too small and worries she will never learn to sing like her brother and her parents.* Guide children through the pictures in the book, stopping to ask questions such as the following: *What do Chuck, Mom, and Pop do under the moon? Who watches them sing? What does Sam do when her family sings? Why do you think Sam looks sad? Why do you think Sam is looking at the star? What does Sam finally learn to do? How do you think she feels?* Have children take turns giving short verbal answers.

GRAPHIC ORGANIZER
Blackline Master 61

Objectives

- To reinforce story characters
- To reinforce key story concepts
- To encourage and support hands-on learning

Materials

One copy of Blackline Master 61 per child; crayons; scissors; paste; craft sticks

Have children color in each of the pictures. Then help them cut out the pictures and paste them to craft sticks to make story puppets. Invite children to work in groups of four, using their puppets to act out the story as you reread it aloud.

As an alternate activity, help children punch small holes into the pictures after they've colored them, then thread the pictures with yarn to make necklaces. Have children discuss how each owl is similar to and different from the others.

III. BUILD SKILLS

Phonics and Decoding

REVIEW *ch, wh, nk*
Blackline Master 62

Objectives

- To review *ch, wh, nk*
- To use illustrations
- To encourage creative thinking
- To follow directions

Materials

One copy of Blackline Master 62 per child; pencil

Explain to children that the person in the picture is working in a studio to make sounds effects that will go with the sounds needed in some cartoons. The first cartoon needs a *whish!* sound for the firefly. The second cartoon needs a *crunch!* sound for the mouse to make while he eats a nut. The third cartoon needs the *plink! plunk!* sound a nut might make when falling from a tree. Have children draw a line matching each cartoon to an object that could make the necessary sound.

INFORMAL ASSESSMENT

To assess children's recognition of the blends *wh, ch,* and *pl,* have them work in pairs. Turn to page 88, and ask each team to identify and write a /wh/ word, *whish.* Then turn to page 89 and have teams write down the /pl/ words, *plink* and *plunk.* Finally, turn to page 90 and ask teams to write down the /ch/ word, *Chuck.* When children are done writing, call on different teams to read their words aloud.

© McGraw-Hill School Division

Phonics and Decoding

REVIEW *ch, wh, nk*
Blackline Master 63

Objectives

- To reinforce use of *ch, wh, nk*
- To reinforce spelling skills
- To support critical thinking

Materials

One copy of Blackline Master 63 per child; pencil

Have children choose and write a blend from the top of the page that will complete each word. When children are finished writing, call on children to answer the questions at the bottom of the page.

INFORMAL ASSESSMENT

Turn to the illustration on page 72 and ask children what object in the picture has *-ch* at the end of its name. *(branch)* Then turn to the picture on page 74 and ask children which owl has a name that starts with *Ch-*. *(Chuck)* Next, turn to the picture on page 84 and ask children what the star does that ends in *-nk. (wink)* Finally, turn to page 88, and ask what sound that starts with *wh-* the firefly makes. *(whish, whish)* Allow children to answer the last question in chorus.

Comprehension

REVIEW COMPARE AND CONTRAST
Blackline Master 64

Objectives

- To use illustrations to compare and contrast
- To reinforce critical thinking

Materials

One copy of Blackline Master 64 per child; pencil; crayons

Help children read each question. Then have them circle the picture in each pair that correctly answers the question. Children may wish to color all the pictures when they are done.

INFORMAL ASSESSMENT

To assess children's understanding of similarities and differences, help them find the text and illustration on page 90. Invite children to read the text aloud, then ask: *How is Sam like the mouse?* (He is small.) *How is he different from the mouse?* (He has feathers; the mouse does not, and so on.) Now have children work in pairs to compare similarities and difference. Children can also repeat this exercise on other pages. For instance, on page 93, children might want to compare and contrast the four owls.

Vocabulary Strategy

INTRODUCE CONTRACTIONS
Blackline Master 65

Objectives

- To reinforce understanding of contractions
- To develop word identification
- To recognize word meanings

© McGraw-Hill School Division

Materials

One copy of Blackline Master 65 per child; scissors

Explain to children that when two words are put together with an apostrophe and some letters from the words are taken out, the new word is called a contraction. Help children cut out the puzzle pieces and mix them up. Then challenge them to match the pieces again to show each contraction with the two words that formed it.

INFORMAL ASSESSMENT

To assess children's recognition of contractions, turn to page 76, and tell them to look for the contraction that means *it is.* Repeat the exercise on page 83, asking children to identify the contraction that means *let us.* Invite children to find other contractions in the story.

© McGraw-Hill School Division

Name_______________________________ Date_______________

Story Puppets

© McGraw-Hill School Division

Name________________________________ Date________________

Sound Effects

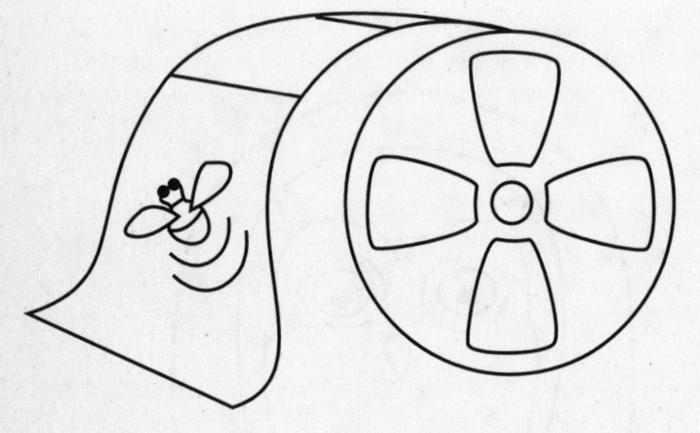

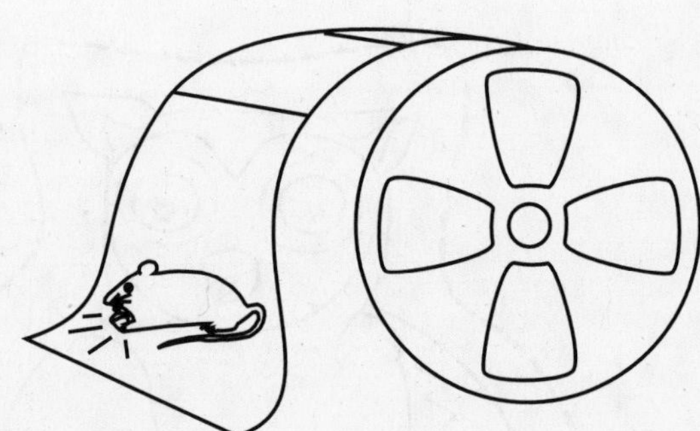

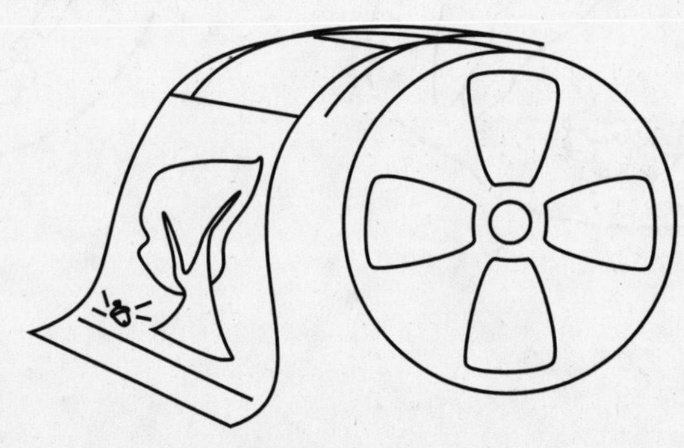

© McGraw-Hill School Division

Name_______________________ Date_____________

Questions and Answers

-ch	-nk	Wh-	Ch-

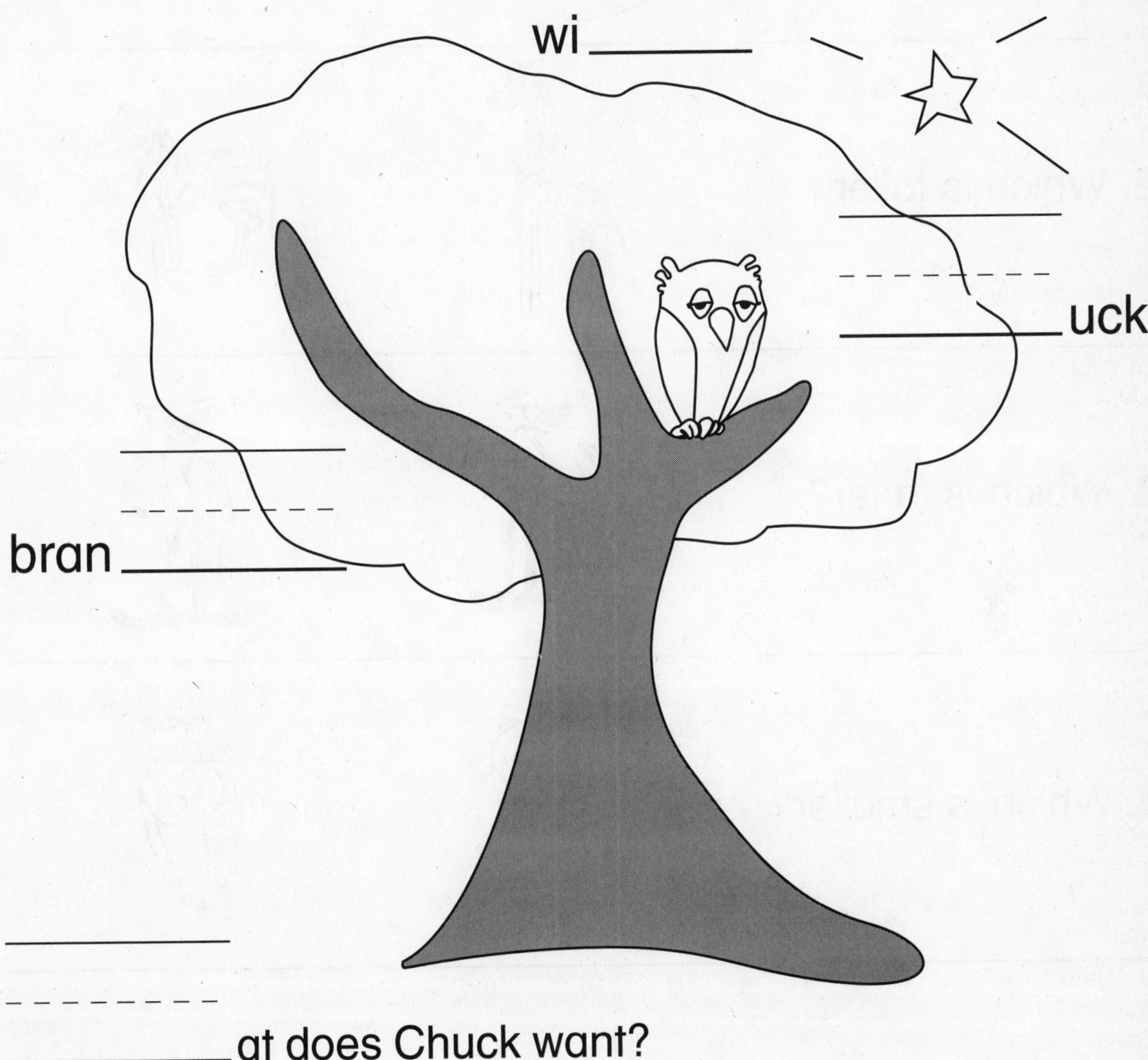

______at does Chuck want?

______ere is Chuck sitting?

© McGraw-Hill School Division

Name________________________ Date____________

Sizes

I. Which is bigger?

2. Which is taller?

3. Which is fatter?

4. Which is smaller?

5. Which is shorter?

© McGraw-Hill School Division

Name________________________________ Date______________

Contractions

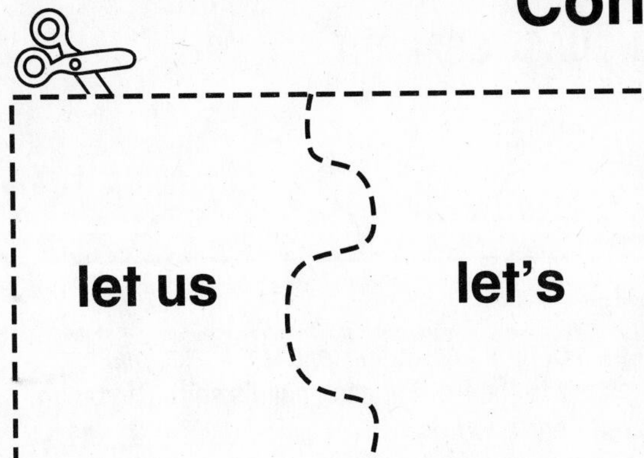

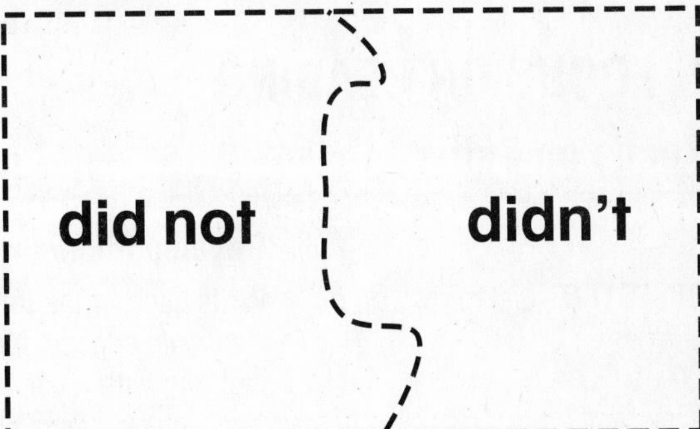

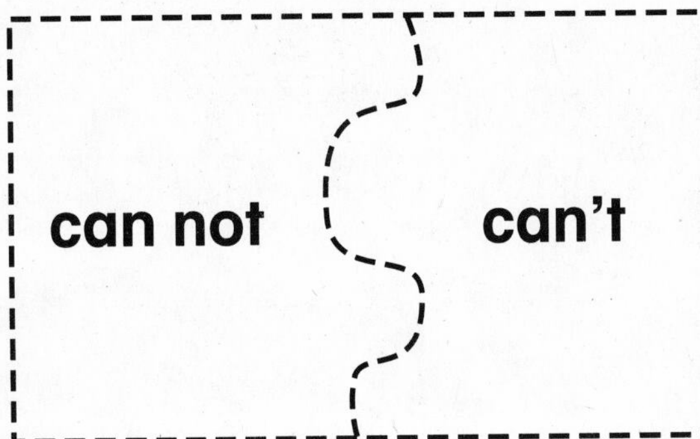

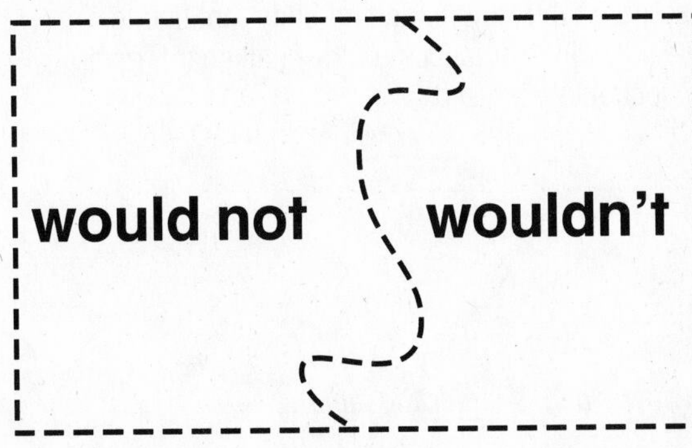

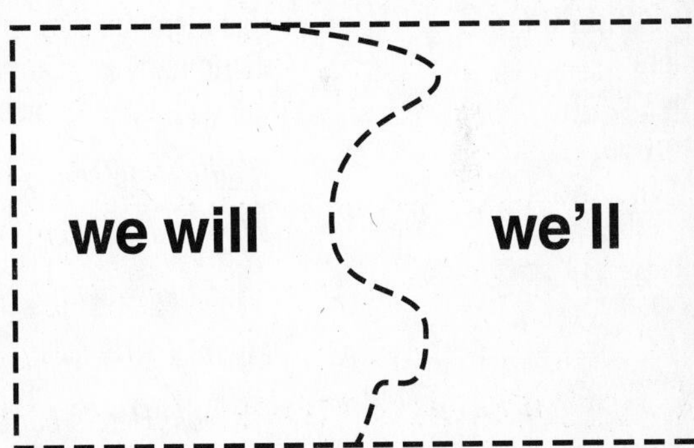

it is

it's

© McGraw-Hill School Division

SNAKES pp. 100–121

Written by Frances Minters

BUILD BACKGROUND FOR LANGUAGE SUPPORT

I. FOCUS ON READING

Focus on Skills

OBJECTIVE: Listen for Long *a: a_e*

Develop Phonological Awareness

Write each of the following words on a different card: *snake, cake, shake, plane, crane, lane, gaze, haze, maze.* Pin a card to the front of each child's shirt. (If you are working with more than nine children, repeat words.)

After you read each child's shirt, ask them to repeat the word. Then help children organize themselves into groups of rhyming words. Guide them to say aloud the words in each group.

TPR
After discussing each word's meaning, invite children to demonstrate their words with sound effects or motions as other children try to guess the words.

II. READ THE LITERATURE

VOCABULARY
where
why
know
under

Vocabulary

Use a stuffed dog, small ball, classroom table, and hand and body motions to demonstrate vocabulary. Write the following sentences on the chalkboard, read them aloud, and discuss how the vocabulary is used.

Where is my dog?

Why is she under the table?

I don't know why she is there.

My dog is under the table.

Oh look! Here's her ball! That's why my dog is under the table.

Ask children to take turns using gestures and facial expressions to act out each sentence. You may want to demonstrate the first sentence by, for example, looking confused and holding hands shoulder-level, palms up, as you say: *Where is my dog?*

Finally, review each sentence, asking children to underline vocabulary words with colored chalk. Give children the opportunity to make up some new sentences; write them on the chalkboard and ask them to underline the vocabulary word in each one.

© McGraw-Hill School Division

CONCEPT
reptiles

Evaluate Prior Knowledge

For each pair of children in your class, you'll need to bring in two copies of at least six different photographs or illustrations of reptiles.

After discussing the pictures with children, invite them to play "Go Reptile", a version of the classic game "Go Fish". Start by helping children create a playing deck of six matching reptile cards (twelve cards altogether). Partners shuffle the deck and deal three cards each. Children should place the remaining cards in a pile at the center of their playing surface.

Develop Oral Language

Players take turns asking one another if they have a certain reptile in their hands. If a player has the requested card, he or she must give it away to the opponent. If a player does not have a requested card, the person must "fish" from the center pile of cards. When all the cards are gone, the person with the most pairs, wins.

nonverbal prompt for active participation

- Preproduction: *Show me* (point to self) *your reptile cards.*

one- or two-word response prompt

- Early production: *Do you have a* (name reptile) *in your cards? Do you have a* (name another reptile) *in your cards?*

prompt for short answers to higher-level thinking skills

- Speech emergence: *What kind of reptiles are in your card deck? What game do you play with the cards? How do you play?*

prompt for detailed answers to higher-level thinking skills

- Intermediate fluency: *What does a* (name reptile) *look like? How would you feel if you saw a* (name reptile)*?*

Guided Reading

Preview and Predict

Tell children that, in this story, they will learn about snakes from all over the world. Explain that this story shows where snakes live, how they eat, how they shed their skin, and how they hatch from eggs when they are babies. Tell children: *Snakes are reptiles. They live in all kinds of places, like deserts and forests. Most snakes do not hurt people, but some are dangerous. Snakes are different from other land animals because they do not have legs.* Then invite children needing language support to work in pairs with English-speaking children as you lead them on a picture walk through the story. Pause at the pictures to ask questions such as: *In what kinds of places do these reptiles live? What do you think snakes eat? How do snakes move around? What does a snake do with its old skin? How do baby snakes hatch? What do you think baby snakes will grow to be like?* Have language-support children offer verbal responses as their partners write them down.

GRAPHIC ORGANIZER
Blackline Master 66

Objectives

- To encourage critical thinking
- To develop understanding of comparisons and contrasts
- To develop understanding of key concepts

Materials

One copy of Blackline Master 66 per child; pencil; crayons

Tell children to look at the left column labeled *same.* As they read, they will draw or write one or two phrases that show how all snakes are the same. In the right column labeled *different,* they will draw or write a phrase that shows how snakes can be different.

© McGraw-Hill School Division

III. BUILD SKILLS

Phonics and Decoding

INTRODUCE LONG *a: a_e*
Blackline Master 67

Objectives

- To introduce long *a: a_e*
- To develop print awareness
- To practice following directions

Materials

One copy of Blackline Master 67 per child; scissors; paste

Help children cut out both snakes along the dotted lines. Then have them paste the a snake along the grass path on the left and the e snake along the grass path on the right. Invite children to read aloud the words that are formed and to use each word in a sentence of their own.

INFORMAL ASSESSMENT

To assess children's understanding of the long *a: a_e* sound, direct their attention to page 104. Identify the words *snakes* and *harm* and say the words aloud. Invite children to work in pairs to decide which word contains the long *a: a_e* sound. Repeat the exercise on page 107 with the words *make* and *mouth.*

Phonics and Decoding

REVIEW BLENDS: LONG *a: -ake*
Blackline Master 68

Objectives

- To practice blending skills
- To review long *a: -ake*
- To practice following directions

Materials

One copy of Blackline Master 68 per child; scissors

Help children cut out the letter strip and cut along the dotted lines of the oven. Show them how to thread the letter strip through the slits and move it to form different *-ake* words. Have them read each *-ake* word they form.

INFORMAL ASSESSMENT

Turn children's attention to the text on page 111 and explain that there are two words that contain *-ake.* Have them work in pairs to find and write the words *lake* and *snake.* When they are finished writing, call on teams to name the *-ake* words.

© McGraw-Hill School Division

Comprehension

REVIEW SETTING
Blackline Master 69

Objectives

- To reinforce understanding of setting
- To support hands-on learning
- To encourage creative thinking

Materials

One copy of Blackline Master 69 per child; crayons

Remind children that *setting* is the word used to describe where a story takes place. Invite them to draw themselves or another character in each of the three settings shown on the page. When they are done, ask children to share a story that may go with the setting and the character they have created. You may also wish to encourage children to draw and tell about other settings.

INFORMAL ASSESSMENT

To assess children's understanding of settings, turn, for example, to page 103 and ask children to identify the setting in each photograph. (desert; forest) Repeat the exercise on other pages.

Vocabulary Strategy

REVIEW CONTRACTIONS
Blackline Master 70

Objectives

- To reinforce understanding of contractions
- To follow directions
- To reinforce word identification

Materials

One copy of Blackline Master 70 per child; scissors

Help children cut out the apostrophe squares at the top of the page. Ask them to read aloud each word, then cover the dark part with an apostrophe. Prompt them to read the words again, guiding them to see that the new form, called a *contraction*, is a shorter way to say the words they read before.

INFORMAL ASSESSMENT

Turn to page 107 and ask children to identify the two words that could form the contraction, *that's.* (that is) Then turn to page 108 and have children identify another contraction (can't) and tell from which two words the contraction is made. (can not)

© McGraw-Hill School Division

Name____________________________ Date________________

Something About Snakes!

Snakes

Same	**Different**

© McGraw-Hill School Division

Name_______________________________ Date____________

Snakes in the Grass

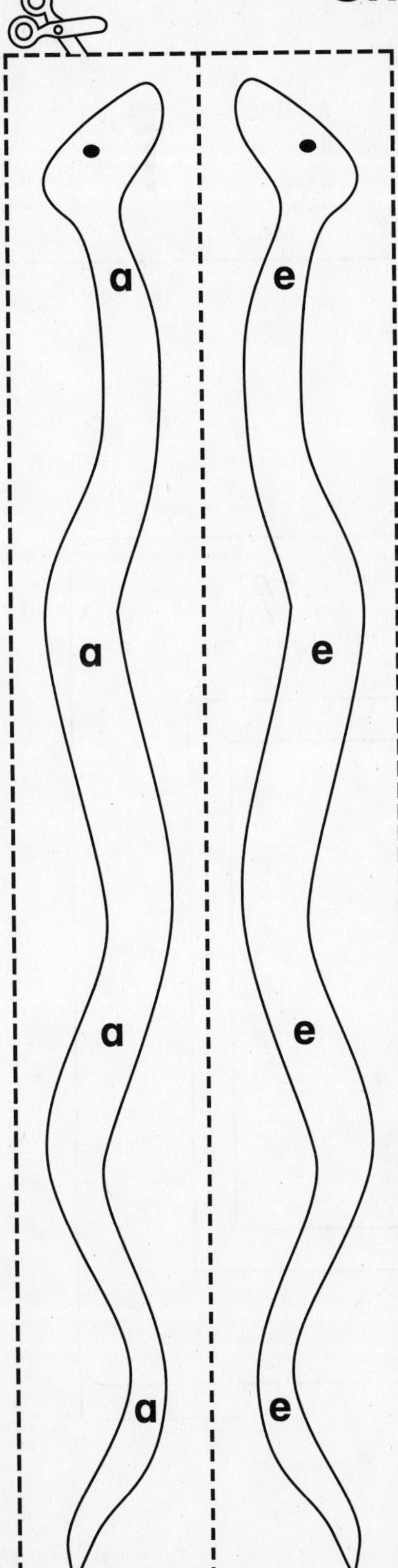

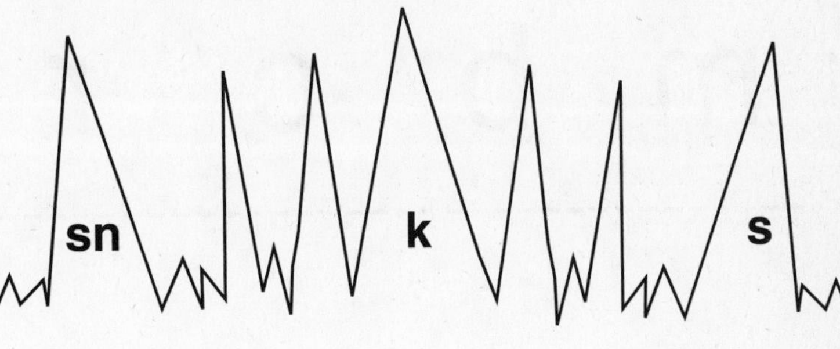

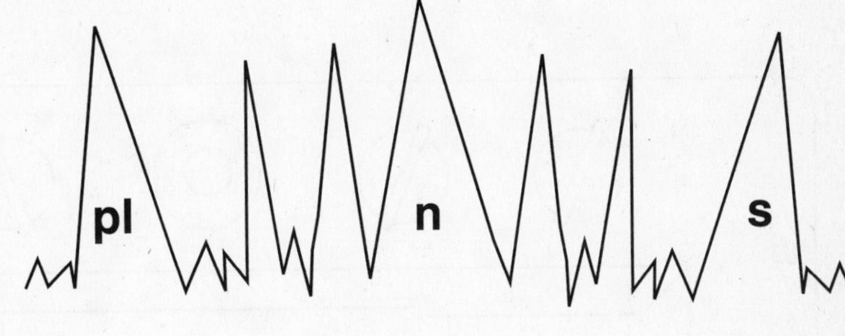

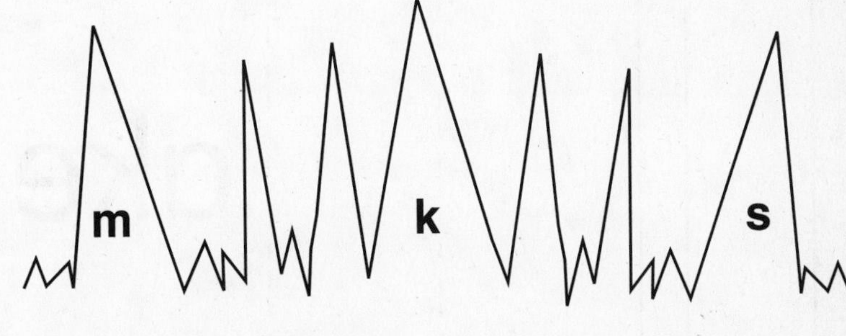

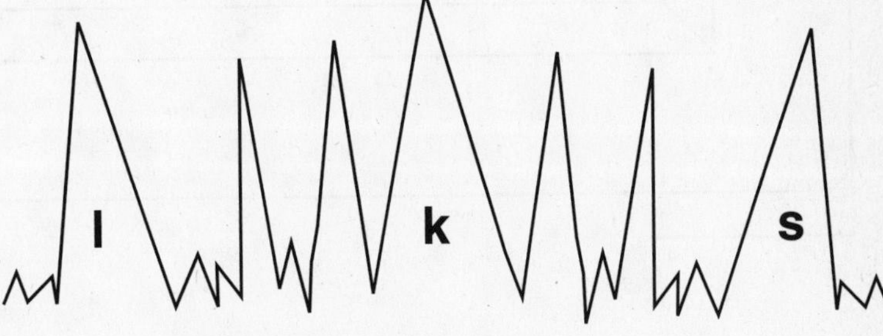

© McGraw-Hill School Division

Name______________________ Date____________

Letter Strips

m b c r l f

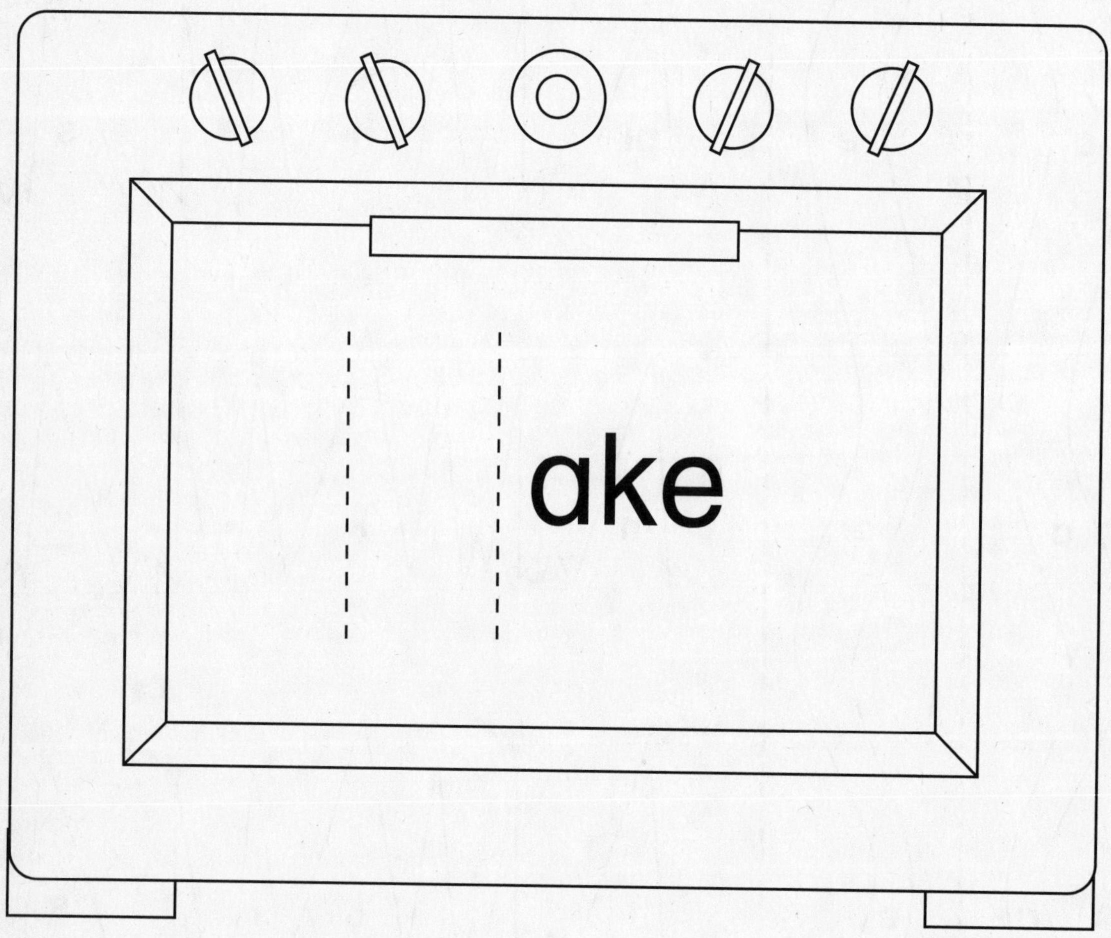

© McGraw-Hill School Division

Name________________________________ Date______________

Get Set

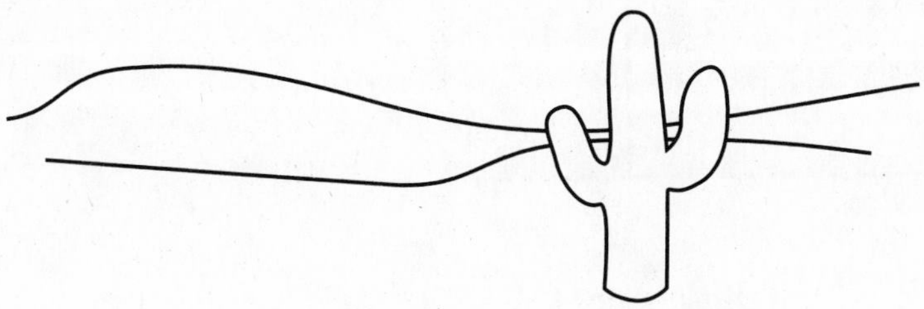

© McGraw-Hill School Division

Name________________________________ Date______________

Shorter Words

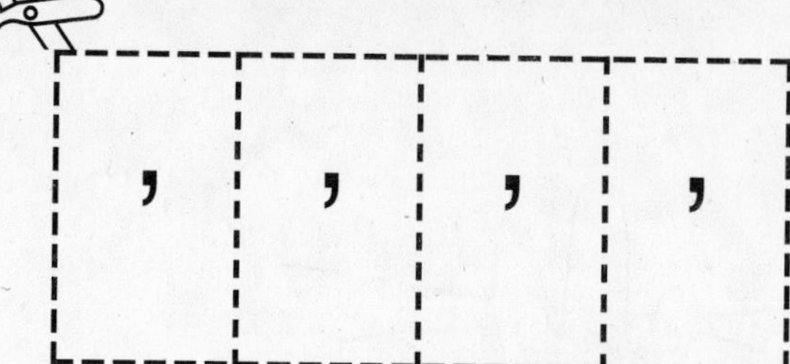

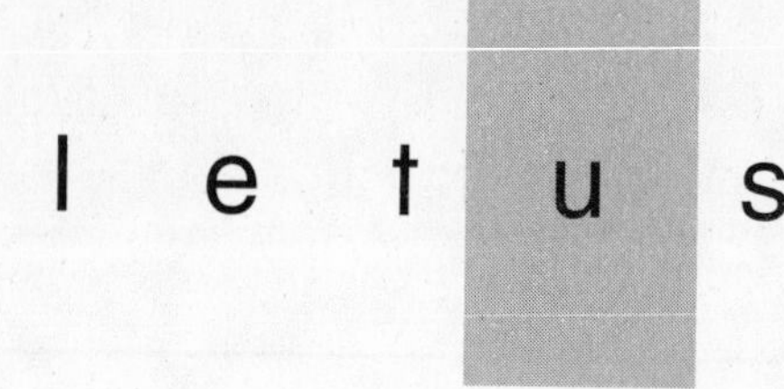

l e t u s

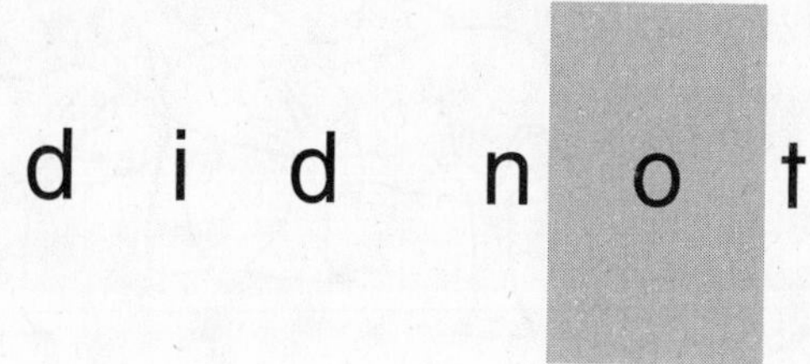

d i d n o t

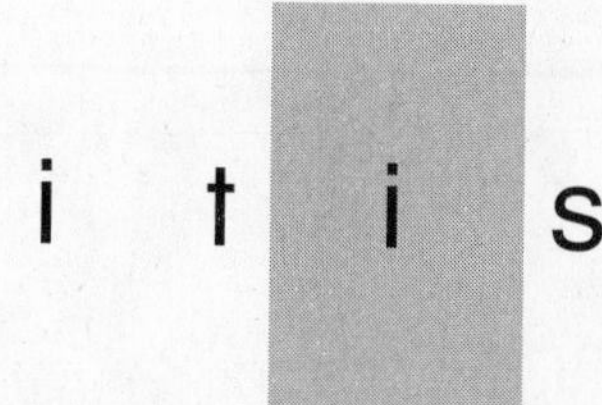

i t i s

c o u l d n o t

© McGraw-Hill School Division

LET'S CAMP OUT PP. 128–135

Time For Kids

BUILD BACKGROUND FOR LANGUAGE SUPPORT

I. FOCUS ON READING

Focus on Skills

OBJECTIVE: Listen for long *a: a_e; ch, wh, nk* blends

TPR
Students can use colored chalk to draw circles around words with the same blend.

Develop Phonological Awareness

Write the word shake on the chalkboard and read it to children. Demonstrate how to shake your legs, head, arms, and so on, and have children mimic you. Say *bake, make, hat, snake, bike, lake, cake,* and *sand.* Then ask children to shake a part of their bodies each time they hear a word that rhymes with *shake.*

Review blends by writing the following words on the board: *lunch, chat, branch, white, whale, sink, skunk.* Read each word, emphasizing the sound the blend represents. Help children identify words that contain the same blend.

II. READ THE LITERATURE

VOCABULARY
under
old
eat
try

Concept
camping

Vocabulary

Write the following sentences on the chalkboard. Read the sentences and pantomime the action of each.

Let's eat by that rock.

Oh no! There's something under the rock!

Let's try to pick it up to see!

Look! It's an old map!

Ask children to identify the vocabulary words, and let one child come to the board and underline them.

Provide props, and guide two children to pantomime the actions while you read the sentences aloud.

Evaluate Prior Knowledge

Bring in books about camping or camping equipment and photographs of outdoor scenes (especially in national or state parks) and wild animals. Help children see the common elements in all of the pictures. They may also be able to share personal camping experiences.

Develop Oral Language

Invite small groups to draw and label pictures of what they would take and what they might see on a camping trip. Let each group present their "camping trip" to the class, using their pictures as aids.

For children who have never been on a camping trip, adjust the following questions to address their "fantasy" camping trips.

© McGraw-Hill School Division

nonverbal prompt for active participation	• Preproduction: *Show us* (point to class and self) *where you go camping. Show us the animals you see.*
one- or two-word response prompt	• Early production: *Do you bring a tent on your trip? Do you go with friends? Do you see some animals?*
prompt for short answers to higher-level thinking skills	• Speech emergence: *What are some things you do on your camping trip? Where do you like to camp?*
prompt for detailed answers to higher-level thinking skills	• Intermediate fluency: *Why do you like to camp? What is hard about camping? Where would you like to go camping the next time?*

Guided Reading

Preview and Predict

Tell children that this is a story about camping out. Explain that it shows what you need to take and what you can do while camping. Tell children: *There are many things to see while camping. There are animals and birds. There are trees and rocks. At night there are stars. It is also fun to sit by the fire and eat outside.*

Then pair English-speaking children with children needing language support. Lead children on a picture walk using the story illustrations to reinforce the concept of camping. Have the English-speaking children record the answers of their partners as you ask the following questions: *What is the family doing at the beginning of the story? What does the family do when they get to the campsite? What does the family see on their hike? How do they make a fire? How do you think they feel as they eat around the campfire? What does the family see at night? What do you think they will see tomorrow?*

GRAPHIC ORGANIZER
Blackline Master 71

Objectives

- To encourage creative thinking
- To use illustrations
- To develop concept of camping

Materials

One copy Blackline Master 71 per child; crayons

Have children draw pictures in each circle of the web to show things people might see or do while camping. When they are done, invite children to share and talk about what they drew and why.

To reinforce the concept of setting, have children draw four different places where people might go camping. For instance, children might draw a seashore setting in one circle.

© McGraw-Hill School Division

III. BUILD SKILLS

Comprehension

REVIEW COMPARE AND CONTRAST
Blackline Master 72

Objectives

- To reinforce understanding of compare-and-contrast
- To use illustrations
- To reinforce concept of camping
- To use critical thinking

Materials

One copy Blackline Master 72 per child; scissors; paste

Help children understand that camping out can be both similar to and different from living at home. Ask them to cut out the pictures at the top of the page. Then read the questions at the bottom of the page and tell children to paste each picture on the chart beneath either the tent or the building.

INFORMAL ASSESSMENT

To assess children's understanding of comparisons and contrasts, turn to the photograph on page 133 and ask: *What are these people doing that they would also do at home?* (They are eating together.) *How is it different from eating at home?* (They are eating around a campfire instead of at a table.) Repeat the exercise on page 135, asking about how bedtime is the same and different while camping.

Comprehension

REVIEW SETTING
Blackline Master 73

Objectives

- To reinforce understanding of setting
- To encourage critical thinking

Materials

One copy Blackline Master 73 per child; crayons

Remind children that the setting of a story is when and where the story takes place. Invite them to complete each picture, adding whatever details they wish, to create story pictures of the two children that might take place in the past, present, and future. Encourage children to use their drawings to tell a story about each setting.

INFORMAL ASSESSMENT

To assess children's recognition of settings, turn to the photograph on page 129 and ask where the story is taking place here. (a city)Then turn to the next page and ask about this setting. (woods or a country environment) You may also wish to ask children what time of day it is in the beginning and at the end of the story. (daytime; nighttime)

© McGraw-Hill School Division

Vocabulary Strategy

REVIEW POSSESSIVES
Blackline Master 74

Objectives

- To reinforce understanding of possessives
- To encourage hands-on learning
- To reinforce word identification

Materials

One copy Blackline Master 74 per child; scissors; paste

Explain to children that each picture on the right side of the page belongs to the words on the left side of the page. Have them cut out each square at the top of the page and paste it in the appropriate space to make a sensible phrase. Invite children to read each of the phrases aloud. Help them realize that these are things they might see while camping.

INFORMAL ASSESSMENT

Turn to the photograph of the bird's nest on page 131 and ask children: *Whose nest is this?* (a bird's nest) On page 133, repeat the exercise by pointing to a bowl one of the people is eating from and ask: *Whose bowl is this?* (the mother's bowl; the father's bowl, and so on) Finally, on page 135, ask: *Whose tent is this?* (the family's tent)

Vocabulary Strategy

REVIEW CONTRACTIONS
Blackline Master 75

Objectives

- To develop hands-on learning
- To practice following directions
- To reinforce understanding of contractions

Materials

One copy Blackline Master 75 per child; scissors; tape

Help children cut out the contraction machine on the right side of the page. Have them roll it into a cylinder, tape it together, and stand it on end. Next, help children cut out the circle and square word cards. Have them place a circle card "into" the machine, pretend to turn it on, then choose a square contraction card that might "come out of" the machine.

INFORMAL ASSESSMENT

To assess children's understanding of contractions, turn to page 129 and ask them to identify the contraction that means *let us*. Then invite children to use the contraction *let's* in sentences of their own.

© McGraw-Hill School Division

Name________________________________ Date______________

A Camping We Will Go

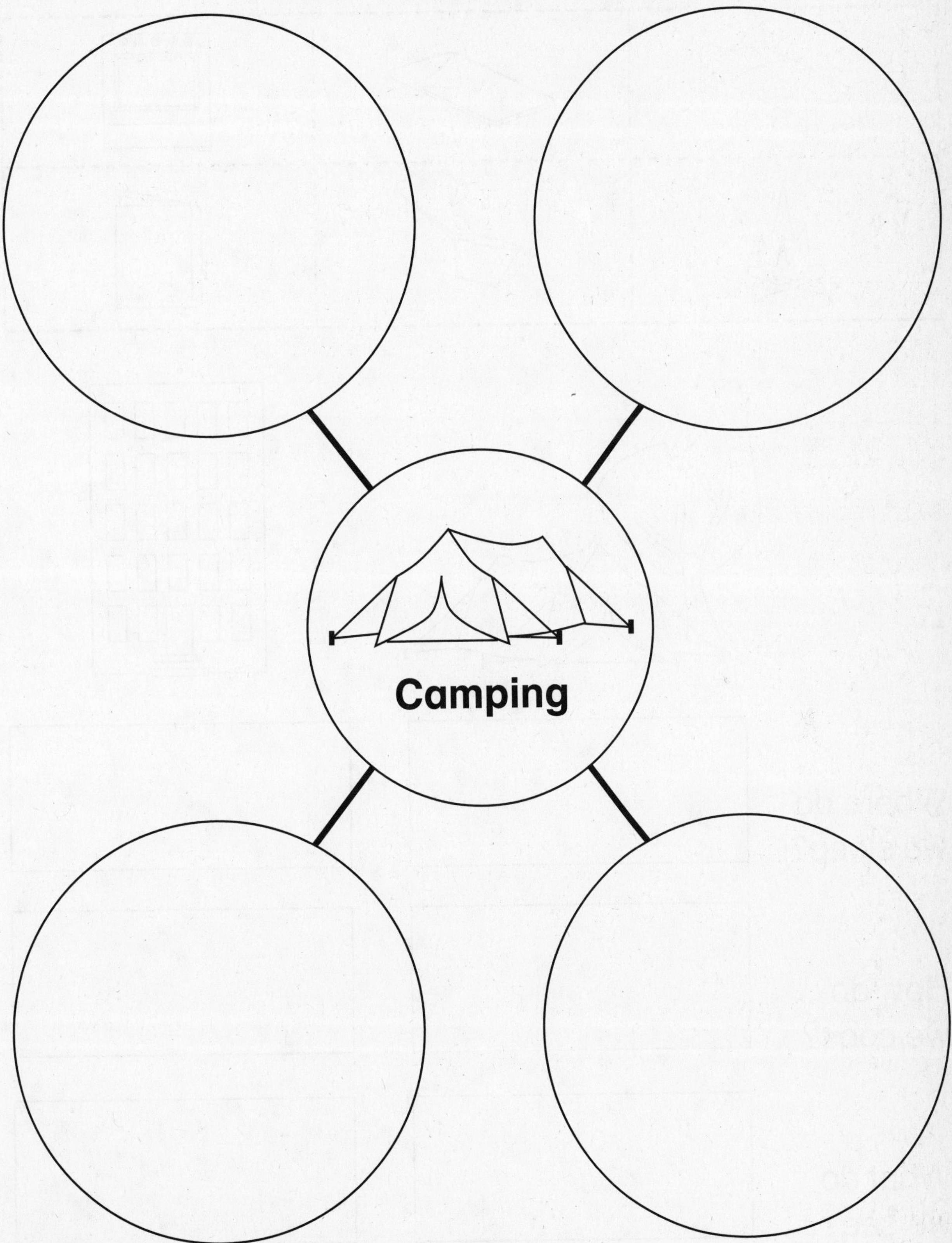

© McGraw-Hill School Division

Name_______________________________ Date_______________

At Home in the Woods

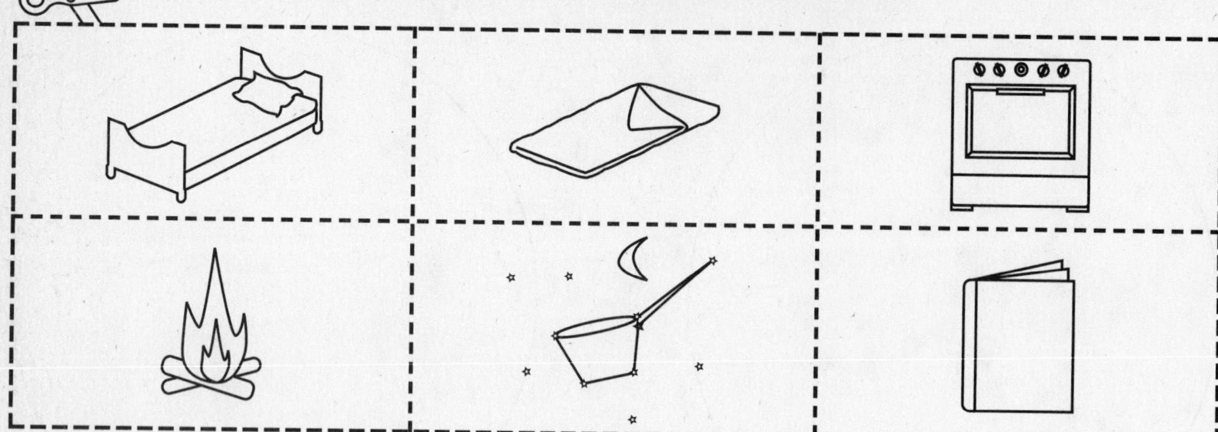

Where do we sleep?

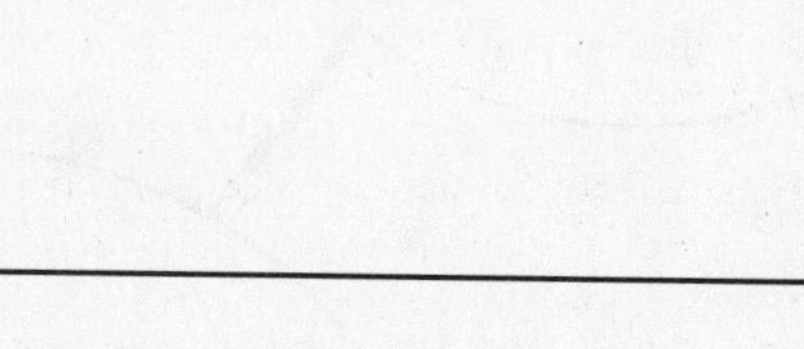

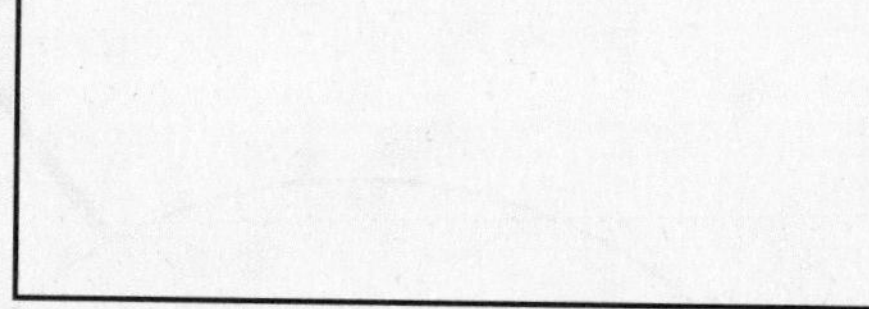

How do we cook?

What do we see?

© McGraw-Hill School Division

Name________________________________ Date______________

When Did It Happen?

A Story of Long Ago

A Story of Today

A Story of the Future

© McGraw-Hill School Division

Name ______________________ Date ____________

On a Hike

’s branch	’s track	’s skin
’s nest	’s spots	

a tree ____________________

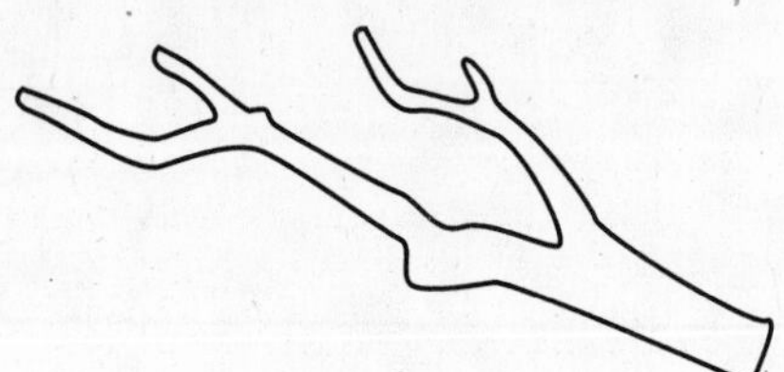

a deer ____________________

a snake ____________________

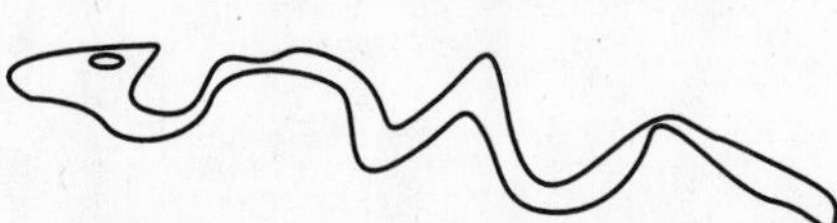

a bird ____________________

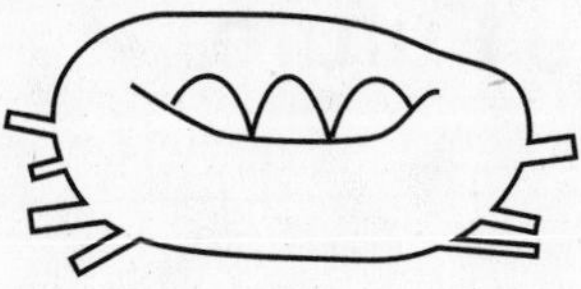

a ladybug ____________________

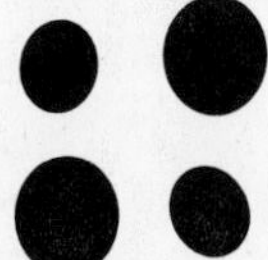

© McGraw-Hill School Division

Name_________________________ Date_______________

Making Contractions

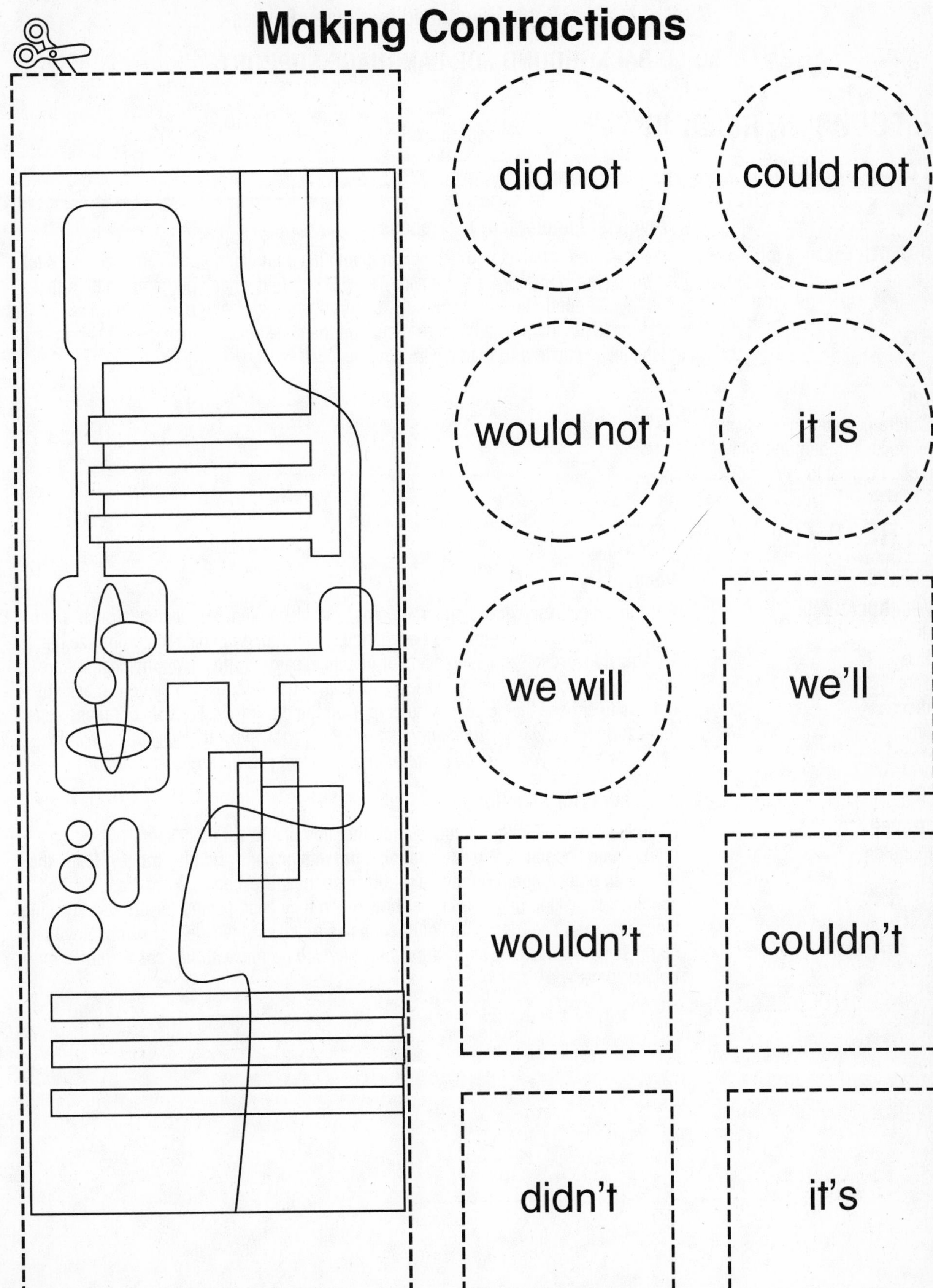

© McGraw-Hill School Division

THE SHOPPING LIST pp. 8A–37R

Written by Gary Apple Illustrated by Shirley Beckes

BUILD BACKGROUND FOR LANGUAGE SUPPORT

I. FOCUS ON READING

Focus on Skills

Develop Phonological Awareness

OBJECTIVE: Listen for long *i*

Have children listen as you recite a shopping list containing many long *i* words, such as *limes, pie, a tie, a kite,* and *a bike.* Tell children that when you name an item that has the /i/ sound, they should repeat the word, say *Fine!,* and make a thumbs-up gesture. Write the words children repeat on the chalkboard. When the list is complete, invite children to read it with you.

TPR
Children engage in physical responses to demonstrate recognition of long *i.*

II. READ THE LITERATURE

Vocabulary

VOCABULARY
always
blue
were
after
who

Print the vocabulary words on large cards, and place them on the chalk tray. As you give the following prompts, use body language and tone of voice to emphasize the vocabulary word in each sentence. For instance, say *I always hang my coat in here,* indicating the closet where you keep your coat. After saying each sentence, ask volunteers to choose the correct word card from the chalk tray. Try some of these sentences: *Show us what you do after school. Point to where we always hang our coats. Who sits next to you? Touch something blue. Were you hungry this morning?*

Evaluate Prior Knowledge

CONCEPT
shopping

Bring in some fruit, canned goods and other items, and set up a "store" where children can go shopping. Provide shopping baskets or bags and play money. Enlist the help of an older student or another adult to be the storekeeper. Dramatize selecting some items, asking the storekeeper how much they cost, paying for them, and taking them away in a bag. Verbalize your actions as much as possible. For example, you might say: *I need to buy some apples. How much do these apples cost? Here is one dollar. Thank you!*

© McGraw-Hill School Division

Develop Oral Language

Now invite children to shop for things in the store. Use prompts appropriate to their linguistic levels. For example:

nonverbal prompt for active participation

- Preproduction: *Pick up something you want to buy. Give the storekeeper one dollar.* (Model for children if necessary.)

one- or two-word response prompt

- Early production: *What do you want to buy? Do you have any more money?*

prompt for short answers to higher-level thinking skills

- Speech emergence: *What will you do with these things you buy? Do you want to buy something that is not here?*

prompt for detailed answers to higher-level thinking skills

- Intermediate fluency: *If you could buy anything you wanted, what would you buy? Why? Where would you buy it?*

Guided Reading

Preview and Predict

Tell children that in *The Shopping List,* Mike is sent to his dad's store with a list of things his mom wants him to buy. Explain that writing down what you need on a list can help you remember to get everything. Tell children: *Mike wrote some of the things his mom needed on his list. But there was something else he was supposed to get that he forgot to write down.* Then pair English-speaking children with those needing additional language support.

Lead children on a picture walk using the illustrations in the story to reinforce the concept of shopping. Have one child answer the questions as the fluent speaker records answers on paper. Ask questions such as: *How does the store look at the beginning of the story? What does Mike get for his mom? Why do you think Mike's dad and the others are taking other things off the shelves? What is happening to the store? What do you think Mike might have forgotten?*

GRAPHIC ORGANIZER
Blackline Master 76

Objectives

- To reinforce understanding of story details
- To support hands-on learning

Materials

One copy of Blackline Master 76 per child; colored pencils or crayons; student copy of *The Shopping List*

Look at the blackline master with children, asking them to identify the items on each shelf, as well as brainstorm other items that might belong there. As you read the story, stop to let children draw in items that are mentioned in the text but are missing from the blackline. (You may need to identify these items in the illustrations.) At the end of the story, have children draw what Mike had forgotten. (his dad) Encourage students to brainstorm reasons it might have been so difficult for the customers to figure out what Mike had forgotten.

© McGraw-Hill School Division

III. BUILD SKILLS

Phonics and Decoding

LONG *i*
Blackline Master 77

Objectives

- To form long *i: i_e* words
- To read long *i: i_e* words

Materials

One copy of Blackline Master 77 per child; scissors

Help children cut out the shapes on the page. Have them match up similar shapes and identify the letters on each. Explain that matching shapes will fit somewhere in the word frame *(_i_e)* to make a long *i* word. (For instance, *s* and *d,* both circles, can be arranged in the first frame to form the word *side.*) Ask students to work alone or with a partner to make long *i* words.

INFORMAL ASSESSMENT

To assess recognition of words with /i/: *i_e,* have children work in pairs to examine page 14 of the story. Encourage them to identify as many /i/:*i_e* words as they can. Have each team read the words they found.

Phonics and Decoding

REVIEW LONG *i* AND LONG *a*
Blackline Master 78

Objectives

- To identify words with long *i* and long *a* sounds
- To form words with the *i_e* and *a_e* spelling patterns

Materials

One copy of Blackline Master 78 per child; scissors; paste or glue

Have children identify the letters at the top of the page and cut them out. Now ask them to name the pictures on the page. Point out that each blank in the words beneath the pictures stands for missing letters. To complete each word, have children paste an *i* or an *a* on the first blank line of each word to represent the vowel sound they hear. Then help them place an *e* at the end of each word to signify the silent letter that makes the first vowel say its name. Ask children to read the completed words to a partner, then make their own word cards to substitute other long vowels (such as *o*) in certain words.

INFORMAL ASSESSMENT

Write two words on the chalkboard, one with a long *i* sound, and one with a long *a* sound (such as *pine* and *pane*). Ask children to help you sound out the words, underline the vowels, and repeat each vowel sound they hear. Now direct children to page 31. Ask them to identify the words with the long *i* sound. *(Mike, wide, smile)* Then turn to page 18 and challenge students to find the long *a* word. *(grapes)*

Comprehension

CAUSE AND EFFECT
Blackline Master 79

Objectives

- To recognize cause and effect
- To recall story details

© McGraw-Hill School Division

Materials

One copy of Blackline Master 79 per child; colored pencils or crayons; scissors; paste or glue

Invite children to describe Mike's dad at the beginning and end of the story. Discuss what happened to cause Mike's dad to look different in each section. Now help children identify the items at the top of the page and then color the items and the picture. Tell them to cut out the items and paste them into the picture to show the mess that made Mike's dad upset. Challenge children to tell what caused the mess, by having them complete the following sentence: *There was a big mess in the store because* ________________.

INFORMAL ASSESSMENT

Tell children to look at the illustrations on pages 17 and 18. Ask them why Dad was showing Mike the fish and the grapes. (He wanted to help Mike remember what else he was supposed to get at the store.)

Vocabulary Strategy

REVIEW INFLECTIONAL ENDINGS *-s, -es*
Blackline Master 80

Objectives

- To review making words plural by adding *-s* and *-es*
- To practice following directions

Materials

One copy of Blackline Master 80 per child; scissors; paste or glue

Ask students to recall how words can be changed to show more than one of something. Remind them that the endings *-s* and *-es* can be added to words to show "more than one."

INFORMAL ASSESSMENT

Have children cut out the letters at the top of the page. Demonstrate how *-es* adds another part or syllable to a word, by clapping out each syllable as you say the words *dress* and *dresses.* Now read the first sentence as it is written, pointing out the reason the word *grape* must be made plural. Ask children to position their ending cards accordingly. Have them repeat the words *grape* and *grapes,* clapping on each syllable. Since *grapes* does not have an added syllable, children should paste an *-s* on the first line. Repeat with the other sentences. Students can brainstorm other words that take *s* and *–es* endings, using their letter cards to make words plural.

Direct children to page 21, and have them name something in the illustration that shows "more than one." (potatoes, boxes) Write the singular noun on the chalkboard. Have children repeat each word, then say the plural; help them decide whether the word ends in *-s* or *-es.* Ask for a volunteer to add the correct ending. Continue with other items shown in the illustration.

© McGraw-Hill School Division

Name________________________________ Date______________

Dad's Store

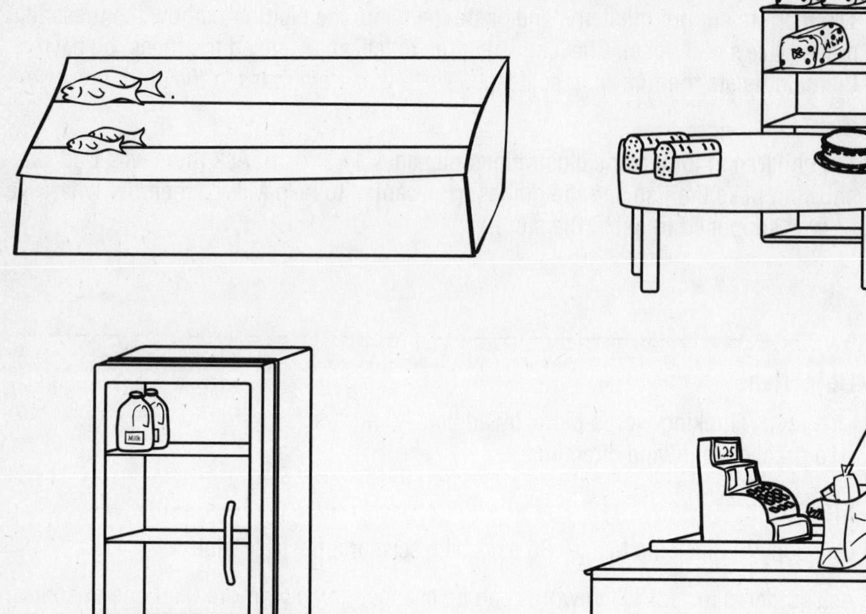

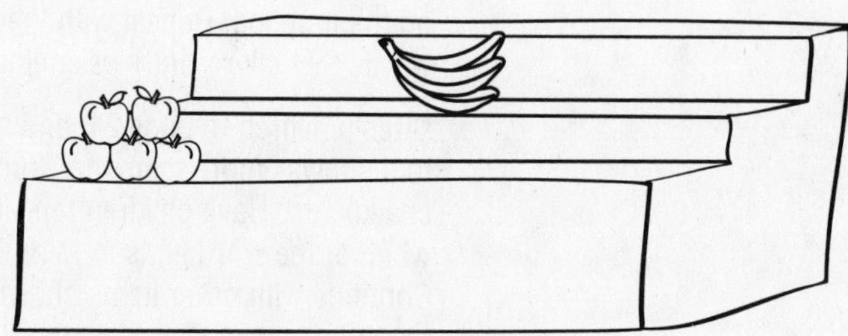

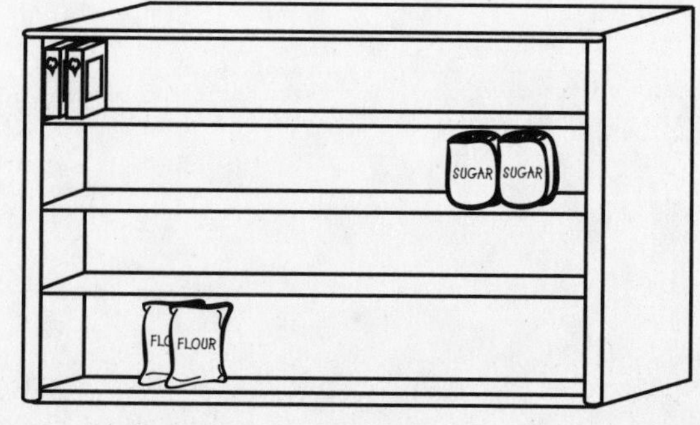

© McGraw-Hill School Division

Name_______________________________ Date_______________

Word Frame in a Can

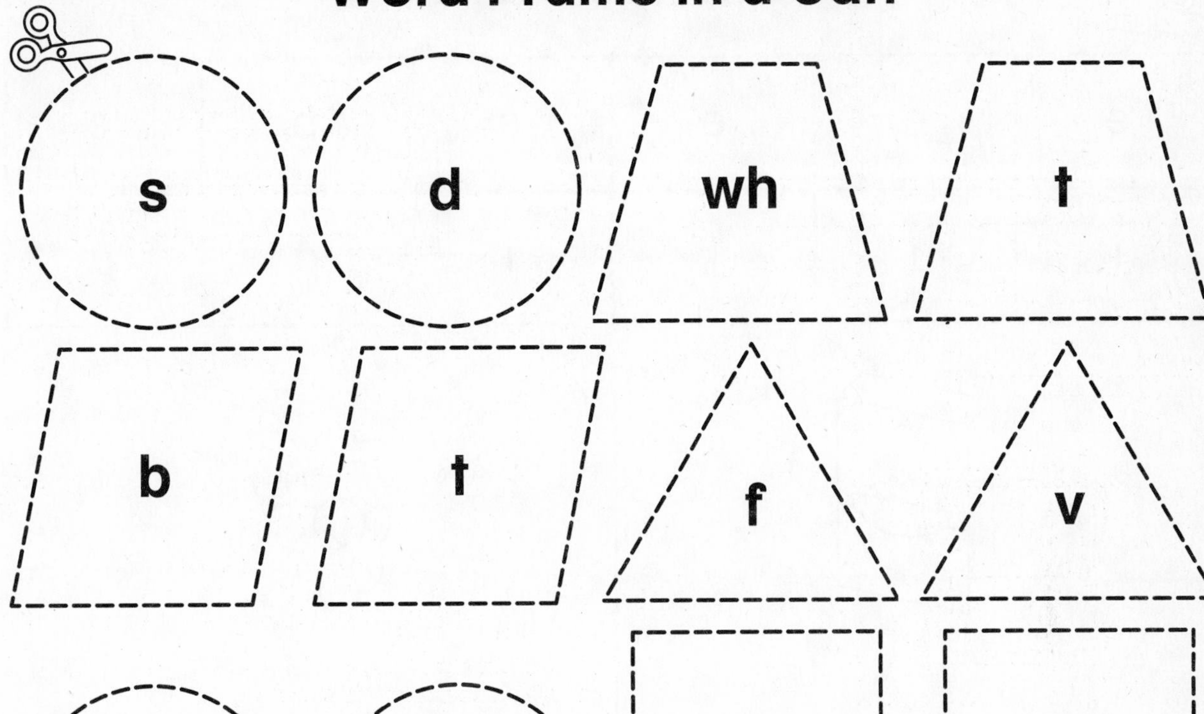

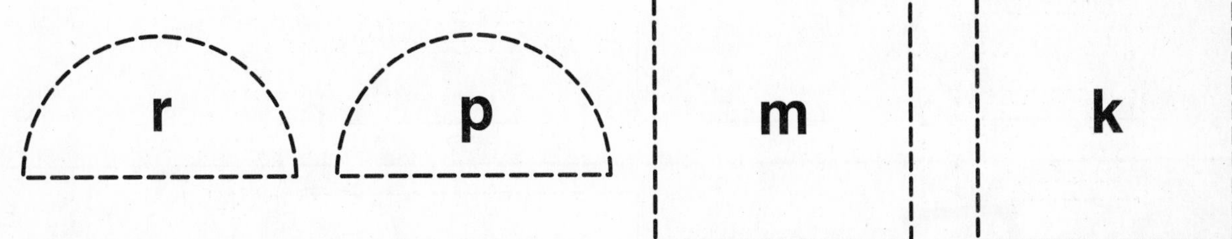

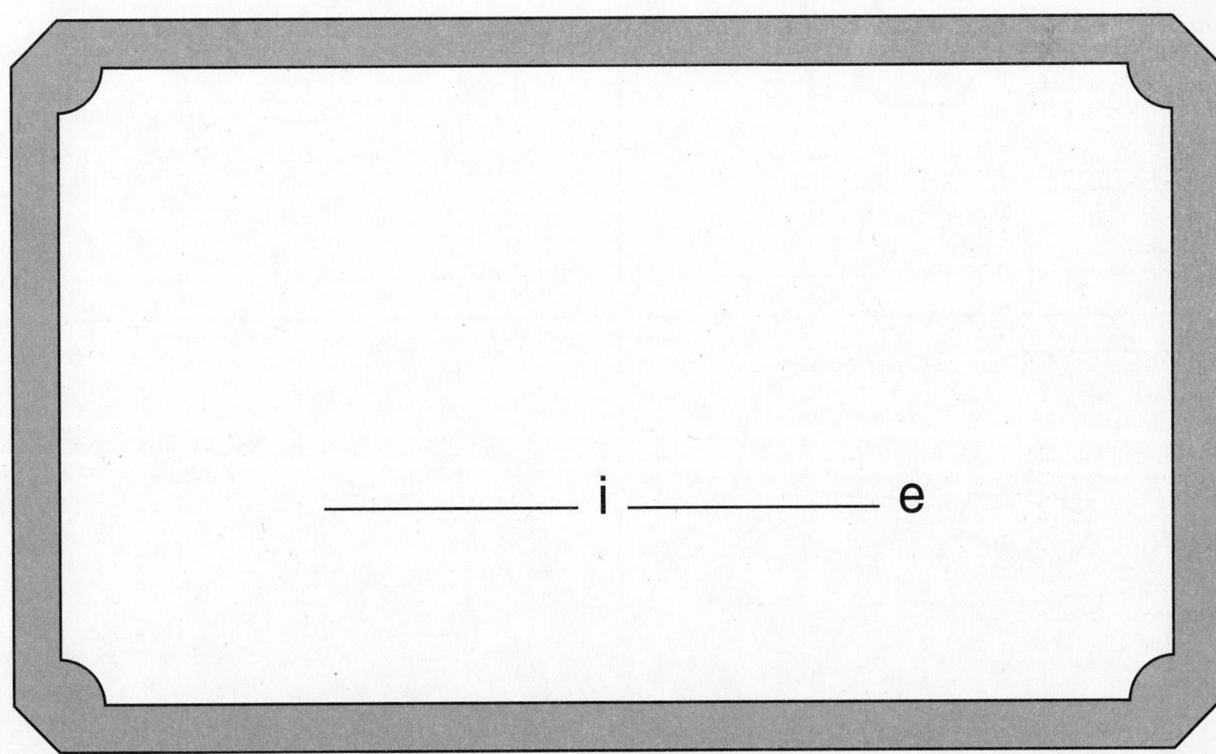

© McGraw-Hill School Division

Name ______________________________ Date ______________

Name the Picture

e	e	e	e	e	e
i	i	i	i	a	a

r ________ c ________

gr ________ p ________ s

f ________ v ________

sm ________ l ________

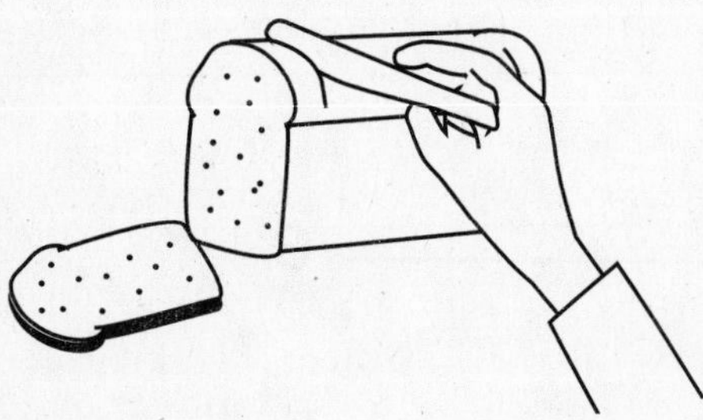

sl ________ c ________

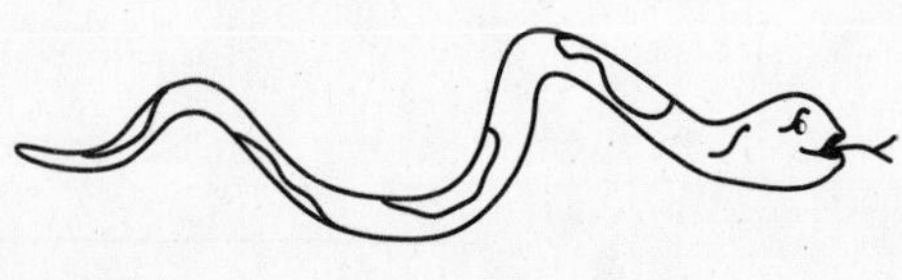

sn ________ k ________

© McGraw-Hill School Division

Name________________________________ Date______________

What Happened Here?

© McGraw-Hill School Division

Name____________________ Date__________

Pick an Ending

s	s	s	es	es

1. 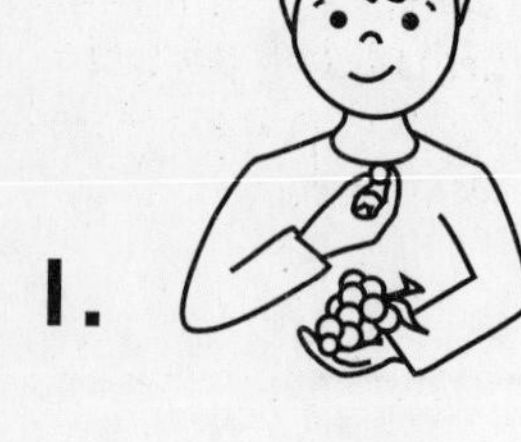 ate the grape__________.

2.  has five can__________.

3.  has two box__________.

4.  takes the ripe plum__________.

5.  puts away a can of peach__________.

© McGraw-Hill School Division

YASMIN'S DUCKS pp. 38A–65R

Written by Barbara Bottner Illustrated by Dominic Catalano

BUILD BACKGROUND FOR LANGUAGE SUPPORT

I. FOCUS ON READING

Focus on Skills

OBJECTIVE: Listen for long *o*

TPR

Develop Phonological Awareness

Show children pictures illustrating a variety of rhyming words that have the long *o* sound (for example: *phone, rose, stone, bone, nose*). Have children repeat the name of items as you display them. Distribute the pictures, one to each child or pairs of children. Children attempt to find other classmates' pictures that rhyme with their own. Call on children to show their pictures and say the rhyming words.

II. READ THE LITERATURE

VOCABULARY
found
buy
some
work
because

Vocabulary

Print each vocabulary word on a large card and help children read them. Ask children to dramatize words after they read them. Try these suggestions:

- hide the card that reads *found*, and ask a child to find it as you say: *Ana found the card;*
- invite a child to take one crayon, and another to take some crayons;
- have children dramatize doing *work;*
- have children demonstrate pretending to buy something;
- take out an umbrella and ask students to state why you might have it using the word *because*.

Ask children to brainstorm and give other prompts using these words.

CONCEPT
teaching something new

Evaluate Prior Knowledge

Tell children you are going to teach them something new. Then teach a simple game, song or art activity. As you teach, say: I *am teaching you how to* [name activity], *and you are learning how to* [name activity]. When the activity is finished, discuss the concept of teaching. Because some children may think that teaching is something done only by teachers in school, help them identify other people who have taught them things. Ask questions such as: *What did your family teach you? Did your mother or father teach you how to talk? Who taught you how to tie your shoes? If you have brothers or sisters, what did they teach you? Have your friends taught you things? What? What have you taught your friends?* Introduce the idea that we don't just learn from other *people,* but that *things* can teach us, as well. Ask: *Can a book teach you things? Can television teach you? What other things can teach?*

© McGraw-Hill School Division

Develop Oral Language

Invite children to teach something to the rest of the group. They can teach other children how to make something, how to play a game, how to say something in another language, and so on. Non-English speakers can teach something in their native language while modeling or using rebus drawings to explain steps in a process.

nonverbal prompt for active participation

- Preproduction: *Teach us* (point to self and class) *how to* (name something the child knows how do).

one- or two-word response prompt

- Early production: *What will you teach us? Do you like to do this? Will it be hard or easy for us to do?*

prompt for short answers to higher-level thinking skills

- Speech emergence: *What are you going to teach? What will we need? What is it like to teach this?*

prompt for detailed answers to higher-level thinking skills

- Intermediate fluency: *What are you going to teach us? How did you learn it? Why do you want to teach us this?*

Guided Reading

Preview and Predict

Tell children that this story is about a girl who likes ducks. Read the title and the author's and illustrator's names as you track the print. Have children identify Yasmin on the first page. Lead a picture walk, encouraging children to make predictions about the story. Use the illustrations to reinforce the concept of teaching.
Ask questions such as: *Why do you think the children are showing each other their pictures? What do you think each child might be saying? What do you think Yasmin might be teaching the other kids at her house? Do you think the other children learn about ducks from Yasmin? Why do you think this?* Invite children to name some skills they imagine each character in the story might be able to teach.

Objectives

GRAPHIC ORGANIZER
Blackline Master 81

- To practice identifying cause and effect
- To reinforce story details
- To encourage higher-level thinking skills

Materials

One copy of Blackline Master 81 per two children; pencils

Go over the Cause and Effect chart, reading the headings together. Then pair children needing language support with fluent English speakers. As they reread the story, help children fill in the left side of the chart with story events. They can decide with their partners why these events occurred, and enter these causes on the right side of the chart. When their charts are finished, call on teams to share their work.

To review the concept of cause and effect, ask children questions they can answer by looking at their charts. For example, you might say: *Why did Tim draw fish?*

© McGraw-Hill School Division

III. BUILD SKILLS

Phonics and Decoding

LONG *o*
Blackline Master 82

Objectives

- To identify long *o* words
- To practice word identification
- To support hands-on learning

Materials

One copy of Blackline Master 82 per child; scissors

Children identify the letters at the top of the page, and cut them out. Say, or hold up, a picture that illustrates one of the following long *o* words: *hope, home, nose, joke, rope, robe, rose.* Children complete the words by placing the correct letters in the shapes. Have children read the word they made.

INFORMAL ASSESSMENT

Have children turn to page 47. Write the words *rocket* and *globe* on the chalkboard. Frame each word as you read it aloud. Ask children to identify the word that has the same long *o* sound as *phone*. Underline the *o* and *e* in *globe.* Repeat with words on other pages, each time selecting a word with *o_e* and one with a different vowel sound.

Phonics and Decoding

REVIEW *o_e, i_e, a_e*
Blackline Master 83

Objectives

- To review o_e, i_e, a_e
- To reinforce story vocabulary
- To practice following directions

Materials

One copy of Blackline Master 83 per child; scissors

Have children identify the pictures from the story. Then help them cut out the strips and the slits. Demonstrate how to thread the numbered strips through the corresponding slits. Ask children to move the strips to create words that match the pictures on the page (dive, wipe, home, globe, lake, brave), then help children read the words.

INFORMAL ASSESSMENT

Direct children to page 45. Have them find a word with the same long *a* sound as in *lake* and read it aloud. (made) Now ask them to find a long *i* word (five) and a long *o* word (hope) on the same page. Have them read these words aloud, brainstorming rhyming words for each one.

Comprehension

CAUSE AND EFFECT
Blackline Master 84

Objectives

- To practice identifying cause and effect
- To recall story details
- To support hands-on learning

© McGraw-Hill School Division

Materials

One copy of Blackline Master 84 per child; scissors; paste or glue

Have children describe what is happening in each picture at the top of the page. Then tell them to cut out the pictures. Help children read the first sentence in the *What?*, or effect, column. Then prompt them to find the cut-out picture that shows the cause of the first sentence, and paste it in the *Why?* column. Guide children to repeat this process for the other sentences.

INFORMAL ASSESSMENT

Have children describe the picture on pages 54–55. Ask: *Do both bags get wet when Yasmin puts water on them?* Then invite children to tell why one bag gets wet but the other doesn't.

Vocabulary Strategy

INFLECTIONAL ENDING *-ed*
Blackline Master 85

Objectives

- To reinforce understanding of inflectional ending *-ed*
- To practice word identification
- To support cooperative learning

Materials

One copy of Blackline Master 85 per child; scissors; paste or glue

Have children cut out the word cards at the top of the page. Say each word and have children hold up the correct word card. Then let children work with a partner to read the rebus sentences and paste the correct words in the blanks.

INFORMAL ASSESSMENT

Direct children to page 50. Read this sentence, *"What did you learn?" Kate asked.* Ask children to change *learn* to *learned* and use it in a new sentence to tell what Yasmin discovered. Explain that this change indicates that something has already happened. Repeat with the words *wipes* and *rolls* on page 52, having children change each word to one with *–ed,* then use it in a sentence.

© McGraw-Hill School Division

Name______________________________ Date______________

What and Why

What Happens	Why It Happens

© McGraw-Hill School Division

Name________________________ Date______________

Miss Rome's Word Frame

h g j n r

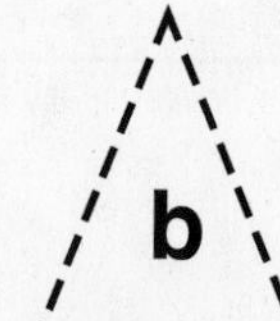

p b s m k

□ o △ e

© McGraw-Hill School Division

Name________________________________ Date______________

1, 2, 3 Letter Strips

1	2	3
h		m
w		p
	o	
d		v
	i	
l		b
	a	
gl		k
br		

-------	-------	-------	
1	2	3	e
-------	-------	-------	

© McGraw-Hill School Division

Name________________________ Date____________

What and Why

What? **Why?**

 get wet.

 don't get wet.

 knows a lot about ducks.

 can't get  to eat in the fall.

© McGraw-Hill School Division

Name ____________________ Date ______________

Picture Sentences

rolled	dripped	wiped	learned

1.  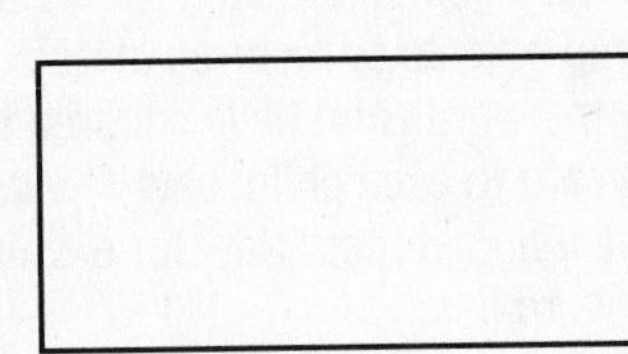 why  don't get wet.

2.  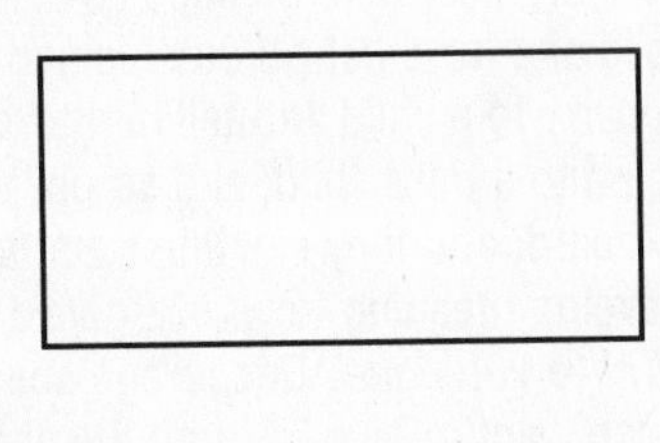 

on a .

3.  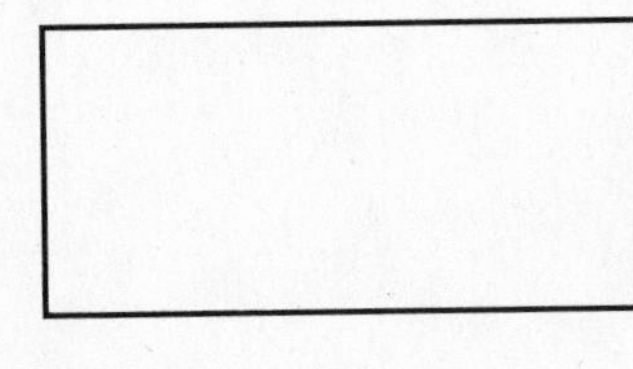 on the 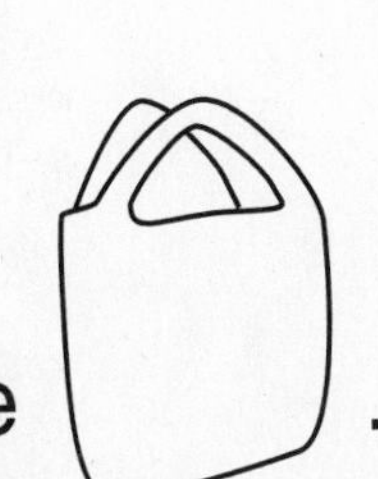 .

4. The 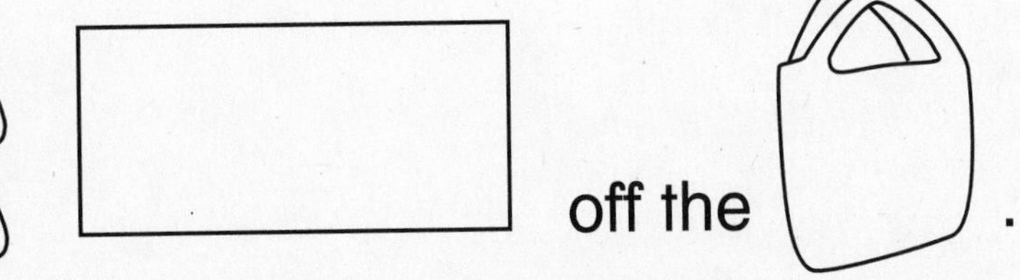 off the .

© McGraw-Hill School Division

THE KNEE-HIGH MAN pp. 66A-95R

Adapted by Ellen Dreyer Illustrated by Tim Raglin

BUILD BACKGROUND FOR LANGUAGE SUPPORT

I. FOCUS ON READING

Focus on Skills

Develop Phonological Awareness

OBJECTIVE: Listen for long *u*

TPR

Draw a cube on the board and tell children to listen for the long *u* sound. Say *cube,* emphasizing the long *u.* Hold up objects or pictures of objects that have the long *u* sound. (tube, mule, glue) Say the words and have children repeat them after you. After distributing a small blue card to each child, say: *Please hold up your blue card when you hear a word with the long* u *sound.* Say, for example: *deck, fix, cube, hat, bag.* Continue with additional word lists.

II. READ THE LITERATURE

Vocabulary

VOCABULARY
clean
carry
far
done
been

Print the vocabulary words on large cards to be used as children dramatize their meanings. Give *been* to a child and have her go outside and come back in. Ask: *Where have you been?* Give *carry* to a child and tell him to *carry* the card to another child, who then carries the card to a third child, and so on. Volunteers can demonstrate how to *clean* the chalkboard, and they can illustrate *far* by standing across the room from each other. To develop meaning for *done,* give a few children a task to do. When they finish, ask: *What have you done?* Encourage children to repeat each vocabulary word. You may also want to give children the chance to make up their own commands or questions using the vocabulary words.

Evaluate Prior Knowledge

CONCEPT
self-acceptance

To help children focus on the concept of self-acceptance, sing the following song to the tune of "Are You Sleeping?". Sing and act out the song several times, encouraging children to join in.

I like me, (2x)

Yes, I do, (2x)

I am kind and brave,

I can help my mother,

I like me. (2x)

© McGraw-Hill School Division

Develop Oral Language

Invite volunteers to substitute their own words for the third and fourth lines. Sing and act out the new verses with the class, encouraging children to pantomime or tell one thing they like about themselves. Use prompts appropriate for the linguistic level of the children. For example:

nonverbal prompt for active participation

- Preproduction: *Show us* (point to class and self) *something you* (point to student) *like about yourself* (point to same student and smile).

one- or two-word response prompt

- Early production: *What do you like about yourself? Is there something else you do that makes you feel good about you? What is it?*

prompt for short answers to higher-level thinking skills

- Speech emergence: *What is special about you? What can you do that makes you feel proud?*

prompt for detailed answers to higher-level thinking skills

- Intermediate fluency: *What do you like about yourself? Why is this special? Is this something you can do, or do you like something about the way you are?*

Guided Reading

Preview and Predict

Preview the story together. While tracking the print, read aloud the title and author/illustrator's name. Direct children to the first illustration, and help them identify Sam, the Knee-High Man. Discuss the term *knee-high*. Let children use their hands to measure about how tall *knee-high* is in relation to other objects. (See page 157 for other size-comparison activities.) Ask children how Sam seems to be feeling in the first illustration. Explain that he is unhappy because he doesn't like being small. Walk through the illustrations and use them to talk about how Sam is feeling about himself.

Ask children what they want to find out as they read the story. Model setting a purpose: *Sam is not happy because he is so small. I see him go to different animals and try to act like them. I want to know why he does that. I also want to know if Sam still feels badly about himself at the end of the story.*

GRAPHIC ORGANIZER
Blackline Master 86

Objectives

- To reinforce understanding of cause and effect
- To recall story details
- To support hands-on learning

Materials

One copy of Blackline Master 86 per child; colored pencils or crayons

Children color in the first picture showing the cause of an event or action. Help them identify what Sam is doing. (eating corn) Then ask: *What happened in the story because Sam ate too much corn?* (His tummy hurt, his legs hurt, and he got mad.)

Children draw one of these "effects" in the empty square next to the illustration of the cause.

Children can create story comic strips by continuing to draw effects for causes on the pages, and coloring them. Encourage children to use the comic strips both to retell the story and identify other cause and effect situations in the story. For example, ask: *Why did Sam eat so much corn? Why did Sam ask for help from the animals?*

© McGraw-Hill School Division

III. BUILD SKILLS

Phonics and Decoding

LONG *u: u_e*
Blackline Master 87

Objectives

- To reinforce understanding of long *u: u_e*
- To develop print awareness
- To practice following directions

Materials

One copy of Blackline Master 87 per child; scissors; paste or glue

Help children identify the letters at the top of the page, and cut them out along the dotted lines. Identify the woman in the first picture as June. Tell children to paste the letters for the sounds they hear at the beginning and end of *June* in the spaces beneath the picture. Repeat with *mule.* Give children clues such as whistling a little tune and pointing to a rule chart, to help them complete the two words without illustrations: *rule* and *tune.*

INFORMAL ASSESSMENT

Direct children to pages 70 and 71, and have them work with a partner to identify at least one long *u: u_e* word. Call on teams to share their words, and challenge the others to find it on the page.

Phonics and Decoding

REVIEW LONG *u_e, i_e, o_e, a_e*
Blackline Master 88

Objectives

- To review long *u_e, i_e, o_e, a_e*
- To reinforce sound/symbol correspondence
- To practice word identification
- To support hands-on learning

Materials

One copy of Blackline Master 88 per child; colored pencils or crayons; scissors

Help children identify the letters at the top of the page, as well as the name for each picture. Then tell children to listen for the long vowel sound they hear in each word and paste the appropriate letter in the empty box. Have children read the words they made.

INFORMAL ASSESSMENT

Write the words *lime* and *flute* on the board, and read them aloud. Then have children work together to find a word on page 81 that rhymes with each word on the chalkboard. (time, brute) Repeat, using words from other pages.

© McGraw-Hill School Division

Comprehension

MAKE INFERENCES
Blackline Master 89

Objectives

- To practice making inferences based on partial information
- To identify story characters
- To practice following directions

Materials

One copy of Blackline Master 89 per child; scissors; paste or glue

Help children identify the names in the boxes at the top of the page. Then tell them to study the pictures at the bottom of the page. Explain that only part of each character is shown. Ask questions such as *Who has feet like this? Whose hand is this?* Then have children cut out the character names and paste them below the correct characters.

INFORMAL ASSESSMENT

Have children look at the illustrations as you reread pages 90–91. Ask if they think Sam is now happy that he is small. Challenge children to show or tell how they know this.

Vocabulary Strategy

INFLECTIONAL ENDINGS
-er, -est
Blackline Master 90

Objectives

- To reinforce understanding of inflectional endings *-er* and *-est*
- To practice word identification
- To recall story characters

Materials

One copy of Blackline Master 90 per child; scissors; paste or glue

Help children read the words in the boxes at the top of the page before cutting them out. Then ask children to identify the story characters in each group. Help them compare the character indicated by the arrow to the other character or characters in the group. Ask questions like: *Is Kate Owl bigger or smaller than Max Mule? Which is tallest: June, the tree, or Sam?* Tell children to paste the correct word in the box below each group.

INFORMAL ASSESSMENT

Ask children to think about your earlier discussion of the term, *knee-high.* Have them use their hands to measure the distance from the floor to the their own knees. Children use this standard, as well as their general knowledge of real animals represented in the story (an owl, a mule, and a bull), to compare the sizes of these characters to the Knee-High Man using *–er* and *–est* words.

© McGraw-Hill School Division

Name________________________________ Date______________

The Knee-High Man

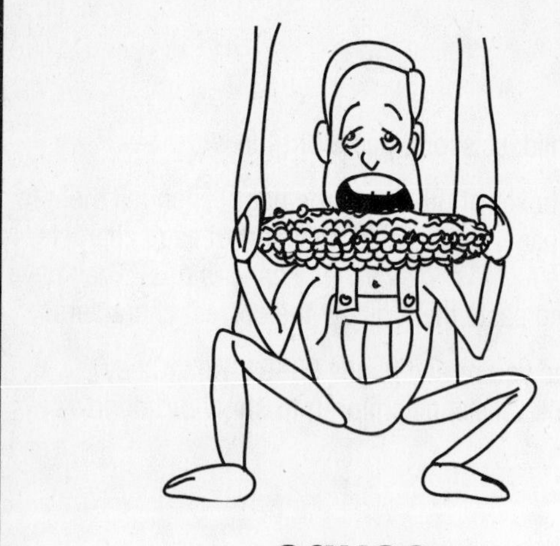 cause	 effect
 cause	effect
 cause	effect

© McGraw-Hill School Division

Name________________________________ Date________________

Word Frame

J n m l

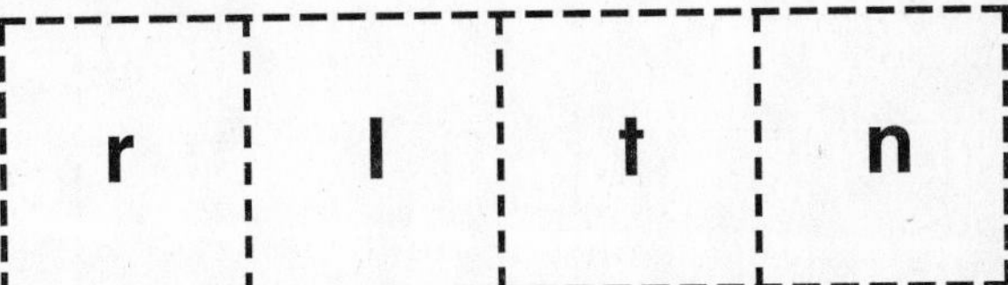

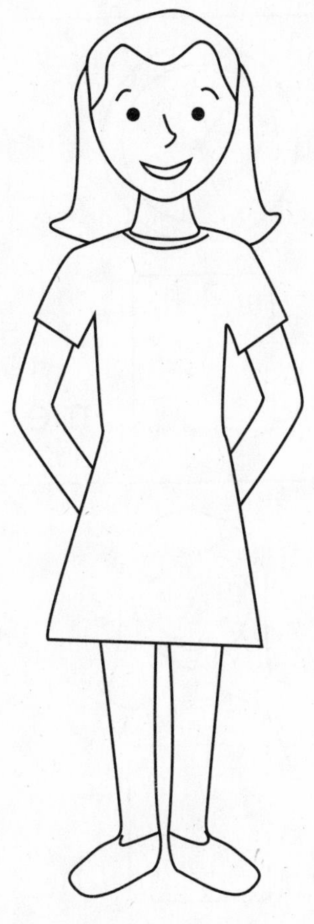

u e

u e

u e

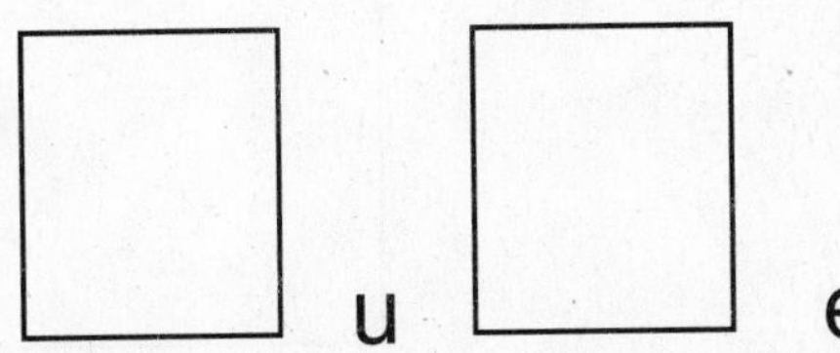

© McGraw-Hill School Division

Name______________________________ Date______________

What Is It?

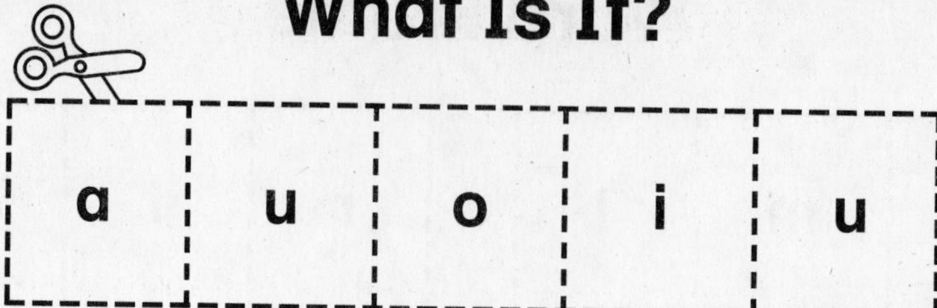

r ☐ pe

t ☐ me

m ☐ le

J ☐ ne

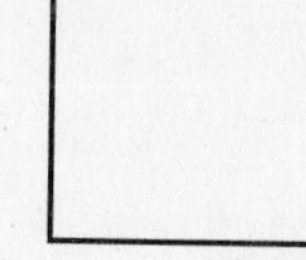

K ☐ te

© McGraw-Hill School Division

Name________________________ Date____________

The Name Game

Max	Bob	Kate
June	Sam	

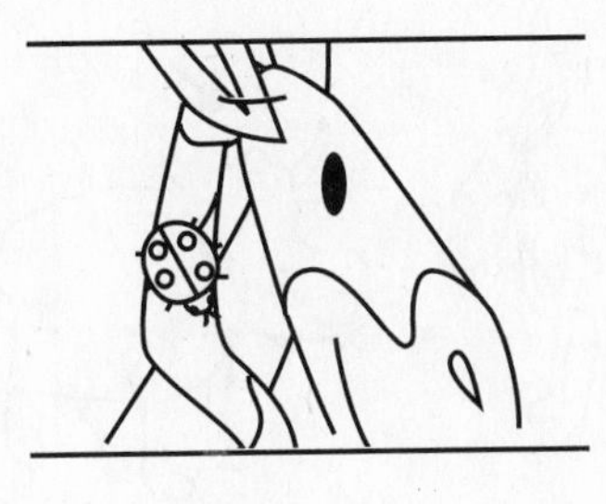
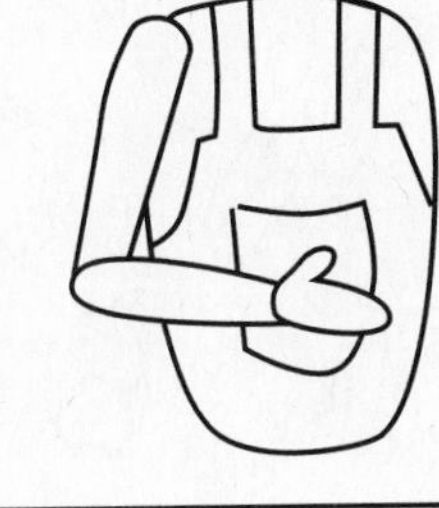

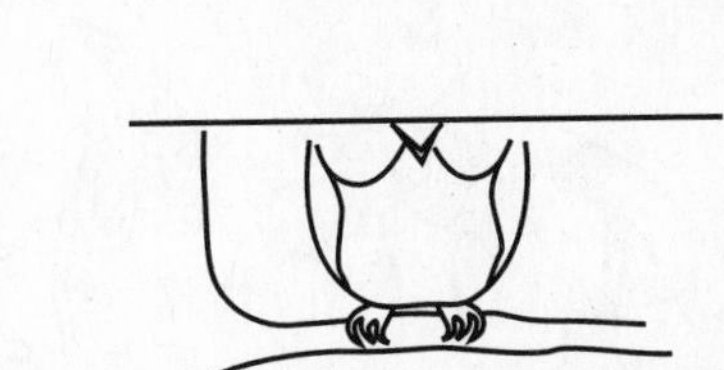
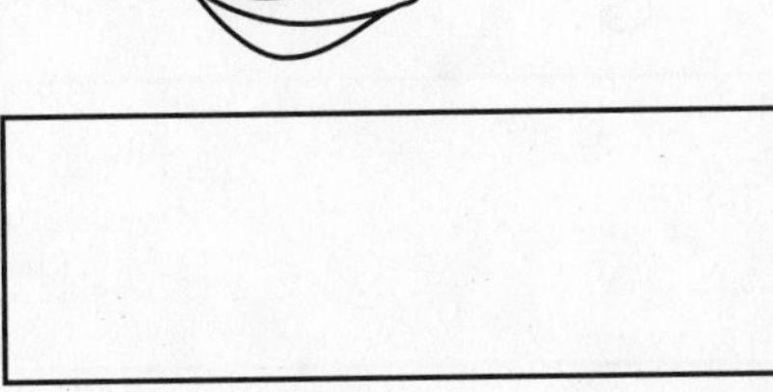

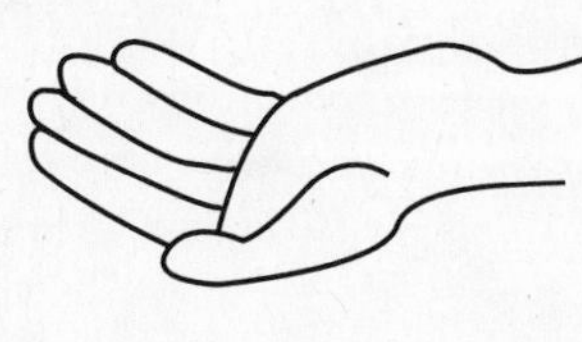

© McGraw-Hill School Division

Name________________________________ Date________________

Characters Big, Tall and Small

smaller	smallest	bigger
biggest	taller	tallest

© McGraw-Hill School Division

JOHNNY APPLESEED pp. 96A–123R

Written by Mary Pope Osborne Illustrated by Michael Steirnagle

BUILD BACKGROUND FOR LANGUAGE SUPPORT

I. FOCUS ON READING

Focus on Skills

OBJECTIVE: Listen for long *a*

TPR

Develop Phonological Awareness

Bring in a variety of items (or photographs of items) with the long *a: ai, ay* sound. (For example: *mail, tail, nail, hay, tray,* and so on.) Label each item, prompting children to repeat the words after you. Then ask children to create sentences, silly or otherwise, using as many of the words as possible. For instance, *I will put the mail on the tray.* Write sentences on the chalkboard, asking children to help you underline the *ai* words and circle the *ay* words. Finally, children can act out the sentences using whatever actual items are available as props, or pointing to those items represented in photos.

II. READ THE LITERATURE

VOCABULARY
pretty
little
light
how
live

Vocabulary

Print the vocabulary words on the chalkboard and read them with children. Underline the word *how,* and frame it and the other words as you use them in the following prompts. Ask children volunteers to point to words in the prompts below as you read each one and children answer or respond to them. Say: *Show us how you turn off the light. Show us how you draw a pretty flower. Show us how you draw a little house.* Then ask: *What else do you know how to do?* Prompt children to demonstrate a skill and say, for example, *I know how to jump.* Then ask: *How can you show us where you live?* (draw a picture, point out the window, and so on)

Concept
trees

Evaluate Prior Knowledge

Prepare an apple tree from construction paper or felt to be used on a bulletin board or flannel board. The tree should have the following detachable parts: roots, trunk, branches, leaves, fruit, seeds. Display the tree and several pictures of real trees. You may want to bring in examples of leaves, needles, and perhaps an apple which you can cut open to reveal the seeds.

Direct children's attention to the tree. As you read each of the following statements, have children come up and point out the parts of the tree indicated by each underscore: *This is a tree. A tree has roots. A tree has a trunk and branches. Some trees have leaves. Other trees have needles. A tree grows from a seed. Sometimes the seed is inside a fruit.* You may also want to briefly describe the different functions of various tree parts.

© McGraw-Hill School Division

Develop Oral Language

Now distribute parts of the construction paper tree to children, and invite them to rebuild the tree, part by part. Use prompts appropriate for the child's linguistic level. For example:

nonverbal prompt for active participation

- Preproduction: *Show us* (point to class and self) *your part of the tree.* (point to the part the child has) *Put the* (name of tree part) *on the tree.*

one- or two-word response prompt

- Early production: *Show us your part of the tree. What part is it? Does it grow under the ground? Does it hang from a branch? Where does it go?*

prompt for short answers to higher-level thinking skills

- Speech emergence: *What part of the tree do you have? What does it look like? Where does* (name of tree part) *go? What other parts of the tree does it touch?*

prompt for detailed answers to higher-level thinking skills

- Intermediate fluency: *What part of the tree do you have? Tell us something about* (name of tree part). *Where does* (name of tree part) *go? What can you tell us about other parts of the tree?*

Guided Reading

Preview and Predict

Tell children that this story is about a man named John Chapman who lived long ago. Read aloud the title as you track the print. Walk through the illustrations and use them to encourage children to make predictions about the story and to reinforce ideas about trees. Ask questions such as: *What is John Chapman planting? What is he giving these people to plant near their new homes? Why would people want apple trees? Why do you think John Chapman was called Johnny Appleseed? What else does Johnny Appleseed do? Do you think he liked to help others? Do you think he is kind?* Now pair a fluent English- speaking student with a child needing extra language support, and ask pairs to draw or write what additional details they hope to discover from reading the story. Invite children to share their illustrations with the rest of the class.

GRAPHIC ORGANIZER
Blackline Master 91

Objectives

- To practice making inferences
- To reinforce the main story character
- To practice following directions

Materials

One copy of Blackline Master 91 per child; colored pencils or crayons

Reread the story, pausing each time Johnny Appleseed helps someone. Instruct children to draw a picture of that person or animal in an apple. When all the apples are full, ask children to decide what kind of person they think Johnny Appleseed was. Write *Johnny Appleseed* on the chalkboard, and ask children to brainstorm a list of words that describe this character.

Have children write *Johnny Appleseed* on the first line of their Tree Charts, and copy some words that tell about him on the lines below.

© McGraw-Hill School Division

III. BUILD SKILLS

Phonics and Decoding

LONG *a: ai, ay*
Blackline Master 92

Objectives

- To identify long *a: ai, ay*
- To practice word identification
- To reinforce selection vocabulary

Materials

One copy of Blackline Master 92 per child; scissors; paste or glue

Help children identify the letter pairs at the top of the page, and cut them out. Then have them paste the letters in place to complete the following words from the story: *rain, always, quail, days, wait, stayed.* Try giving clues or sentences from the text to help children identify the words. For example: *This is wet, and falls from the sky.* (rain) *Johnny Appleseed fixed the wing of a ____.*(quail) When children have filled in all of the blanks, encourage them to read the words aloud.

INFORMAL ASSESSMENT

To assess recognition of long *a: ai, ay* words, have children work in pairs. Direct them to a page in the text where they will find one of the words from the blackline master (for instance, page 108). Challenge them to find other words from the black-line master in the text. Call on teams to share the word(s) they found, and to tell if it is spelled with the letters *ai* or *ay.*

Phonics and Decoding

REVIEW *ai, ay; u_e, o_e*
Blackline Master 93

Objectives

- To review *ai, ay; u_e, o_e*
- To reinforce selection vocabulary
- To support hands-on learning

Materials

One copy of Blackline Master 93 per child; colored pencils or crayons; scissors; oak-tag; paste or glue

Help children identify each picture, and read the words. Then have them color the pictures and paste the whole page onto oaktag. When the paste is dry, children can cut apart the pictures and words to make word puzzles. Tell them to mix up the puzzle pieces, and then match the correct word with each picture.

INFORMAL ASSESSMENT

Direct children to page 103. Ask them to find the word that has the same long *a* sound as *jay.* (day) Have them read *day* aloud. Repeat, asking children to identify a long *a: ai* word (sailed) and an *o_e* word (those) on page 104, and a *u_e* word (mules) on page 106.

© McGraw-Hill School Division

Comprehension

REVIEW MAKE INFERENCES
Blackline Master 94

Objectives

- To practice making inferences
- To recall story details
- To support higher level thinking

Materials

One copy of Blackline Master 94 per child; colored pencils or crayons

Prompt children to look at the first picture and identify what is happening. Help them make inferences by pointing out details and asking questions. Say, for example: *Johnny Appleseed is on a raft in the river. He is waving. To whom do you think he is waving?* Then ask children to draw people on the shore to whom Johnny is waving.

Repeat this exercise with the remaining pictures, having children add seeds that Johnny is planting and apples that Johnny is picking.

INFORMAL ASSESSMENT

Have children look at the illustration of Johnny Appleseed on page 100 to figure out if Johnny was rich or poor. Have them identify details in the picture that helped them answer the question.

Vocabulary Strategy

REVIEW INFLECTIONAL ENDINGS *-er, -est*
Blackline Master 95

Objectives

- To practice applying inflectional endings *-er, -est*
- To reinforce vocabulary development
- To support cooperative learning

Materials

One copy of Blackline Master 95 per child; scissors

Read the words on the page, prompting children to point to and repeat each word after you. After they've cut apart the word cards, children can work with partners to use the cards to make comparisons. They might compare classroom objects, pictures from the story, or themselves. Invite teams to share their comparisons with the rest of the group.

INFORMAL ASSESSMENT

Have children work in small groups. Give each group a set of word cards, and have them find pictures from the story that illustrate the words. Invite teams to show the pictures they chose, and read the word card which applies.

© McGraw-Hill School Division

Name________________________ Date____________

Tree Chart

© McGraw-Hill School Division

Name____________________ Date__________

Make the Words

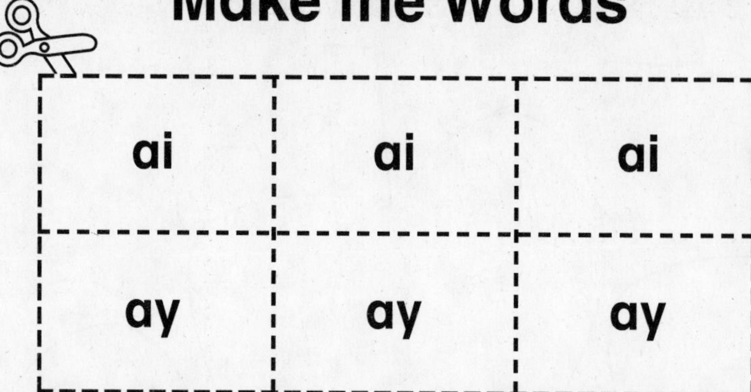

r ☐ n

w ☐ s

qu ☐ l

d ☐ s

w ☐ t

st ☐ ed

© McGraw-Hill School Division

Name______________________________ Date______________

Johnny Appleseed Puzzle

© McGraw-Hill School Division

Name_______________________________ Date______________

You Finish It

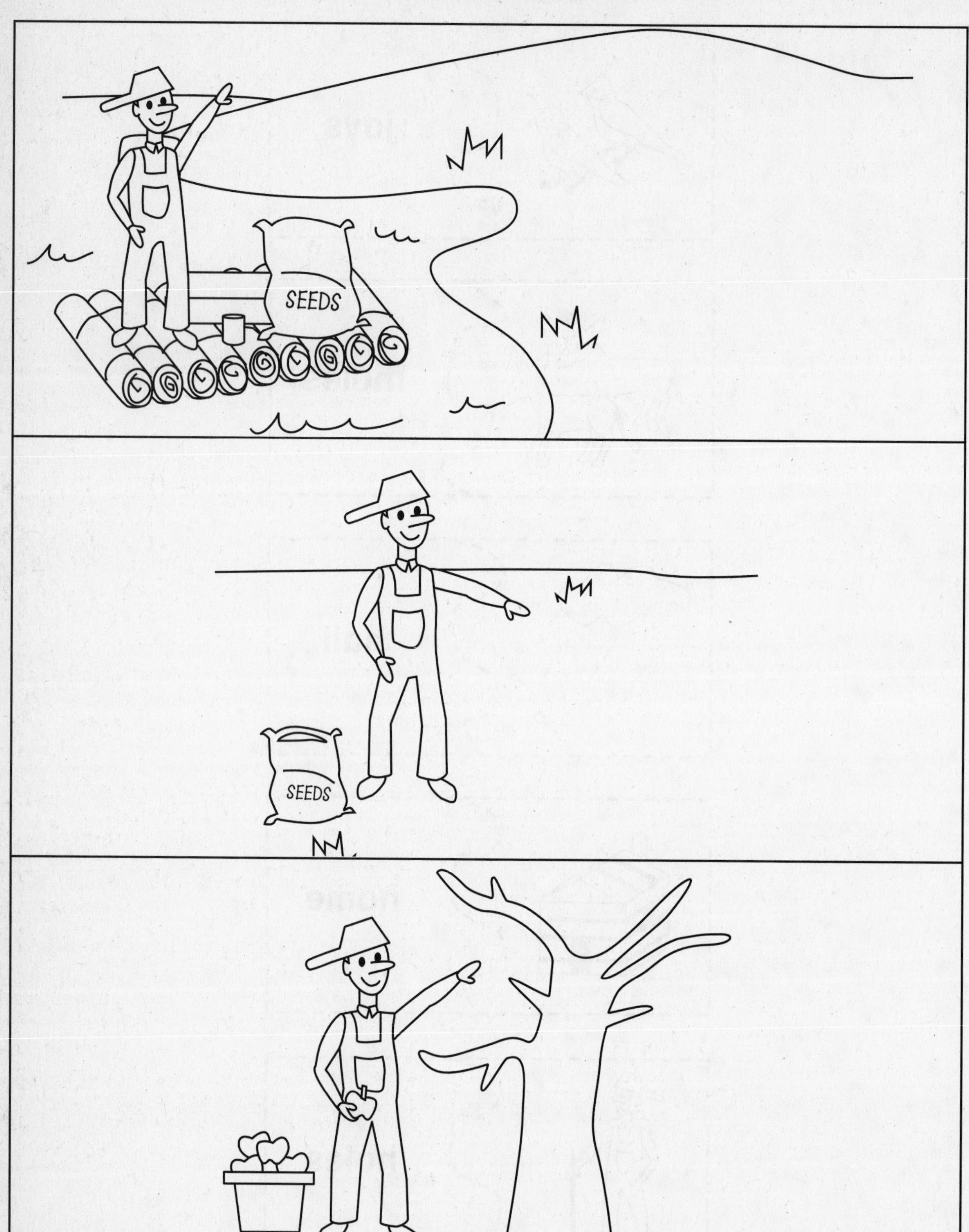

© McGraw-Hill School Division

Name________________________________ Date_______________

Look Around

old	older	oldest
pink	pinker	pinkest
big	bigger	biggest
little	littler	littlest

© McGraw-Hill School Division

RING! RING! RING! PUT OUT THE FIRE! pp. 124A–133R

Time For Kids

BUILD BACKGROUND FOR LANGUAGE SUPPORT

I. FOCUS ON READING

Focus on Skills

OBJECTIVE: Listen for long *a*, *i*, and *o*

TPR

Develop Phonological Awareness

Have on hand a foam ball or beanbag. Organize children into three groups, and assign each group one of the following names: *Fire, Smoke, Flame.* Have students help you establish the long vowel sound in each word. Let teams line up facing you. Say a word with either a long *a*, *i*, or *o*, and toss the ball into the air. The first child in line on the team with the same vowel sound as the word you said catches the ball and repeats the word. Repeat until all children have had a turn.

II. READ THE LITERATURE

VOCABULARY
work
done
always
clean
how

Vocabulary

Print the vocabulary words on the chalkboard, and read each one with the children. Use the following suggestions to dramatize each word without saying it, making a specific gesture (such as both palms up) to indicate blanks in sentences. Have children name the word, and invite a volunteer to point to it on the board. Suggestions:

Always: Act out driving a car, saying: *I drive my car to school every day, and I drive my car home every day. I ____________ drive my car.*

Clean: Dramatize sweeping, wiping tables, and so forth.

Done: Dramatize eating a meal. Wipe your mouth, saying: *I've finished eating. I'm ____________.*

How: Shake hands with several children, saying: *Good morning. ____________ are you?*

Work: Dramatize digging, hammering, or some other physical work, saying, for example: *I ____________ very hard in my garden.*

Encourage children to create and dramatize their own sentences using the words as other children guess the missing vocabulary word.

CONCEPT
properties of fire

Evaluate Prior Knowledge

Hold up a picture of a lit candle. Point to the flame, and say, *fire.* Say: *Fire gives light.* Hold your hand out to the flame in the picture, then pull it back as if burned and say: *Fire is hot!* Show children pictures of fire in various contexts, such as being used for cooking, campfires, candles or lanterns, and so forth. Say: *Fire can help us.* Now show a picture of a forest fire or house fire and say: *Fire burns things. Fire can be dangerous, too.*

© McGraw-Hill School Division

Develop Oral Language

Working with a partner, invite children to dramatize a situation involving the use of fire (such as making a campfire). Use prompts appropriate for the linguistic level of children.

nonverbal prompt for active participation

- Preproduction: *Show us* (point to class and self) *one way* (hold up one finger) *we use fire* (point to candle flame).

one- or two-word response prompt

- Early production: *Where have you seen fire? Is fire helpful when it is used in this way, or is it dangerous?*

prompt for short answers to higher-level thinking skills

- Speech emergence: *When do we use fire? What can happen if we are not careful around fire?*

prompt for detailed answers to higher-level thinking skills

- Intermediate fluency: *How does fire help us? How should we be careful around fire? What might happen if we are not careful?*

TPR

Guided Reading

Preview and Predict

Tell children that they will be reading about firefighters. Explain that firefighters are people who put out fires that might hurt people, animals, or things. While tracking the print, read the title of the selection. Explain that the word *ring* in this context means the sound of a bell or alarm. As you take a picture walk through the story, help children identify unfamiliar items in the photographs. Reinforce the concept of fire by asking questions such as: *What are the firefighters wearing? Why do they need special clothing to put out fires? Why do firefighters need ladders to put out fires? Why do you think this firefighter is sliding down a pole instead of walking downstairs? Why do you think she is moving quickly?* Ask children what they hope to learn as they read the story. Write their questions on a chart.

GRAPHIC ORGANIZER
Blackline Master 96

Objectives

- To reinforce understanding of story details
- To support vocabulary development
- To support hands-on learning

Materials

One copy of Blackline Master 96 per child; scissors

Have children cut out the firefighter's clothes and equipment on the dotted lines. As you read about these items in the story, have children name the appropriate cutouts, and place them on or near the firefighter and his truck. After reading the story, invite children to use the cutouts and work with a partner to tell what they learned. Reread their chart of questions from the previous activity to see if each one was answered. Help children make inferences by asking them the following types of questions as they cut out each piece of equipment or clothing: *Why does a firefighter wear a hat? Why is the water hose so long?*

© McGraw-Hill School Division

III. BUILD SKILLS

Comprehension

CAUSE AND EFFECT
Blackline Master 97

Objectives

- To practice identifying cause and effect
- To demonstrate understanding of story details
- To support hands-on learning

Materials

One copy of Blackline Master 97 per child; scissors; paste or glue

Discuss with children what is happening in each "effect" picture at the top of the page. Have children cut out these pictures. Help children identify what is happening in the "cause" pictures in the bottom three rows. Finally, challenge children to paste the correct "effect" cards next to their corresponding "causes."

INFORMAL ASSESSMENT

Have children look at the photographs on page 129. Ask them to tell what happened in the story that caused the firefighter to slide down the pole. Ask what they think will happen after the fire truck races to the fire.

Comprehension

MAKE INFERENCES
Blackline Master 98

Objectives

- To practice making inferences
- To reinforce word identification
- To support cooperative learning

Materials

One copy of Blackline Master 98 for every two children; scissors; paste or glue

Instruct children to work with partners to cut out the sentences at the top of the page. They can then look at the first picture and discuss the clues that indicate what is happening. You may need to point out details such as the fire in the window of the house.

INFORMAL ASSESSMENT

Have children read their cut-out sentences and paste the one that describes the picture in the box below it. Repeat this process for each of the other pictures.

Direct children to page 128, and reread the sentence *The fire trucks have to be clean and ready to go.* Have children tell why fire trucks always need to be ready to go.

© McGraw-Hill School Division

Vocabulary Strategy

INFLECTIONAL ENDINGS
-ed, -s, -es
Blackline Master 99

Objectives

- To practice applying inflectional endings *-ed, -s,* and *-es*
- To practice word identification
- To practice following directions

Materials

One copy of Blackline Master 99 per child; scissors; paste or glue

Have children cut out the words at the top of the page. Then discuss what is happening in each picture, encouraging the use of the cut-out words. Demonstrate how to complete the word math problems by doing the first one on the board. Have children identify the correct answer by holding up the word card. Encourage children to complete each word problem and paste the correct word in each box. Discuss why each word was changed. For instance, a *p* and *-ed* was added to *drip* to show something that already happened. An *-es* was added to *branch* to make it more than one. An *-s* was added to *firefighter* to make it more than one.

INFORMAL ASSESSMENT

Have children turn to page 127. Working with a partner, challenge them to find as many words as they can that have an added *-s* or *e-s* to show more than one, or an added *-ed* ending to show something that already happened. Call on teams to read the words they found.

Vocabulary Strategy

INFLECTIONAL ENDINGS
-er, -est
Blackline Master 100

Objectives

- To practice applying inflectional endings *-er, -est*
- To support vocabulary development
- To encourage creative thinking

Materials

One copy of Blackline Master 100 per child; scissors; paste or glue

Help children read the words at the top of the page, and then cut them out. Do the first word math equation together, asking children to hold up the correct answer before pasting it on the proper line. Help children note that these words help make comparisons. Continue until all words have been fitted on their corresponding lines. When all the words are in place, have partners use the words to create sentences about the pictures. They can point to each word as they use it in a sentence.

INFORMAL ASSESSMENT

Ask children to find the word *fast* on page 129. Ask students to add the endings *-er* and *-est* to the word, then use the new forms of the word to describe scenes in the story. For instance, *This firefighter was* faster *than this firefighter sliding down the pole, but this firefighter was the* fastest*!*

© McGraw-Hill School Division

Name______________________________ Date______________

Ring! Ring! Ring!

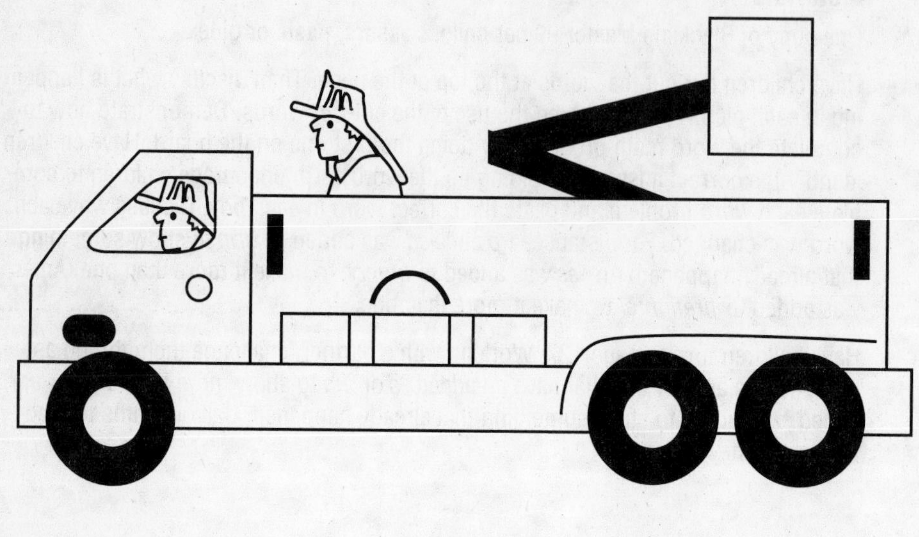

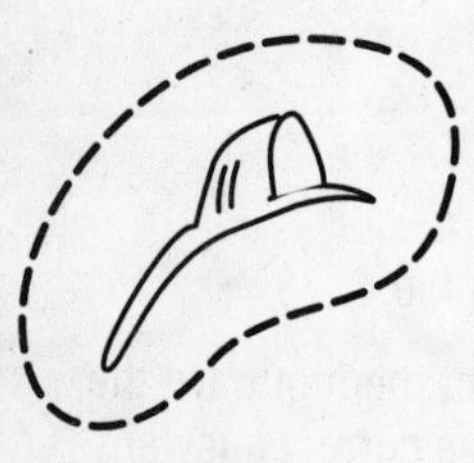

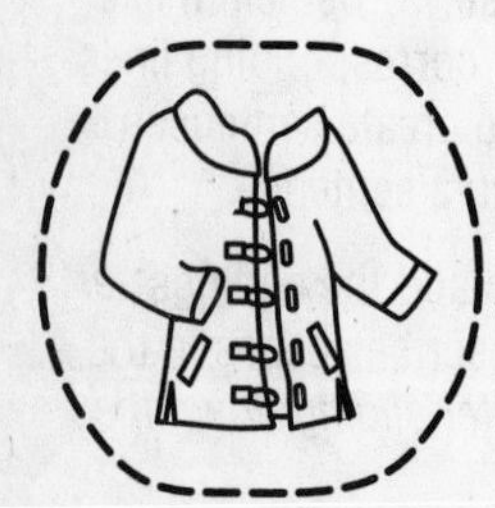

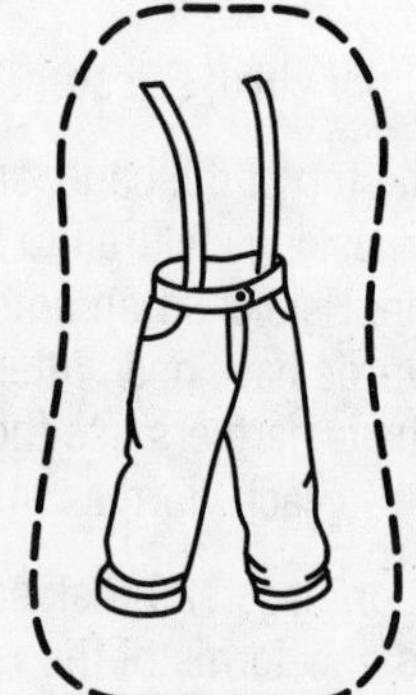

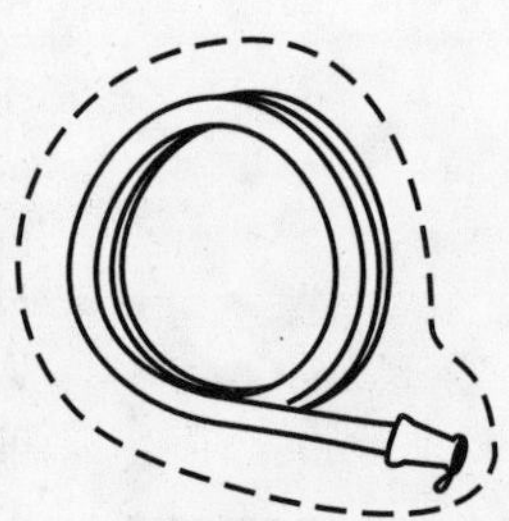

© McGraw-Hill School Division

Name________________________ Date______________

Show What Happened

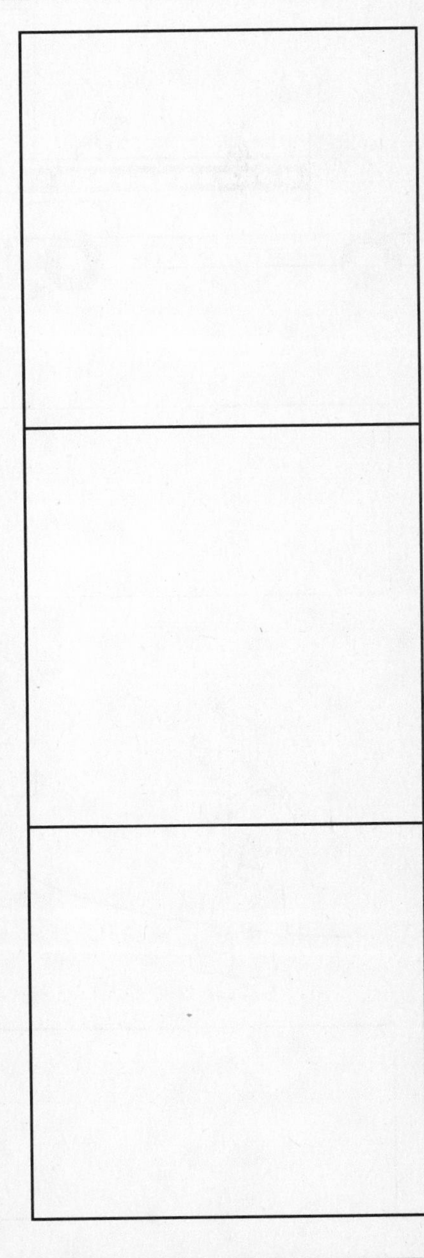

© McGraw-Hill School Division

Name____________________________ Date______________

Look For Clues

There is a fire.	The fire is out.
The smoke is bad.	Get the ladder.

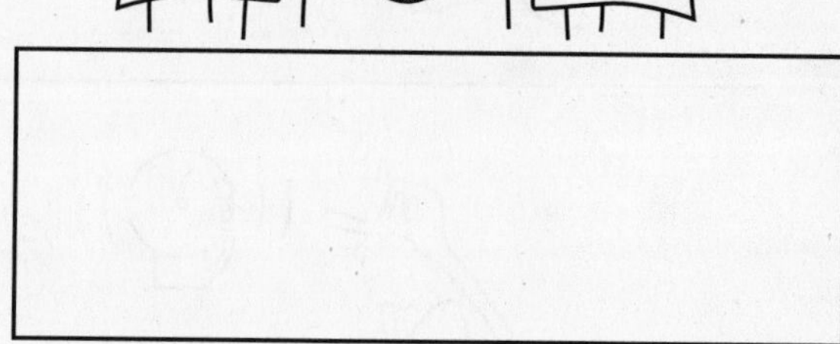

© McGraw-Hill School Division

Name ____________________ Date __________

Word Math

saved	branches	firefighters	dripped

drip + p + ed = ☐

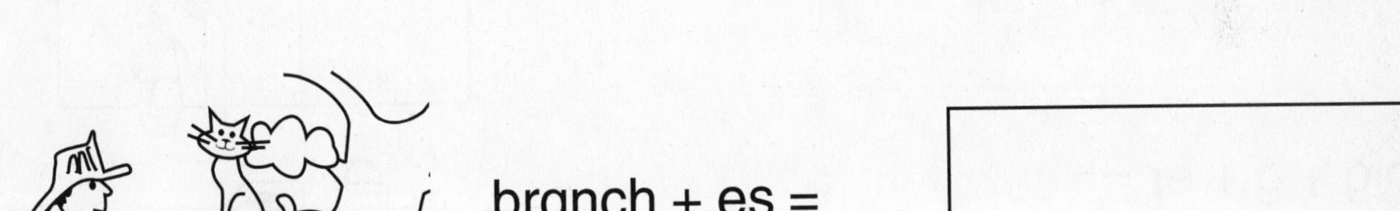

branch + es = ☐

save - e + ed = ☐

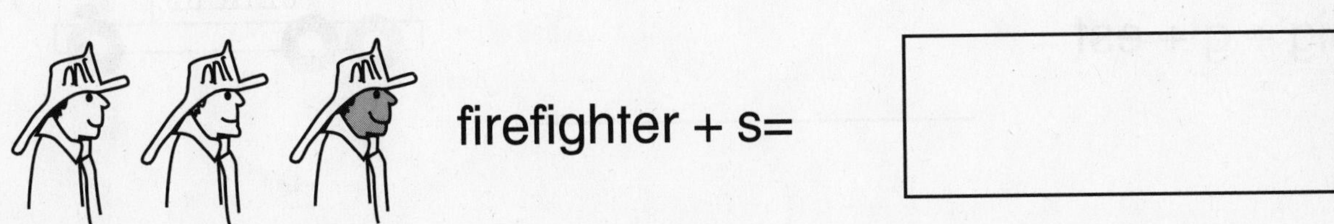

firefighter + s= ☐

© McGraw-Hill School Division

Name________________________________ Date______________

More Word Math

smaller	smallest	bigger	biggest

small + er =

____

big + g + er =

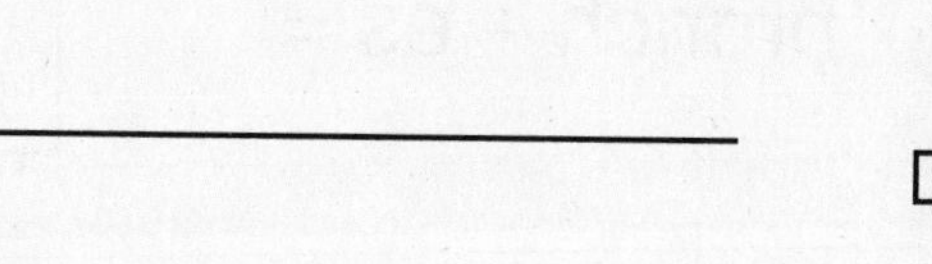

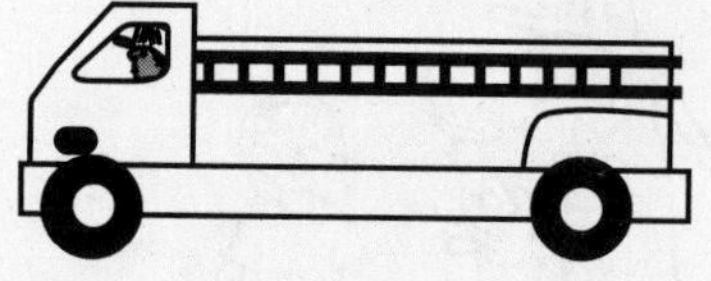

small + est =

____

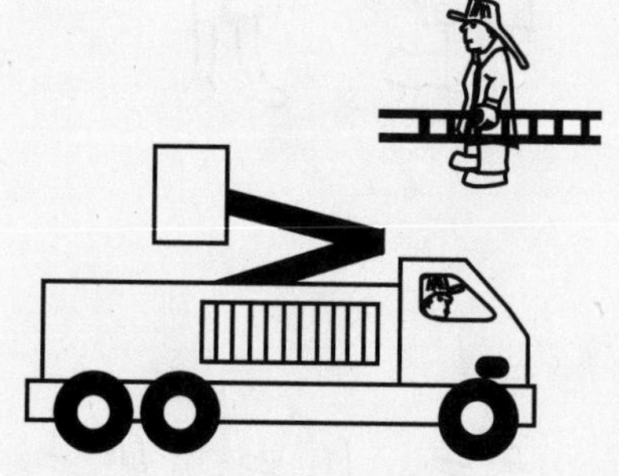

big + g + est =

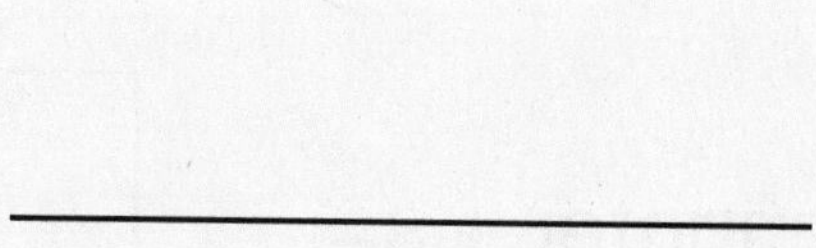

© McGraw-Hill School Division

SEVEN SILLIES pp. 10A–45R

Written by Joyce Dunbar Illustrated by Chris Downing

BUILD BACKGROUND FOR LANGUAGE SUPPORT

I. FOCUS ON READING

Focus on Skills

OBJECTIVE: Listen for long *e*

TPR

Develop Phonological Awareness

Play Hide and Seek with long *e* words. Collect a variety of pictures of things with long *e* such as *sheep, feet, three, knee, heel, queen, street, creek.* Name each picture, and have children repeat the word after you. Then ask one child to leave the room while you hide one of the pictures. When the child returns, she or he looks for the picture. Have the other children whisper the name of the picture when the seeker is far away from it, and say the word louder and louder as the seeker gets closer. When she or he finds the picture, the seeker should name it. Repeat with other pictures until all children have had a turn. Then read the poem "Hide-and-Seek." Have children raise their hands every time they hear a word that rhymes with *seek.*

II. READ THE LITERATURE

VOCABULARY
all
four
many
over
so

Vocabulary

Print the vocabulary words on the chalkboard. Frame each word as it is used in the following activities. Use repetition and body language to increase understanding. Tell children to find a partner, then ask: *Do you all have partners?* Have children respond: *Yes, we all have partners.* Ask: *How many hands do you and your partner have all together?,* encouraging children to say: *We have four! That's how many!* Say: *Hold your hands over your partner's head.* Have children say: *My hand is over your head.* Now say: *Hold out your hand so your partner can shake your hand.* Ask children to say: *We are friends, so we will shake hands.*

CONCEPT
looking in the mirror

Evaluate Prior Knowledge

Show children a mirror you have brought in. Tell them what it is, and ask if they know what it is used for. Look into the mirror and say: *I see* (your name). Smile. Then say: *I see a happy person in this mirror.* Make a silly face. Say: *I see a silly person in this mirror. I see my face in the mirror, but I am not in the mirror.* Lay the mirror on a table. Hold up the story so that the picture of the pig is reflected in the mirror. Ask: *What do you see in the mirror? Is the pig really in the mirror? No, the pig's image is reflected in the mirror. Is it a handsome pig? Is it a silly pig?* Hold up the other animal's pictures so that they are reflected in the mirror. Have children talk about what they see in the mirror.

Develop Oral Language

Invite children to take turns looking into the mirror and describing what they see. Use prompts appropriate for children's linguistic level.

nonverbal prompt for active participation

- Preproduction: Model and say: *Who do you see in the mirror? Show us a happy girl (boy). Show us a silly girl (boy).*

one- or two-word response prompt

- Early production: *Who do you see in the mirror? What is the girl (boy) in the mirror wearing? What color hair does she (he) have? What color are her (his) eyes?*

© McGraw-Hill School Division

prompt for short answers to higher-level thinking skills

- Speech emergence: *Look in the mirror and tell us what you see. Make a silly face. What do you see in the mirror now? When do you use a mirror?*

prompt for detailed answers to higher-thinking skills

- Intermediate fluency: *Tell us about the image you see in the mirror. What happens in the mirror when you smile? What happens when you shake your head? Why do people use mirrors? What else can you tell us about mirrors?*

Guided Reading

Preview and Predict

Tell children this story is about some animals. Read the title and the author's and illustrator's names as you track the print. Take a picture walk, naming the animals and using the story illustrations to reinforce the concept of looking in the mirror. Explain that the still water in a pond can reflect images just like a mirror. Encourage children to make predictions by asking questions such as: *What is the pig doing in this picture? What do you think he sees in the pond? What is the goat looking at in the pond? What do you think the goat says? Why do you think the animals jump into the pond?* Help children set a purpose for reading by directing them back to the title page. Say: *The title of this story is* Seven Sillies. *Who do you think the seven sillies are? What do they do that makes them silly?*

GRAPHIC ORGANIZER
Blackline Master 101

Objectives

- To reinforce key story concepts
- To encourage dramatic interpretation
- To develop oral language

Materials

One copy of Blackline Master 101 per child; ovals of tinfoil cut to fit inside the mirror; paste or tape; colored pencils or crayons (optional)

Help children paste or tape the tinfoil to the mirror with the shiny side up. They may color the mirror frame if desired. As you read the story, stop after each animal comments on its reflection, and calls to the next animal. Have children role play each animal's reaction to seeing its reflection. Encourage them to use a different voice for each animal.

© McGraw-Hill School Division

III. BUILD SKILLS

Phonics and Decoding

REVIEW LONG *e: e, ee*
Blackline Master 102

Objectives

- To identify words with the long *e* sound spelled *e, ee*
- To blend and read long *e* words spelled *e, ee*
- To reinforce sound/symbol correspondence

Materials

One copy of Blackline Master 102 per child; scissors

Have children cut along the dotted lines to make an *eep* card and six letter cards. Then say or hold up a picture of each of the following words: s*heep, sleep, peep, cheep, beep, creep.* Have children make each word by placing the correct letter card in front of their *eep* card. Encourage children to read each word they make and to demonstrate the word when possible.

INFORMAL ASSESSMENT

Tell children to look at the illustration on pages 40–41 and have them name the animals they see. Write the name of each animal mentioned on the chalkboard. Ask children to name the animal that rhymes with *sleep.*

Phonics and Decoding

REVIEW LONG *e, ee; LONG ai*
Blackline Master 103

Objectives

- To review */ē/ e, ee; /ā/ ai*
- To blend and read long *e* and long *a* words
- To support vocabulary development

Materials

One copy of Blackline Master 103 per child; scissors; paste or glue

Go over the pictures together, having children name each one. Guide children to cut out the letters at the top of the page, identifying the sounds they make. Then have them paste the letters in the boxes to complete the word that names each picture.

INFORMAL ASSESSMENT

Have children look at the illustration on pages 36–37. Write *tail* on the board and ask children to read the word and tell you who has one in the picture. Then have them turn to page 30 and find two words in the text that are on the blackline master. Call on children to read these words aloud as they point to them in the text. Repeat with other words from the blackline master.

Comprehension

INTRODUCE MAKE PREDICTIONS
Blackline Master 104

Objectives

- To practice using picture clues to make predictions
- To support vocabulary development
- To encourage higher level thinking

Materials

One copy of Blackline Master 104 per two children; scissors; paste or glue

Organize children in pairs, and encourage them to discuss what is happening in each picture box on the left as they cut them out on the dotted lines.

© McGraw-Hill School Division

Then tell children to look at the first picture box on the right and describe what they see. Let them work together to decide what they think will happen next. Encourage them to talk about the clues in each picture. Guide them to paste the cut-out picture box that matches their prediction next to the first picture. Repeat with the other pictures.

INFORMAL ASSESSMENT

Direct children to pages 40–41. After rereading the text and looking at the illustration, invite children to make predictions about what they think will happen next. If necessary, ask them to draw their predictions.

Vocabulary Strategy

INFLECTIONAL ENDING *-ing*
Blackline Master 105

Objectives

- To practice adding the inflectional ending *-ing* to words
- To practice word identification
- To support vocabulary development

Materials

One copy of Blackline Master 105 per child; scissors; paste or glue

Go over the pictures together, having children describe each one. Encourage use of the target words. Then have children read the words and identify the *-ing* endings at the top of the page. Tell them to cut along the dotted lines to make ten cards. Have them paste a word card and an ending card next to each picture. Pairs of children can read the words to each other.

INFORMAL ASSESSMENT

Have children turn to page 36 and find the two words that have the ending *-ing*. Call on children to read aloud the words. Write the last sentence *(They did feel very silly!)* on the chalkboard and have children read it. Below it write *They were ________ very silly!* Ask children to add *-ing* to *feel* to complete the new sentence. Invite them to read the new sentence aloud.

© McGraw-Hill School Division

Name_______________________________ Date_______________

Mirror, Mirror

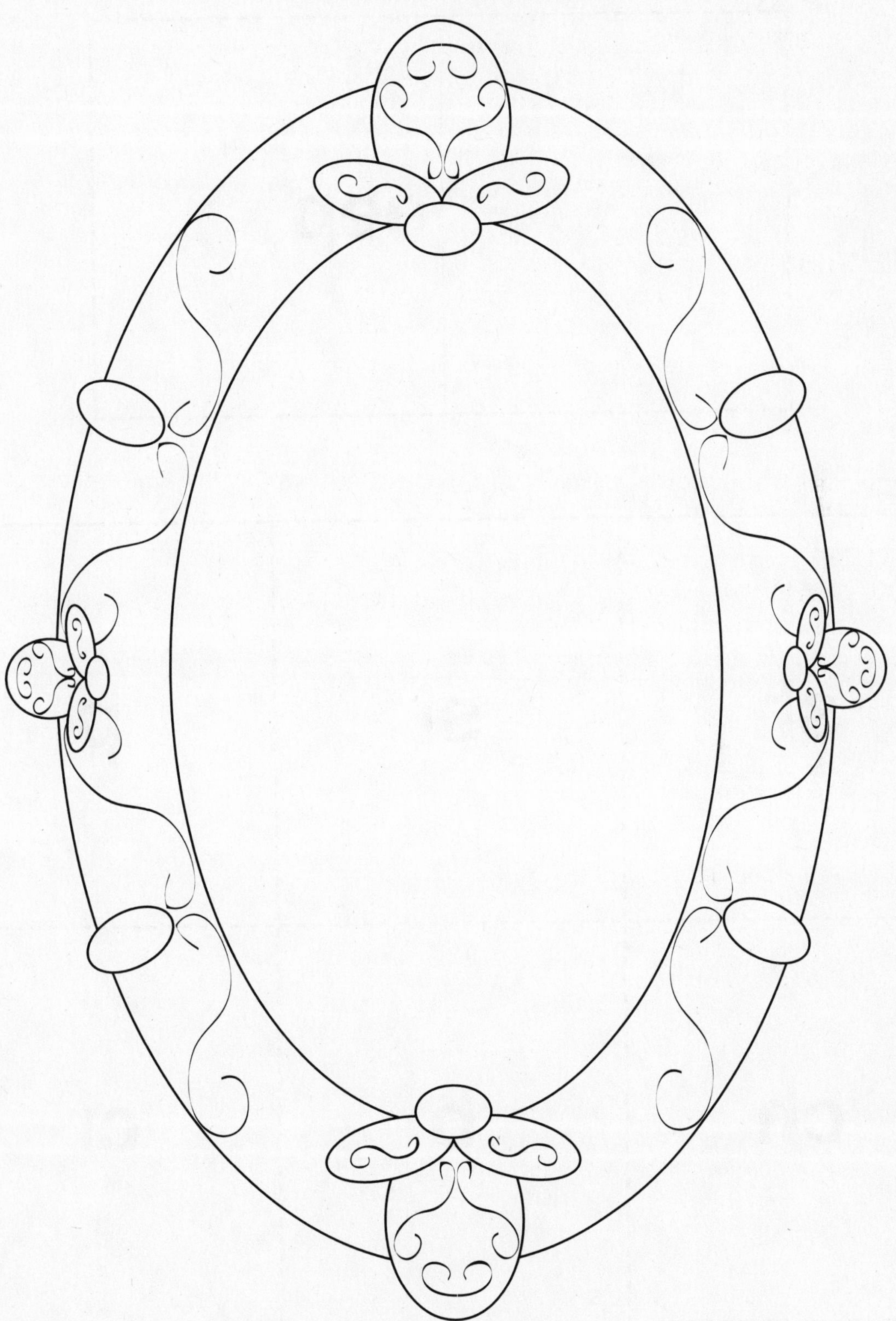

© McGraw-Hill School Division

Name_________________________ Date_____________

Long e -eep

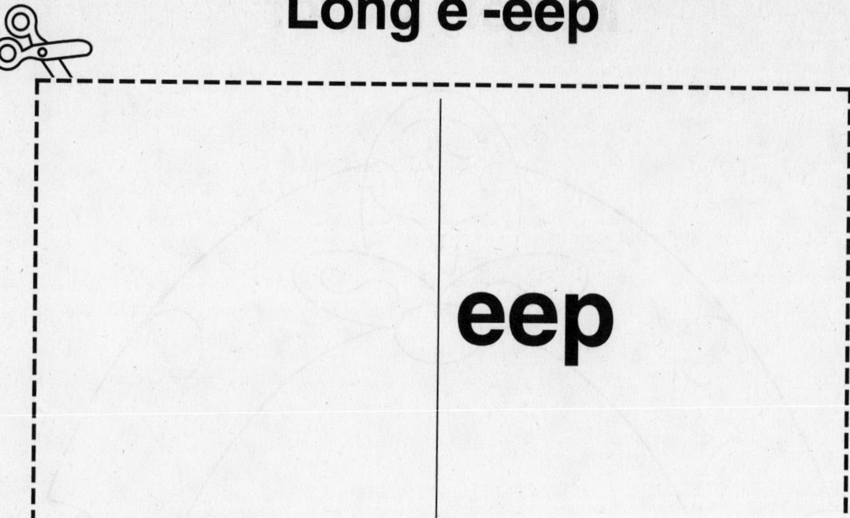

sh	sl	p
ch	b	cr

© McGraw-Hill School Division

Name________________________ Date____________

What's Missing?

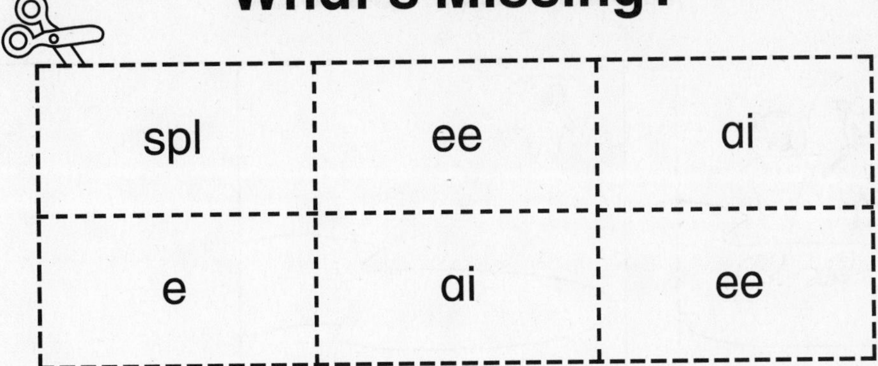

ash

thr

t l

sh p

w

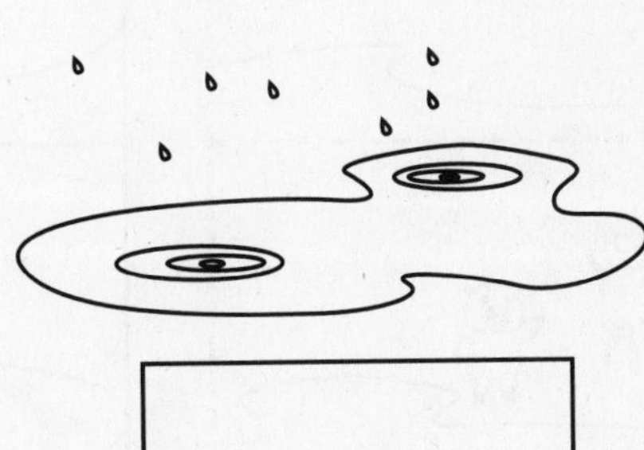

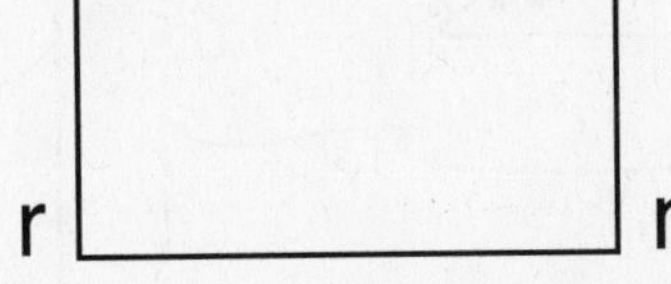
r n

© McGraw-Hill School Division

Name______________________ Date____________

Look and Guess

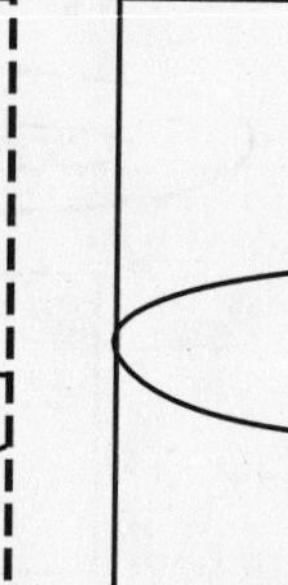

© McGraw-Hill School Division

Name________________________ Date____________

What Are the Animals Doing?

call	look	jump	laugh	count
ing	ing	ing	ing	ing

 1 2 3 4 5		

© McGraw-Hill School Division

SHRINKING MOUSE pp. 46A–81R

Written and Illustrated by Pat Hutchins

BUILD BACKGROUND FOR LANGUAGE SUPPORT

I. FOCUS ON READING

Focus on Skills

OBJECTIVE: Listen for long *e*

TPR

Develop Phonological Awareness

Bring in pictures of words that have the long *e* sound, such as the following: *peach, beach, bean, pea, sea.* Also have some pictures of items that do not have this sound. Hold up one long *e* item and one with a different vowel sound, naming them in this chant: *pen, peach. Reach for the peach.* Have children repeat the word *peach* as they reach for it. Repeat this with other long *e* words by saying, for example, *bean, dog. Reach for the bean.*

II. READ THE LITERATURE

VOCABULARY
right
before
our
come
off

Vocabulary

Print the vocabulary words on the chalkboard. Point to each one as you give the following commands. Encourage children to repeat the vocabulary words after performing each action. Model and say: *Stand up. Clap before you sit down again.* Let children give other commands using the word before. For example: *Hop before you sit down.* Now tell children: *Put your hands on your head. Now take them off your head.* Ask children to say: *My hand is off my head.* Say: *Point to our coats.* Have them say: *These are our coats.* Tell children: *Raise your right hand.* Have children say: *This is my right hand.* Say: *Come to the front of the room.* Ask children to say: *We come to the front.*

CONCEPT
things aren't always as they seem

Evaluate Prior Knowledge

Show children a clear glass wrapped in colored cellophane into which you have placed a white object. Ask children what color they think the object is. Then remove the cellophane. Discuss how the object in the jar is not the color it seemed to be at first. Now let children look at their reflections in a shiny spoon. Have them turn the spoon so the reflections become distorted. Ask them if they really look like what they see in the spoon's reflection. Point out that things are not always as they seem.

Develop Oral Language

Direct children to look at a ball across the playground. Have them compare the size of the distant ball to their thumbs as they stand across the playground, as they move closer and as they finally reach it. Use prompts appropriate for the linguistic level of the children.

© McGraw-Hill School Division

nonverbal prompt for active participation

- Preproduction: Model and say: *Look at your thumb and the ball. Show us which seems bigger. Walk to the ball. Hold your thumb next to the ball. Show us which seems bigger now.*

one- or two-word response prompt

- Early production: *Which seems bigger, your thumb or the ball? What seems to happen to the ball as you move closer? Hold your thumb next to the ball. Which is really bigger?*

prompt for short answers to higher-level thinking skills

- Speech emergence: *What do you see when you look at your thumb and the ball across the playground? Do you think the ball is really smaller than your thumb? What happens as you move closer to the ball?*

prompt for detailed answers to higher-level thinking skills

- Intermediate fluency: *Look at your thumb and the ball, and describe what you see. Why do you think your thumb looks bigger than the ball? What happens as you move closer to the ball? How do you know the ball is really bigger than your thumb?*

Guided Reading

Preview and Predict

Tell children that in this story some animals decide to leave their woods and visit some woods they see in the distance. Read aloud the title and the author/illustrator's name as you track the print. Explain that *shrinking* means to get smaller and smaller. Lead children on a picture walk using the illustrations to reinforce the concept that things seem to get smaller as they move farther away. Ask questions such as: *What seems to be happening to Owl as he flies towards the woods? Why do you think Fox follows Owl? How does each animal seem to change as it goes toward the woods? Do you think the animals are really getting smaller? How do the animals seem to change as they come back to their own woods?* Then ask them to predict what Mouse might be thinking as she sees her friends appear to be shrinking. Invite children to share their predictions.

GRAPHIC ORGANIZER
Blackline Master 106

Objectives

- To practice making predictions
- To support using picture clues
- To encourage higher level thinking skills

Materials

One copy of Blackline Master 106 per child; colored pencils or crayons

After completing the picture walk, ask children to tell whether they think Mouse will really shrink in the story. Encourage them to explain why they think this, or indicate which pictures support their predictions. Have children draw a picture of their prediction in the first box. After reading pages 64–65, ask children if they now think Mouse is a shrinking mouse. Have them draw their revised prediction in the second box. At the end of the story, children draw a picture of what really happened to Mouse, and compare that with their two previous predictions. Discuss the differences between their predictions and the outcome.

© McGraw-Hill School Division

III. BUILD SKILLS

Phonics and Decoding

REVIEW LONG *e: ie, ea*
Blackline Master 107

Objectives

- To identify and review */ē/ ie, ea, e, ee*
- To blend and read long *e* words
- To reinforce spelling skills

Materials

One copy of Blackline Master 107 per two children; scissors

Organize children in pairs, and have them cut out the word frames. Then let the partners choose who will be Mouse and who will be Owl. As you say a word, or hold up a picture that illustrates an *-ie* or *-ea* word, children can make the word by placing the correct word frame on Mouse or Owl. They should make sure the frame fits neatly around the card held by Mouse or Owl. Then children can take turns reading the words to their partners.

INFORMAL ASSESSMENT

Assign each pair of children a page from the story and have them search the picture and text for long *e: ie, ea* words. Call on teams to share the words they found.

Phonics and Decoding

REVIEW LONG *e: ie, ea, e, ee;* LONG *i: -igh;* AND DIGRAPH *-nk*
Blackline Master 108

Objectives

- To review long *e: ie, ea, e, ee*; long *i: -igh*; digraph *-nk*
- To blend and read long *e* and digraph *-nk* words
- To reinforce spelling skills

Materials

One copy of Blackline Master 108 per child; scissors; paste or glue

Help children identify what each picture shows. Then have them cut out the letters at the top of the page, encouraging them to identify the sounds they represent. Children can paste the letters in the correct spaces to complete each word. Let children read their completed words to a friend.

INFORMAL ASSESSMENT

Direct children to turn to pages 72–73. Write the words *fields, trees, leaf* on the chalkboard, and challenge children to read each word and find the object it names in the illustration. Then have children look at the text and find a word with long *e: ea;* (reached) and a word with long *i: -igh* (right). Call on children to read the words they found.

Comprehension

REVIEW MAKE PREDICTIONS
Blackline Master 109

Objectives

- To practice making predictions
- To encourage higher level thinking
- To practice following directions

© McGraw-Hill School Division

Materials

One copy of Blackline Master 109 per child; scissors; paste or glue

Go over the pictures on the left together, encouraging children to tell what is happening in each. Have children cut out the pictures on the right. Then have them paste each cutout next to a picture so that it shows what happens next. Encourage children to discuss the picture clues they see in each one.

INFORMAL ASSESSMENT

Have children turn to the last page in the story. Ask what they think will happen the next time one of the animals runs toward the woods. Call on children to share their predictions.

Vocabulary Strategy

REVIEW INFLECTIONAL ENDING *-ing*
Blackline Master 110

Objectives

- To practice applying inflectional ending *-ing*
- To reinforce story vocabulary
- To practice word identification

Materials

One copy of Blackline Master 110 per child; scissors; paste or glue

Have children describe each picture. Encourage use of target words by supplying frames for children to complete orally such as: *The animals are* ____________ *together. The squirrel is* ____________ *at a nut.* Show children how to follow the addition signs next to each picture. Then have them cut out the words at the top of the page, and paste each one in the correct box.

INFORMAL ASSESSMENT

Direct children to the text on page 51. Have them find the words that end in *-ing*. Call on children to read the words they found. Repeat the process, looking for *-ing* words on other pages.

© McGraw-Hill School Division

Name______________________________ Date____________

What Will Mouse Do?

	Make Prediction
	Revise Prediction
	Confirm Prediction

© McGraw-Hill School Division

Name________________________________ Date________________

Long e Word Puzzles

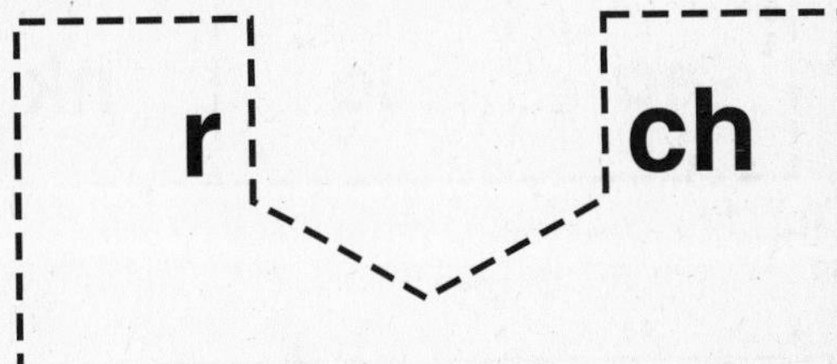

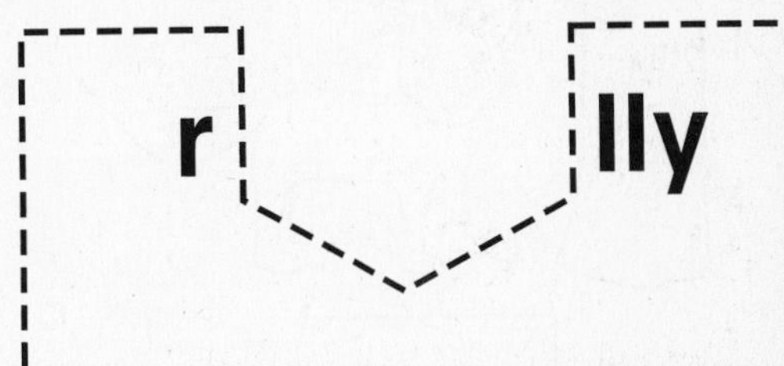

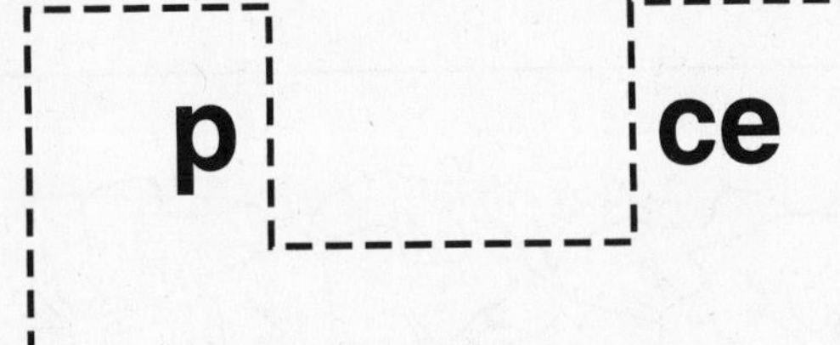

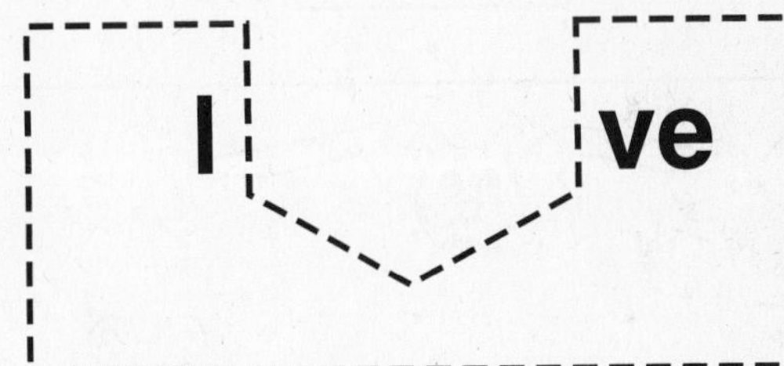

© McGraw-Hill School Division

Name______________________________ Date______________

What's the Word?

ea	ie	nk	i	ea	ee

© McGraw-Hill School Division

Name________________________________ Date__________________

Guess What They Will Do

© McGraw-Hill School Division

Name________________________________ Date________________

Follow the Signs

following	sitting	flying	looking

sit + t + ing =

look + ing =

fly + ing =

follow + ing =

© McGraw-Hill School Division

YOU CAN'T SMELL A FLOWER WITH YOUR EAR! pp. 82A–117R

Written by Joanna Cole Illustrated by Mavis Smith

BUILD BACKGROUND FOR LANGUAGE SUPPORT

I. FOCUS ON READING

Focus on Skills

OBJECTIVE: Listen for long *o*

TPR

Develop Phonological Awareness

Play Go on O. Tell children you will say a word. If the word has a long *o* sound as in *go*, they can repeat the word and begin walking quietly around the room. As they walk, they must listen for the next word. If it is another long *o* word, they repeat it and keep walking. If the word has a different vowel sound, they must stop. They cannot go again until you say a word with long *o*. Tell children that now they will listen to the poem, "Raindrops." If they hear a word with the long *o* sound they may *go*, by taking one step forward.

II. READ THE LITERATURE

VOCABULARY
high
find
more
kind
by

Vocabulary

Print the vocabulary words on the chalkboard. Read the words and have children repeat them after you.

by: Say to one child: *Tony, come and stand by me.* Tell that child to call on another child and repeat the sentence until all children are standing in a line.

high: Pass a ball over the head of the child next to you and say: *The ball is high over Tony's head.* Have the children pass the ball in the same way repeating the sentence.

kind: Ask the child next to you: *What kind of fruit do you like best?* Have children ask the question, all of the way down the line.

find: Place a small object in one hand and say: *Who can find the ___________?* Then let children play the guessing game with partners.

more: Have a boy count the boys in the room and a girl count the girls. Then ask: *Are there more boys or girls in the room?* Have children respond by using the word more.

CONCEPT
the five senses

Evaluate Prior Knowledge

Bring in the following items: a tape player with a music tape, a banana, cotton balls, perfume, a picture. Use body language and repetition as you do the activities. Play the music and say: *We hear the music with our ears.* Give children a small piece of banana to eat, and say: *We taste the banana with our tongues.* Let children feel the cotton balls as you say: *We feel the cotton with our fingers.* Pass the perfume around for children to smell, and say: *We smell perfume with our noses.* Show the picture and say: *We see the picture with our eyes.*

© McGraw-Hill School Division

Develop Oral Language

To increase children's understanding of the five senses, have them respond to questions and prompts such as those below. Choose those that are most appropriate for their language ability.

nonverbal prompt for active participation

- Preproduction: Model and say: *Look at the chalkboard. You see the chalkboard with your eyes. Point to your eyes. Touch the chalkboard. Show us the part of your body you use to touch the chalkboard.*

one- or two-word response prompt

- Early production: Model and say: *What did you smell? What part of your body did you use to smell the perfume? Could you see the perfume? What part of your body did you use to see it? Could you hear the perfume?*

prompt for short answers to higher-level thinking skills

- Speech emergence: *What did you taste? What part of your body did you taste the banana with? How did it taste? Could you smell the banana? What did you use to smell with? What else could you do with the banana? Why can't you hear a banana?*

prompt for detailed answers to higher-level thinking skills

- Intermediate fluency: *What did you hear? What did you hear the music with? Could you smell or taste the music? Why not? What other things can you hear? Can you see or touch any of them?*

Guided Reading

Preview and Predict

Read the title and ask children what body part they would use to smell a flower. Ask what ears can do if they can't smell things. Tell children that this story is about the five senses: see, hear, smell, taste, and touch. Walk through the illustrations together and use them to highlight key vocabulary and concepts. Help children identify the brain in many of the drawings. Explain that the brain helps you see, hear, smell, etc. Ask: *Which pages will tell us more about the sense of sight? Where will we learn more about the ear? On which pages will we learn more about the sense of touch? What things do you see children smelling? What do you think we'll learn about on the page that has the picture of the tongue?* Invite children to turn to a picture which shows something they would like to know more about. Call on children to share their questions and interests with the rest of the group.

Objectives

GRAPHIC ORGANIZER
Blackline Master 111

- To reinforce understanding of main concept and story details
- To develop print awareness
- To support cooperative learning

Materials

One copy of Blackline Master 111 per child; pencils

Go over the Senses chart with children, having them identify the word and picture for each sense. As you read the story, stop after each section. In small groups have children discuss what they learned about that sense. Help them write words or phrases on their Senses charts that describe what they learned. Invite children to share their completed charts with each other.

To help children practice making predictions, use the chart to encourage pre-reading predictions. Ask questions such as: *What body part do you think we use to taste? With what do you think we smell?* Help children write their predictions on the line next to each picture.

© McGraw-Hill School Division

III. BUILD SKILLS

Phonics and Decoding

LONG *o: o, oa, oe, ow*
Blackline Master 112

Objectives

- To identify /ō/ *o, oa, oe, ow*
- To blend and read long *o* words
- To practice spelling skills

Materials

One copy of Blackline Master 112 per child; scissors; paste or glue

Have children cut out the letters at the top of the page. Direct them to the unfinished words in the first box. As you say a word either demonstrate or hold up a picture that illustrates a long *o* word, help children complete that word by pasting the correct letter or letters in the empty space. When the page is complete, let children check their answers.

INFORMAL ASSESSMENT

Have children turn to page 104. Select a long *o* word and a word with a different vowel sound, for example *soap* and *smell*. Write the words on the chalkboard and ask children to read the word with the long *o* sound. Invite a volunteer to underline the letters that stand for the long *o* sound. Repeat with words on pages 110–111, such as *pillow, cold, snowball, potato.*

Phonics and Decoding

REVIEW *o, oa, oe, ow; ie, ea*
Blackline Master 113

Objectives

- To review long *e; ie, ea;* long *o: o, oa, oe, ow*
- To blend and read long *e* and long *o* words
- To practice word identification

Materials

One copy of Blackline Master 113 per child; scissors; paste or glue

Have children identify the letters at the top of the page and the sounds they represent before cutting them out. Then go over the pictures together, having children name each one. Guide children to complete each word by pasting the correct letter or letters in the empty box.

INFORMAL ASSESSMENT

Have children work with a partner. Assign each pair a word from the Blackline Master, and a page from the text on which they must find the word or an illustration of it. Call on teams to share their answers with the rest of the group.

Comprehension

INTRODUCE DRAW CONCLUSIONS
Blackline Master 114

Objectives

- To practice drawing conclusions
- To encourage higher level thinking
- To practice following directions

© McGraw-Hill School Division

Materials

One copy of Blackline Master 114 per child; scissors; paste or glue

Have children name the pictures at the top of the page and then cut them out. Read the first rebus riddle together. Children answer the riddle by pasting the correct picture in the empty box next to the riddle. Then allow children to work in small groups or with partners to complete the rest of the page. When all the riddles have been answered, let children take turns reading and answering them.

INFORMAL ASSESSMENT

Direct children to page 105. Ask if they think the boy at the bottom of the page likes the way his shoe smells. Encourage them to give reasons for their conclusions. Follow the same procedure with the illustration on page 106, asking children if they think the boy and girl in the picture like the taste of pizza.

Vocabulary Strategy

REVIEW CONTEXT CLUES
Blackline Master 115

Objectives

- To practice finding the meanings of unfamiliar words
- To practice word identification
- To support hands-on learning

Materials

One copy of Blackline Master 115 per child; scissors; paste or glue

Read the words at the top of the page with children, and have them cut out the words. Then invite children to work with partners to read the rebus sentences. They can complete each sentence by pasting the correct word in the empty box.

INFORMAL ASSESSMENT

Have children turn to page 106. Write the word *pizza* on the board, and ask children to use the illustration and the first sentence to identify the word. Repeat with unfamiliar words on other pages.

© McGraw-Hill School Division

Name_______________________________ Date_______________

All About the Senses

tasting

smelling

hearing

feeling

seeing

© McGraw-Hill School Division

Name________________________________ Date______________

Long o Fun

o	oa	oe	ow	o	oa
oe	ow	o	oa	oe	ow

g ☐

h ☐ me

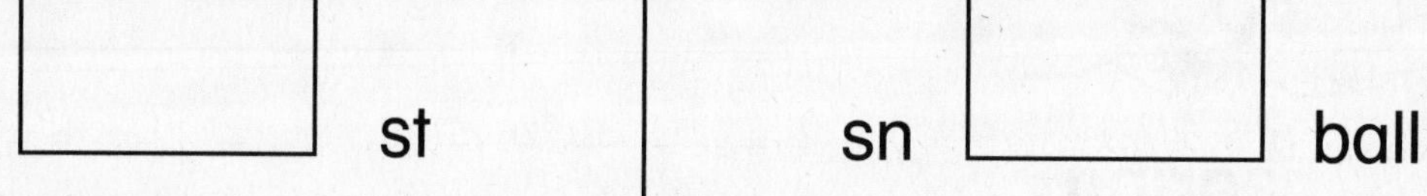

m ☐ st

l ☐

pill ☐

sn ☐ ball

s ☐ p

g ☐ t

b ☐ t

g ☐ s

t ☐ s

h ☐

© McGraw-Hill School Division

Name_________________________________ Date_______________

Something's Missing

o	oa	oe	ow	ea	ea	ie	ie

pill ☐	s ☐ p
blindf ☐ ld	p ☐ ce
☐ t	f ☐ ld
ice cr ☐ m	t ☐ s

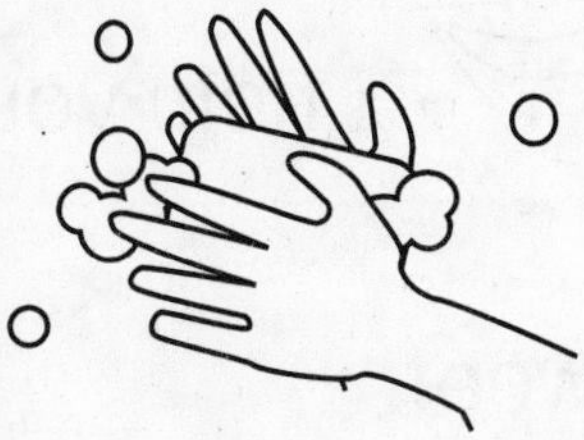

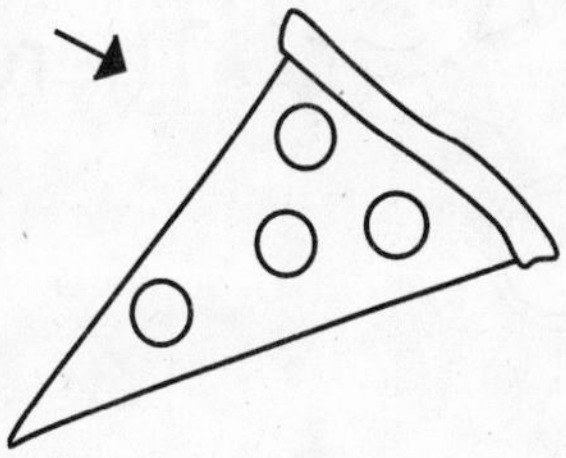

© McGraw-Hill School Division

Name________________________________ Date______________

Riddle Fun

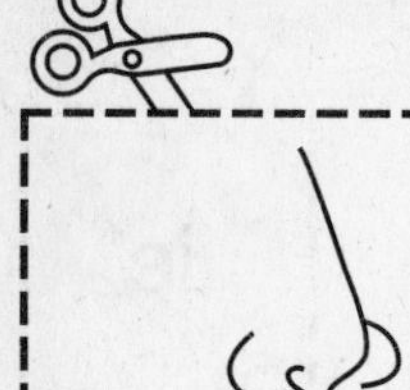

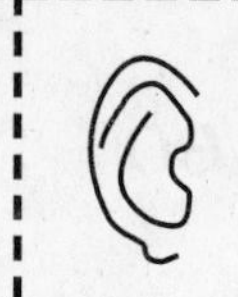   

I am in your . I help you know

if  is sweet.

What am I? 

We are on your . There are 2 of us.

We help you .

What are we? 

We are on your . There are 2 of us.

We help you .

What are we? 

I am between your  and your .

I help you smell .

What am I? 

© McGraw-Hill School Division

Name________________________________ Date______________

Fill in the Blanks

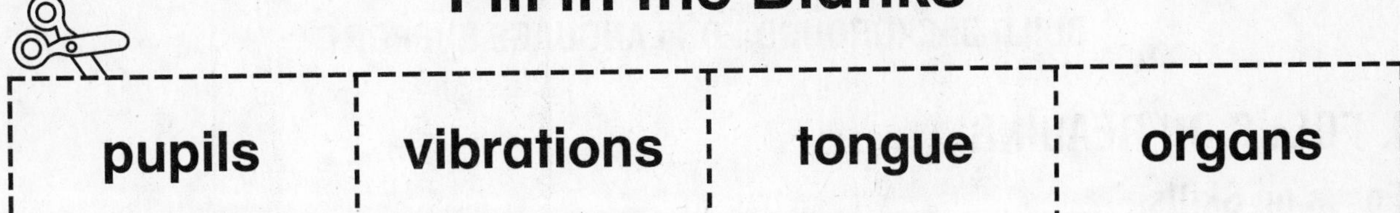

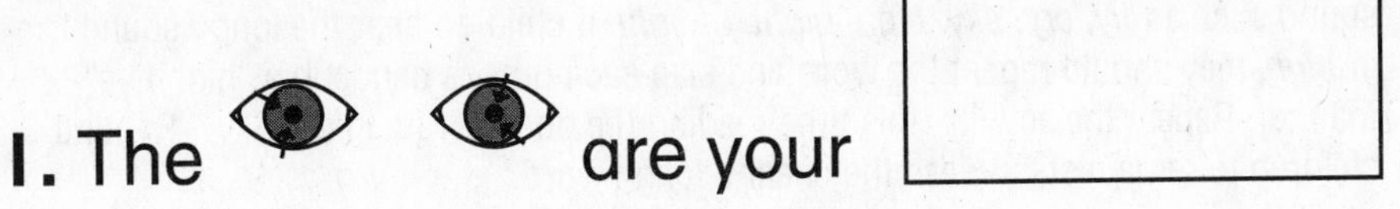

1. The are your ______.

2. Your pick up called ______.

3. You lick an with your ______.

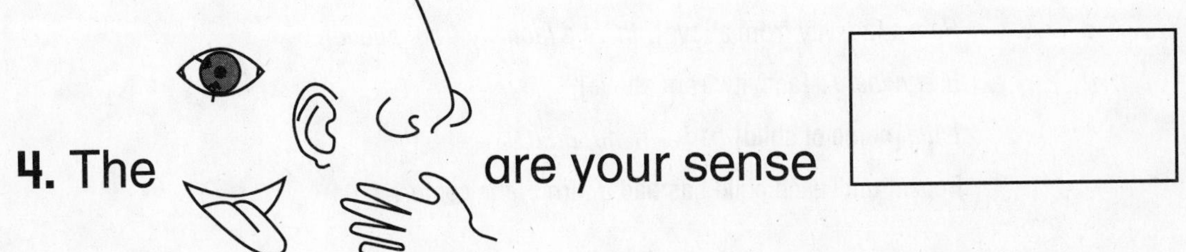

4. The are your sense ______.

© McGraw-Hill School Division

OWL AND THE MOON pp. 118A–141R

Written and Illustrated by Arnold Lobel

BUILD BACKGROUND FOR LANGUAGE SUPPORT

I. FOCUS ON READING

Focus on Skills

OBJECTIVE: Listen for long *i*

TPR

Develop Phonological Awareness

Have each child sit facing a partner. Hold up a picture, or say a word with a long *i* sound such as *fly, cry, sky, high, night,* or *light.* If children hear the long *i* sound like in *high,* they should repeat the word and slap each other's hands in a "high five" manner. Repeat the activity, this time reading the poem, "Kite in the Sky." Remind children to remain still unless they hear a long *i* word.

II. READ THE LITERATURE

VOCABULARY
gone
room
everything
eyes
head

Vocabulary

Print the vocabulary words on the chalkboard, and read the words together. Have children copy each word onto a card. As you demonstrate and discuss each word meaning, have children hold up the correct words. Use body language to increase understanding. Empty a small box of items onto a table and say: *Everything in the box is on the table.* Have children say: *I see everything.* Put the box outside the classroom, saying: *Is the box gone?* Encourage children to answer: *Yes, the box is gone.* Put your head on your desk. Instruct children to do the same, then have them say: *I put my head on my desk.* Point to your eyes and children's eyes, saying: *My eyes are brown, your eyes are green.* etc. Turn off the lights and ask: *Is the room dark?* Have children answer by saying: *Yes, the room is dark.*

CONCEPT
friendship

Evaluate Prior Knowledge

To encourage children to think about the concept of friendship, play the following circle game, sung to the tune of "Old Macdonald Had a Farm." Choose one child to stand in the middle of the circle and sing:

Little [name of child] *had a friend, EIEIO.* [child chooses friend to join her in the center]

And with her friend she liked to [child names activity she does with a friend], *EIEIO.*

With a [activity from above] *here, and a* [activity from above] *there,* [children in center dramatize activity]

Here a [activity from above], *there a [activity from above],*

Everywhere a [activity from above],

Little [name of child] *had a friend, EIEIO.*

Repeat until each child has had a turn in the center.

© McGraw-Hill School Division

Develop Oral Language

nonverbal prompt for active participation

- Preproduction: *Show us* (point to class and self) *how you feel* (point to your face) *when you are with a friend* (point to child's friend).

one- or two-word response prompt

- Early production: *Who is your friend? What do you like to do together? Have you been friends for a long time?*

prompt for short answers to higher-level thinking skills

- Speech emergence: *Tell us about your friend. Is she or he a good friend? Why?*

prompt for detailed answers to higher-level thinking skills

- Intermediate fluency: *How did you become friends with* [name of child]*? Why is she or he your friend?*

Guided Reading

Preview and Predict

Tell children that this story is about a very different friendship. Read the title and author/illustrator's name while tracking the print. As you lead children on a picture walk, encourage them to use the illustrations to make predictions about the story, and to reinforce the concept of friendship. Ask questions such as: *Who do you think Owl's friend is in this story? What does it look like the moon is doing when Owl is walking? What do you think Owl is saying to the moon? Can the moon be a friend? Why or why not?* Help children set a purpose for reading by asking them what they would like to find as they read this story.

Objectives

GRAPHIC ORGANIZER
Blackline Master 116

- To reinforce drawing conclusions
- To practice higher-level thinking skills
- To support cooperative learning

Materials

One copy of Blackline Master 116 per two children; pencils

As you read the story, stop and ask questions when there are opportunities for children to draw conclusions. For example, after reading the first page of the story, ask children if they think Owl is a real owl. Invite them to explain why they think as they do. Then have children work with partners to write a word or phrase about their conclusion. At the end of the story, ask children what Owl believed about the moon. Help them write Owl's conclusions on their charts. Ask why they think Owl believed what he did. Invite children to say whether they think Owl's conclusions were correct.

© McGraw-Hill School Division

III. BUILD SKILLS

Phonics and Decoding

REVIEW LONG *i: i, y, -igh*
Blackline Master 117

Objectives

- To review long *i: i, y, -igh*
- To blend and read words with long *i: i, y, -igh*
- To review initial and final consonants

Materials

One copy of Blackline Master 117 per child; scissors

Have children cut out the letter cards. As you say a word or hold up a picture that illustrates a long *i: i, y,* or *-igh* word, children can use the letter cards and word fragments to form the correct word. Children may work with a partner and take turns making and reading new words.

INFORMAL ASSESSMENT

Have children turn to page 124. Write the sentence *It climbed higher and higher into the sky* on the chalkboard. Ask volunteers to point to and read aloud the words that have the long *i* sound they hear in *night.* Underline the *-igh* in *higher* and the *y* in *sky.*

Phonics and Decoding

REVIEW LONG *i: i, y, igh* AND LONG *o: oa, oe, ow*
Blackline Master 118

Objectives

- To review long *i: i, y, -igh*
- To review long *o: oa, oe, ow*
- To blend and read long *i* and long *o* words

Materials

One copy of Blackline Master 118 per child; scissors; paste or glue

Have children cut out the letters at the top of the page, and identify the sounds they stand for. Say the first word *kind* and have children complete the word by pasting the correct letters in the empty box. Repeat with the rest of the words. Encourage children to read each word as they complete it.

INFORMAL ASSESSMENT

Direct children to turn to page 124. Have them find two words in the text that are on Blackline Master 118. Tell them that one of the words has an *-er* added to it in the text. Call on children to read the words aloud. Repeat with the other words on the Blackline Master.

Comprehension

REVIEW DRAW CONCLUSIONS
Blackline Master 119

Objectives

- To practice drawing conclusions
- To encourage higher-level thinking skills
- To support cooperative learning

Materials

One copy of Blackline Master 119 per two children; scissors; paste or glue

Have children cut out the phrases at the top of the page, and help them read each one. Then read aloud the rebus clues, encouraging children to track the print as you read. Children can answer the question about where Owl or Moon is by pasting the correct phrase in each sentence frame. Call on teams to read the completed riddles and their answers to the class.

© McGraw-Hill School Division

INFORMAL ASSESSMENT Have children turn to pages 130–131. Ask them to tell why Owl climbed to the top of a hill. Encourage them to explain their answers.

Vocabulary Strategy

REVIEW CONTEXT CLUES
Blackline Master 120

Objectives

- To practice finding the meanings of unfamiliar words
- To practice word identification
- To support hands-on learning

Materials

One copy of Blackline Master 120 per child; scissors; paste or glue

Have children cut out the words at the top of the page. Then help them describe each picture as you encourage the use of the target words. Guide children to use the pictures and what they know about letter sounds to paste each word under the picture it names.

INFORMAL ASSESSMENT Have children turn to page 130. On the chalkboard write *Owl climbed to the top of the hill.* Underline the word *climbed.* Have children use the illustration and context clues to read *climbed.* Encourage them to explain how they figured out the unfamiliar word.

© McGraw-Hill School Division

Name______________________ Date__________

All About Owl

© McGraw-Hill School Division

Name ____________________ Date __________

What Words Can You Make?

k	m
f	gr

sk	tr
fl	m

n	l
m	r

☐ ind

☐ y

☐ ight

© McGraw-Hill School Division

Name________________________________ Date________________

What Belongs Where?

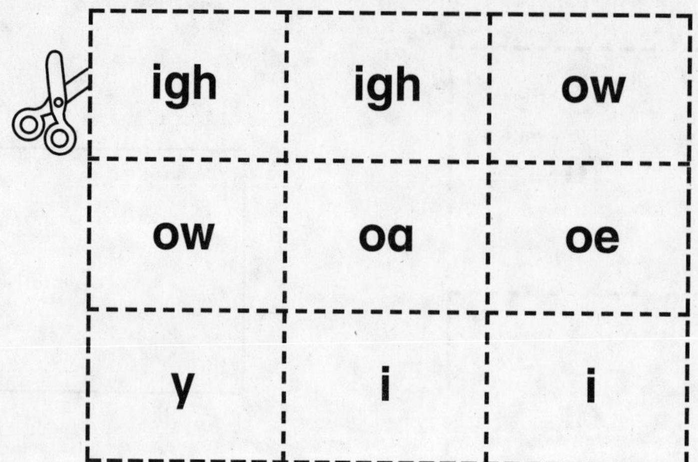

k ☐ nd m ☐ l ☐ t

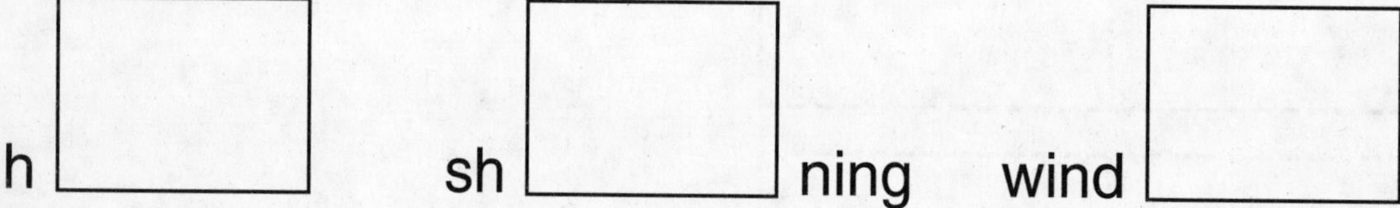

r ☐ d foll ☐ g ☐ s

© McGraw-Hill School Division

Name______________________________ Date______________

Where is Owl? Where is Moon?

at home in bed	behind the clouds	in the sky	at the seashore

Owl sits on a . Owl hears .

Where is Owl?

Owl is ☐.

Owl looks . Owl sees the .

Where is the moon?

Moon is ☐.

Owl sits on top of a .

Owl cannot see the .

Where is the moon?

The moon is ☐.

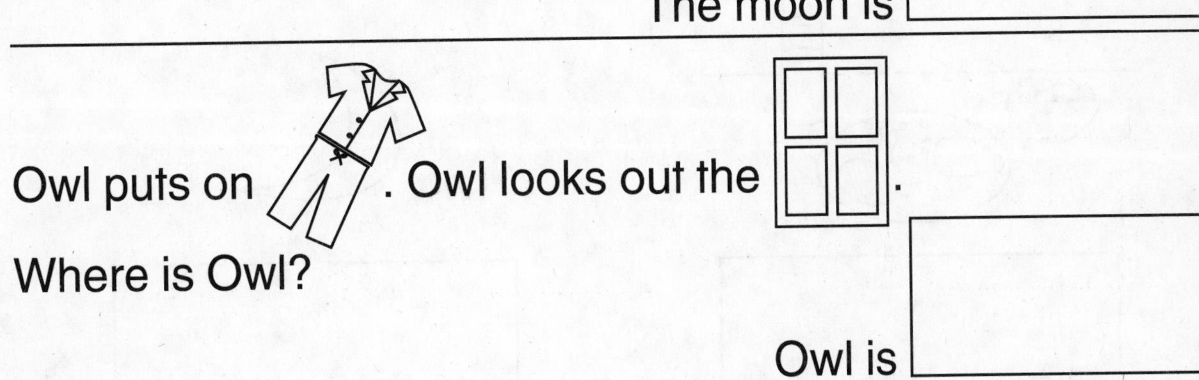

Owl puts on . Owl looks out the .

Where is Owl?

Owl is ☐.

© McGraw-Hill School Division

Name________________________________ Date______________

Picture-Word Match-up

moon	edge	sky
supper	pajamas	pillow

© McGraw-Hill School Division

THE NIGHT ANIMALS pp. 142A–151R

Time For Kids

BUILD BACKGROUND FOR LANGUAGE SUPPORT

I. FOCUS ON READING

Focus on Skills

OBJECTIVE: Listen for long *i*, *o*, and *e*

TPR

Develop Phonological Awareness

Play "Leap, Fly, Row." Say a word or show a picture of an object with either a long *e*, *i*, or *o*. If the word has a long *e* like in *leap*, children should repeat the word as they leap. Children should pretend to fly if the word has a long *i*. They should pantomime rowing if the word has a long *o*. Make sure children repeat each word as they perform the correct actions. Then read the poem, "At Night" to the children and tell them to listen closely for the long *e*, *i*, and *o* words.

II. READ THE LITERATURE

Vocabulary
come
many
find
kind
all
off

Vocabulary

Write the vocabulary words on the board. As you say each word, have them repeat the word after you. Instruct one child to call on another and say, (*child's name*), *Come and turn off the lights*. Then turn the lights on again and repeat until all children have been called on. Then play "All Sit Down." Tell children that when you turn off the lights, they should say: *We all sit down*. They should stand up when you turn on the lights. Show children several small objects. Point to an object. Say: *What kind of object is this?* Then tell children to close their eyes while you hide them. Say: *Now open your eyes and see how many you can find*. Have them respond by predicting: *I think I can find this many*. Children can hold up fingers to indicate number.

Concept
animals at night

Evaluate Prior Knowledge

Bring in pictures of a variety of nocturnal and diurnal animals. If possible, have some pictures showing animals at night. Also have a picture of a night sky on hand, and one showing daytime. Point to an animal in a picture and say: *This is a [raccoon]*. Hold up the night picture and say: *At night the raccoon hunts for food*. Encourage children to join you in dramatizing the raccoon's behavior. Now hold up the daytime picture and say: *The raccoon sleeps during the day*. Have children dramatize the sleeping raccoon. Repeat for the other animals in the pictures.

Develop Oral Language

Give each pair of children a picture of an animal and have them dramatize a situation showing that animal at night. Use prompts appropriate for children's linguistic level.

nonverbal prompt for active participation

- Preproduction: *Show us* (point to self and class) *what the* (name animal and point to it in picture) *does at night* (point to night picture).

one- or two-word response prompt

- Early production: *What is this animal* (point to picture)? *Is it awake at night or during the day? When does it look for food?*

© McGraw-Hill School Division

prompt for short answers to higher-level thinking skills	• Speech emergence: *What is the name of your animal? What does it do at night? What does it do during the day?*
prompt for detailed answers to higher-level thinking skills	• Intermediate fluency: *Tell us about your animal. What does it do at night? Why do you think it does this at night? What does it do during the day? Why do you think it does this? What other animals do you know that are active when your animal is active?*

Guided Reading

Preview and Predict

Have children look at the first page of the story. Read the title while tracking the print. Ask children what they think the story will be about. Lead them on a picture walk, naming any unfamiliar animals. Use the photographs to reinforce the concept of "night animals," and encourage children to make predictions about the story. Ask questions such as: *Do you think it is daytime or nighttime in this picture? How do you know? What do you think the owl is doing? Why do you think the picture of the rat is here? What animals do you think are awake at night? Why do you think they might be awake at night and sleep during the day?* Have children draw pictures of what they hope to learn from the story. Invite them to share their pictures with the rest of the group.

Objectives

GRAPHIC ORGANIZER
Blackline Master 121

- To practice drawing conclusions
- To reinforce understanding of story details
- To encourage higher-level thinking skills

Materials

One copy of Blackline Master 121 per two children; pencils

Go over the Animal Chart with children, reading the headings and the first entries together. As you read the story, stop at the end of each page and have children discuss with their partners what they learned about each animal. Help them enter these facts on their charts. Then prompt them to identify the conclusions they can draw from each fact, and enter these on the chart as well.

To reinforce drawing conclusions, arrange students in pairs. One partner can hold the chart and read some facts about an animal. The other partner can identify the animal and tell what conclusion can be drawn about it.

© McGraw-Hill School Division

III. BUILD SKILLS

Comprehension

REVIEW MAKE PREDICTIONS
Blackline Master 122

Objectives

- To practice making predictions
- To encourage higher-level thinking skills
- To support cooperative learning

Materials

One copy of Blackline Master 122 per two children; scissors; paste or glue

Have children cut out the pictures at the top of the page and set them aside. Then they can discuss the pictures in the first row, and describe what is happening. You may need to point out details such as which direction the sun is moving, and what that indicates. Children should try to predict what will happen next. They can paste the correct cut-out picture in the empty box. Encourage them to tell if their predictions matched the pictures. Repeat with the other rows.

INFORMAL ASSESSMENT

Have children look at the photograph on page 146. Ask them to predict whether the bat will eat the bug. Encourage them to give reasons for their answers by telling what they know or have learned about bats.

Comprehension

REVIEW DRAW CONCLUSIONS
Blackline Master 123

Objectives

- To practice drawing conclusions
- To reinforce story vocabulary
- To encourage higher-level thinking skills

Materials

One copy of Blackline Master 123 per child; scissors; paste or glue

Help children identify the words at the top of the page, and then cut them out. Invite them to read the clues in each row, and answer the riddle by pasting the correct word in each box. Encourage children to read the riddles and their answers to a friend.

INFORMAL ASSESSMENT

Have children turn to page 145. Ask them whether they think owls eat rats. Have them explain their answers.

Vocabulary Strategy

INFLECTIONAL ENDING *-ing*
Blackline Master 124

Objectives

- To practice reading words with the ending *-ing*
- To practice word identification
- To practice following directions

Materials

One copy of Blackline Master 124 per child; scissors; paste or glue

Help children cut out the word cards at the top of the page. Say a base word for one of the word cards, and write it on the board. Have children say the word with the *-ing* ending and hold up the correct card. Ask them to point to the base word on their word cards. Then guide them to paste the word under the picture it describes.

© McGraw-Hill School Division

INFORMAL ASSESSMENT

Direct children to page 146. Ask them to find the word that ends in *-ing* and read it aloud. Have them identify the base word. You may need to point out that some words have the letters *-ing* but the letters are not an ending added to a base word. For example: *sing, wing, something,* etc.

Vocabulary Strategy

REVIEW UNFAMILIAR WORDS
Blackline Master 125

Objectives

- To use context clues to find the meanings of unfamiliar words
- To practice word identification
- To support hands-on learning

Materials

One copy of Blackline Master 125 per child; scissors; paste or glue

Go over the pictures in the third column and help children identify each one. Encourage use of the target words. Have children cut out the pictures. Invite them to use what they know about letter sounds and the picture clues to paste each picture next to the word it illustrates.

INFORMAL ASSESSMENT

Direct children to page 145. On the chalkboard write the sentence *The night owl flies around to find something to eat.* Frame each word as you read the sentence, skipping the word *something.* Ask children to use what they know about the sentence, and letter sounds to read the underlined word. Repeat with other unfamiliar or difficult words in the text.

© McGraw-Hill School Division

Name____________________________ Date______________

Animal Chart

Animal	Fact	Conclusions
owl	Can not see or smell rat, but can hear it.	Owl's hearing is very sharp.
bat		
snake		
some pets		

© McGraw-Hill School Division

Name____________________________ Date______________

What Will Happen Next?

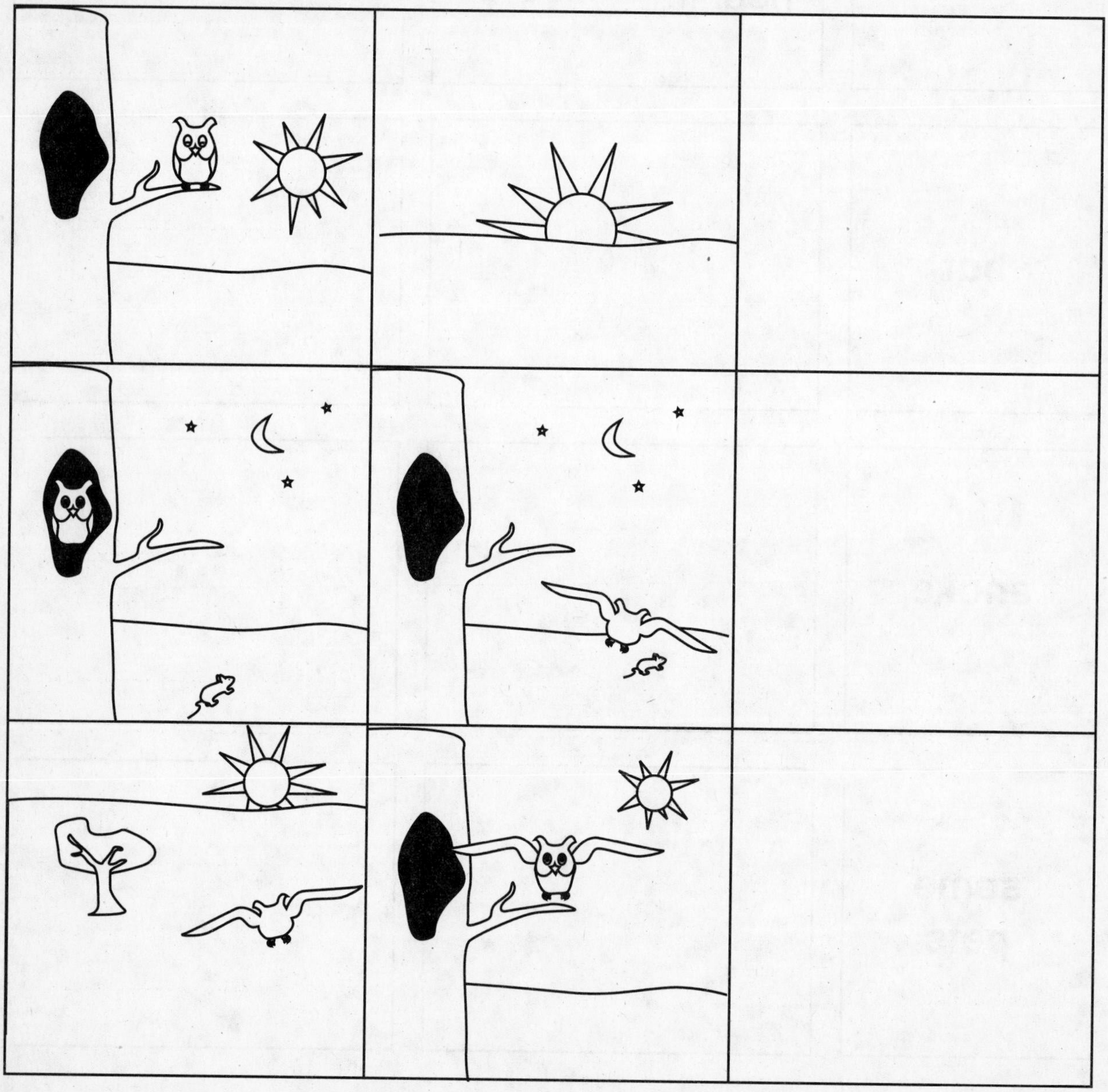

© McGraw-Hill School Division

Name ______________________ Date ____________

What Is It?

daytime	night	pet	bat

It has .

It is not a .

It is a [ ].

You can see .

The is shining.

It is [ ].

It lives with a . It may

be a or a or a .

It is a [ ].

The is up.

You are .

It is [ ].

© McGraw-Hill School Division

Name______________________________ Date______________

What's Happening?

hopping	hunting	sleeping
flying	rubbing	sitting

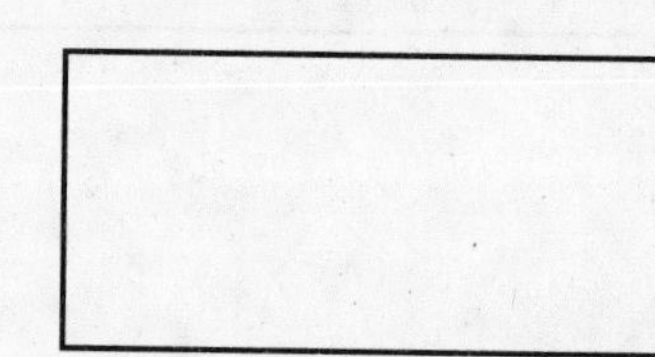

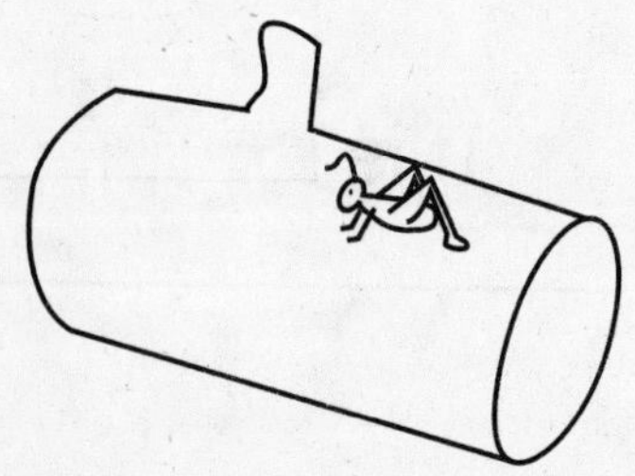

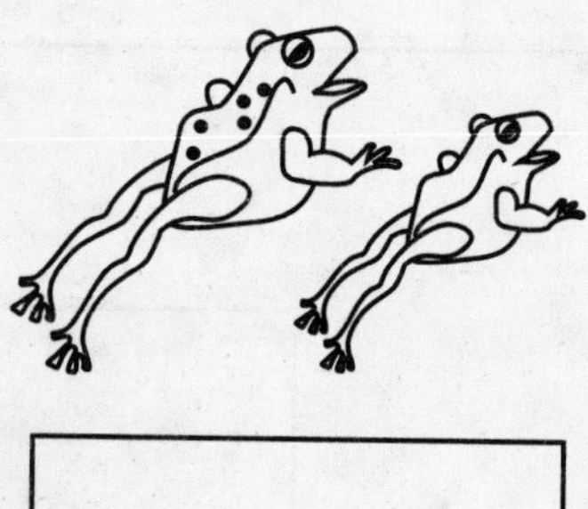

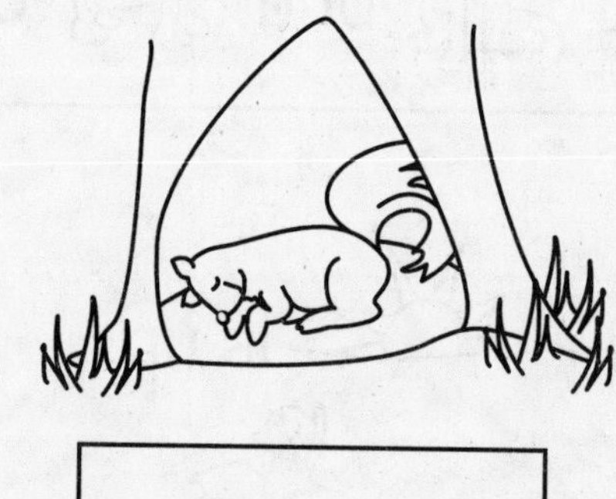

© McGraw-Hill School Division

Name________________________ Date______________

Make a Picture-Word Match

daytime	
bird	
dusk	
mammal	
animals	
wings	

© McGraw-Hill School Division

A FRIEND FOR LITTLE BEAR pp. 156A–191R

Written and Illustrated by Harry Horse

BUILD BACKGROUND FOR LANGUAGE SUPPORT

I. FOCUS ON READING

Focus on Skills

OBJECTIVE: Listen for /ü/ oo

TPR
Encourage children to make the *oo* by making two circles with their thumbs and forefingers every time they hear the /ü/ sound in the poem.

Develop Phonological Awareness

Read aloud the poem "Little Bear's Tooth." Choose a word from the poem, and use the sounds of the word in a game. Say: */g/ /ü/ /s/.* Ask: *What can it be?* Prompt children to blend the sounds, and have them answer with the following response: A *goose, goose, goose. Don't you see?* Change the underlined parts to other /ü/ words (loose, tooth, balloon) from the poem, and repeat the exchange. For example, say: */r/ /ü/ /f/. What can it be?* Prompt children to say: A *roof, roof, roof. Don't you see?*

II. READ THE LITERATURE

VOCABULARY
called
friend
only
these
pulled

Vocabulary

Cut out pictures of two children from a magazine. Assemble a wagon out of a wide rectangle (the base), a long thin rectangle (the handle), and two circles (the wheels) cut from construction paper. Tape the wagon to the chalkboard. Write the following dialogue on the board then, hold up the pictures of the children, and read: *These two children are friends. This one* (raise one picture) *is called* (name the child in the picture), *and this one* (raise the other picture) *is called* (name the child in the picture). *Only one friend could sit in the wagon* (tape one picture above the wagon). *So, the other friend pulled the wagon* (place the other picture beside the handle of the wagon). Let children take turns manipulating the props and repeating the dialogue.

CONCEPT
islands

Evaluate Prior Knowledge

Tell children that an island is land surrounded on all sides by water. Show children examples of islands on a map. Emphasize that each island they see is surrounded by water. Tell children that the story they will read takes place on an island. Invite them to look through books and travel brochures about islands to see what makes an island different from other places. Give children a sheet of dark blue construction paper and a piece of modeling clay. Show them how to flatten the clay into a disk. Then place the clay disk in the middle of the paper. Tell children that the blue paper is water and the clay is an island. Encourage children to use construction paper to create plants, animals, or other objects they might find on or around an island. Have them add these to their paper sea and clay island.

© McGraw-Hill School Division

Develop Oral Language

Invite children to participate in a discussion about their islands. Use prompts appropriate to individual linguistic levels.

nonverbal prompt for active participation

- Preproduction: *Point to the island. Point to the water.*

one- or two-word response prompt

- Early production: *What is this* (point to the island)? *What is this* (point to the water)?

prompt for short answers to higher-level thinking skills

- Speech emergence: *What is special about an island? Would you like to visit an island? Would you like to live on an island?*

prompt for detailed answers to higher-level thinking skills

- Intermediate fluency: *How could people get to this island? Tell why you would or would not like to live on an island.*

Guided Reading

Preview and Predict

Explain to children that this story is about a bear that lived alone on an island. Say: *Little Bear spends all his time alone on the island. He wishes he had something or someone to play with.* Lead children on a picture walk using the story illustrations to reinforce the concept of islands. Ask questions such as: *What do you think Little Bear did when he was alone on the island? What do you think he will find in the water? What do you think Little Bear and the wooden horse will do together? What do you think they will find in the water? What do you think happened to the wooden horse? Why do you think Little Bear is sad? How do you think he feels when he finds the wooden horse again?*

GRAPHIC ORGANIZER
Blackline Master 126

Objectives

- To practice distinguishing between fantasy and reality
- To support hands-on learning
- To reinforce working together cooperatively

Materials

One copy of Blackline Master 126 per child; crayons or colored pencils; scissors; tape; craft sticks or rulers; child copy of *A Friend for Little Bear*

Have children point to and name the supplies needed to make the sock puppets. Invite children to color the Little Bear and wooden horse puppets. Help them cut out the puppets and tape them to craft sticks or rulers. Encourage pairs to use the puppets to retell or summarize various events while they are reading.

© McGraw-Hill School Division

III. BUILD SKILLS

Phonics and Decoding

Variant Vowel /ü/ *oo*
Blackline Master 127

Objectives

- To review variant vowel /ü/ *oo*
- To blend and read /ü/ *oo* words

Materials

One copy of Blackline Master 127 per child; scissors; paste or glue

Read aloud and pantomime the first word at the top of the page. Ask children to model your action while saying the word. Encourage children to cut out the word and paste it below the picture it matches. Repeat the process with the remaining words.

INFORMAL ASSESSMENT

Direct children's attention to page 176. Have them find a word in which *oo* represents the /ü/ sound. Encourage them to use this word in a sentence. For example: *I keep all of my toys in my room.*

Phonics and Decoding

REVIEW /ü/ *oo*; LONG *e: e, ee, ea;* LONG *o: o, oa;* LONG *a: ay*
Blackline Master 128

Objectives

- To review variant vowel /ü/ *oo*
- To review long *e: e, ee, ea;* long *o: o, oa;* long *a: ay*
- To review consonant sounds, including blends and digraphs

Materials

One copy of Blackline Master 128 per child; pencils

Read aloud each sentence indicating the place for the missing word. Prompt children to blend and read the word choices, then circle the word that correctly completes the sentence. Encourage pairs to read the sentences aloud to each other.

INFORMAL ASSESSMENT

Have children turn to page 162. Read the sentence "Little Bear picked it out of the sea." Ask children to identify a word with the long *e* sound. Have them tell how /ē/ is spelled.

Comprehension

Fantasy and Reality
Blackline Master 129

Objectives

- To review distinguishing between fantasy and reality
- To support a hands-on approach to learning

Materials

One copy of Blackline Master 129 per child; scissors; glue or paste; crayons or colored pencils

Tell children that some of these pictures show things that could not really happen. Prompt a discussion of what each picture shows. Then invite children to cut out the words at the top of the page. Tell them to paste the word *yes* below each picture that could happen and the word *no* below each picture that could not happen. Have children tell why the things could not happen.

INFORMAL ASSESSMENT

Direct children's attention to various story illustrations. Have them say, "yes" for events that could really happen and say, "no" for events that could not.

© McGraw-Hill School Division

Vocabulary Strategies

REVIEW Dropping *E* Before Adding *-ING*
Blackline Master 130

Objectives

- Review dropping *e*, before adding *-ing*
- To support a hands-on approach to learning

Materials

One copy of Blackline Master 130 per child; scissors; paste or glue

Have children cut out the words at the top of the page. Print the words *dance, hide, live,* and *pile* on the chalkboard. Read the first word aloud. Erase the *e* and add *-ing.* Have children hold up the card that matches the new word and say the word. Repeat the procedure with the remaining words. Then read aloud each sentence, and prompt children to determine which word completes the sentence. Have them paste the correct word onto the box.

INFORMAL ASSESSMENT

Have children refer to the last page of the story. Direct their attention to the word *danced.* Ask them to identify its root word as *dance.* Then ask them to write the word *dancing.*

© McGraw-Hill School Division

Name_________________________________ Date_______________

Sock Puppet Patterns

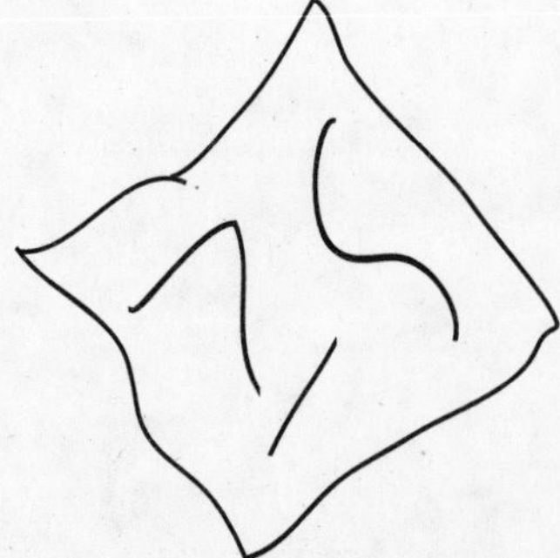

© McGraw-Hill School Division

Name________________________________ Date__________

What Little Bear Sees

boot	spoon	broom	spool

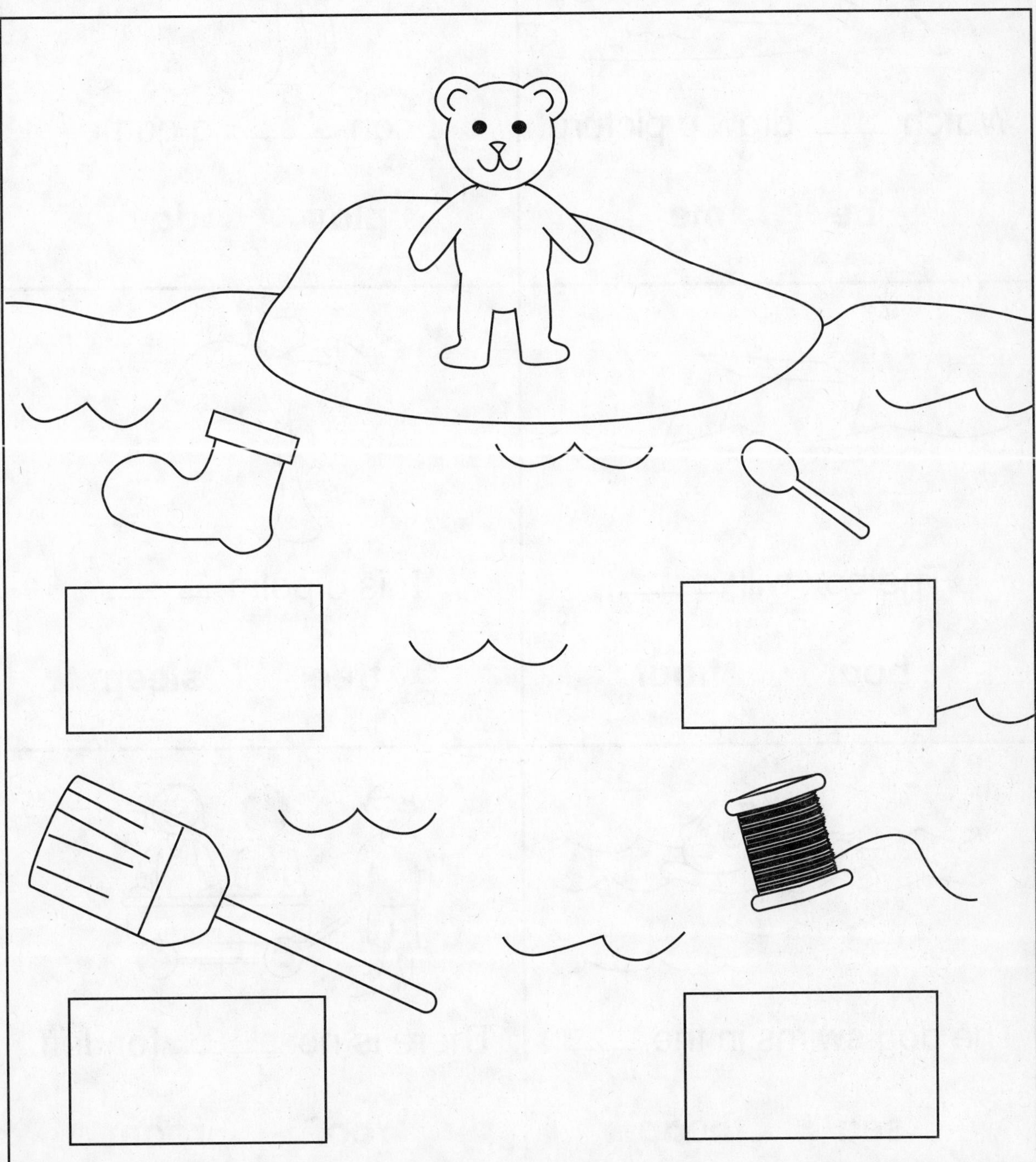

© McGraw-Hill School Division

Name______________________ Date__________

Which Word Fits?

Watch ____ draw a picture.

be **me**

I can _____ a game.

play **day**

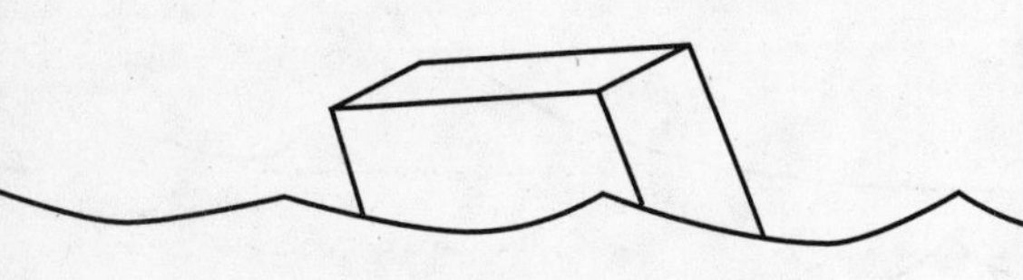

The box will _____.

boat **float**

It is a palm _____.

tree **sleep**

The dog swims in the ____.

sea **heap**

There is no _____ for Jeff.

roof **room**

© McGraw-Hill School Division

Name________________________ Date____________

Could It Really Happen?

yes	yes	no	no

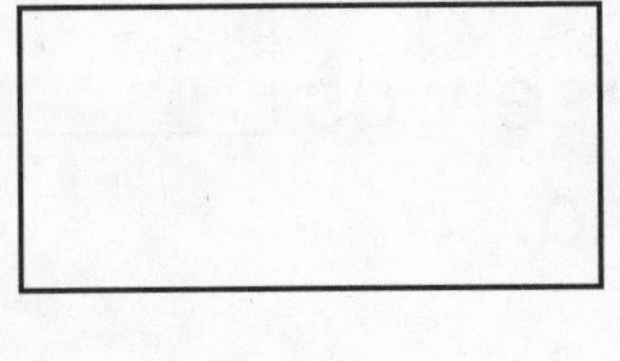

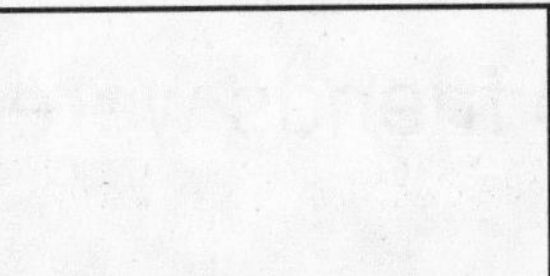

© McGraw-Hill School Division

Name____________________________ Date____________

Add -ing

dancing	hiding	living	piling

Little Bear was ________ alone on the island.

The horse was ________ from his friend.

Little Bear kept ________ boxes on a chair.

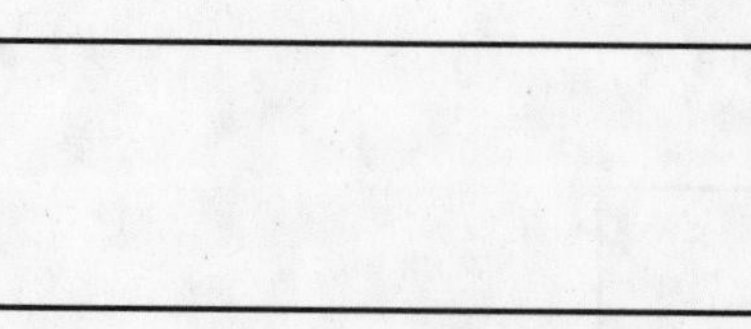

The two friends were ________ for joy.

© McGraw-Hill School Division

NEW SHOES FOR SILVIA pp. 192A–225R

Written by Johanna Hurwitz Illustrated by Jerry Pinkney

BUILD BACKGROUND FOR LANGUAGE SUPPORT

I. FOCUS ON READING

Focus on Skills

OBJECTIVE: Listen for /är/ *ar*

TPR

Develop Phonological Awareness

Print each of the following words from "What is It?" on a card or piece of paper: *carton, harp, scarf, bars, car, parts, dark, stars.* Tell children to listen carefully for these words in the poem. Read the poem aloud to children. Have each child choose one of the words to illustrate on a sheet of paper. Reread the poem, and invite children to stand with their picture when they hear their word.

II. READ THE LITERATURE

VOCABULARY
once
every
morning
took
or

Vocabulary

Print the vocabulary words on the chalkboard. Ask children to put a blue, a black, and a red crayon on their desks. Give the following directions, and point to the vocabulary words on the board when appropriate. Use demonstrations and body language to illustrate word meanings when necessary. Say: *Tap the red crayon on your desk once. Pick up every crayon on your desk. Pick up the black or blue crayon.* Remove the red crayon from each student's desk. Say: *I took your red crayon. Pick up the crayon that is the color of the sky in the morning.* Let children take turns giving the directions to each other, making sure to use the vocabulary words.

CONCEPT
new shoes

Evaluate Prior Knowledge

Place a large sheet of paper on the floor. Divide the paper into four squares, and label each the following: *black, white, brown, other.* Invite children to take off their shoes and place them in the square that has the name of the color of their shoes. Have each child use the following sentence frame to describe their shoes: *My shoes are black.*

Bring in real shoes or pictures of different kinds of shoes. (sandals, sneakers, construction boots, ballet slippers, scuba flippers) Talk with children about the occasion for which each shoe is appropriate. Ask them what kinds of shoes they would like to have and why.

Develop Oral Language

Ask children to think of something they might do with their shoes besides put them on their feet. Encourage children to be creative and even silly. (for example, a toy car for dolls, plant flowers, bookends) Have children draw a picture of their idea, and question children according to their level of language proficiency.

© McGraw-Hill School Division

nonverbal prompt for active participation	• Preproduction: *Point to the shoes in your picture. Point to* [something else] *in your picture.*
one- or two-word response prompt	• Early production: Point to various items in child's picture and say: *What is this? What are the shoes doing?*
prompt for short answers to higher-level thinking skills	• Speech emergence: Point to child's drawing and ask: *Could someone really do this with shoes? Why or why not?*
prompt for detailed answers to higher-level thinking skills	• Intermediate fluency: *Tell us about how these shoes are being used. Would you do this with your shoes? Why or why not?*

Guided Reading

Preview and Predict

Tell children that this story is about a little girl who gets new shoes. Say: *Silvia is waiting to grow into her new shoes. She finds different ways to keep busy as she waits for her feet to grow.* Lead children on a picture walk using the story illustrations to reinforce the concept of new shoes. Ask questions such as: *Who do you think sent Silvia new shoes? How do you think Silvia feels about her new shoes? Who do you think lives with Silvia? What is Silvia doing with her shoes while she is waiting for her feet to grow? How do you think Silvia feels when her new shoes finally fit?*

Objectives

GRAPHIC ORGANIZER
Blackline Master 131

- To practice distinguishing between fantasy and reality
- To support hands-on learning
- To reinforce working together cooperatively

Materials

One copy of Blackline Master 131 per child; child copy of *New Shoes for Silvia;* crayons or colored pencils; glue or paste

Invite children to color the drawing of Silvia if they wish. Point to the small cut-out shoes and have children color them red. As you picture walk through the story, encourage children to write or draw inside the five big shoes on the graphic organizer to show what Silvia does with her new shoes in the story. If necessary, demonstrate by drawing a doll inside the first shoe and writing "bed for doll" underneath. Help children understand that the five uses are not *real* uses for shoes, but pretend, or *fantasy* uses. Then have children cut out the small red shoes. Say, *Show the real use for Silvia's shoes.* If necessary, prompt children to glue or paste the shoes onto Silvia's feet.

© McGraw-Hill School Division

III. BUILD SKILLS

Phonics and Decoding

REVIEW /är/ *ar*
Blackline Master 132

Objectives

- To review variant vowel /är/ *ar*
- To reinforce following directions

Materials

One copy of Blackline Master 132 per child; pencils; crayons or colored pencils

Tell children that the boy at the top of the page is named *Carlos*. Explain that he sees some objects on his way to the post office to mail a letter. Help children read each word under the title aloud, listening for words that have the /är/ sound as in *Carlos*. Tell them to circle the words with the /är/ sound then color the pictures of words in which they hear /är/. Invite children to write each word on the line below the appropriate picture.

INFORMAL ASSESSMENT Have students turn to page 197 and find a word with the /är/ sound. (far)

Phonics and Decoding

REVIEW /är/ *ar*, /ü/ *oo*; LONG *i, a*
Blackline Master 133

Objectives

- To review /är/ *ar;* /ü/ *oo;* long *i: igh, y;* long *a: ay, ai*
- To review initial and final consonants

Materials

One copy of Blackline Master 133 per child; pencils

Prompt children to describe each picture. Read the sentences aloud with children. Then help children sound out the words below each sentence. Invite them to circle the word that completes the sentence and then read the sentence, using the correct word.

INFORMAL ASSESSMENT Direct children's attention to the following pages and have them find each of these words: *bright* (p. 198); *you, are, away* (p. 201); *by* (p. 208). Have children match each word with a rhyming one on their graphic organizers.

Comprehension

REVIEW FANTASY AND REALITY
Blackline Master 134

Objectives

- To practice distinguishing between fantasy and reality
- To support a hands-on approach to learning

Materials

One copy of Blackline Master 134 per child; scissors; glue or paste

Invite children to describe what is happening in each picture. Ask children to decide if the event is real or not. Then instruct them to cut out the four boxes at the top of the page and glue the word *yes* below events that could really happen and *no* beside the event that couldn't really happen. Ask them to tell you how they know that the event could not happen.

INFORMAL ASSESSMENT Have children identify one event from the story that could really happen and one that could not. (A girl could get new shoes. A doll doesn't really fall asleep.)

© McGraw-Hill School Division

Vocabulary Strategy

REVIEW INFLECTIONAL ENDING *-ing*
Blackline Master 135

Objectives

- To review inflectional ending *-ing*
- To review doubling the final consonant before adding *-ing*
- To review dropping the *-e* before adding *-ing*

Materials

One copy of Blackline Master 135 per child; pencils; crayons or colored pencils

Have children cut out the words at the top of the page. Print on the chalkboard the words *ride, run, write,* and *set.* Read aloud the first word, erasing the *e* and adding *-ing.* Have children hold up the card that matches the new word. Repeat the procedure with the remaining words, doubling the final consonant or dropping the final *e.* Read aloud each sentence, and prompt children to determine which word completes the sentence. Tell them to paste the correct word onto the box and then ask them to read the sentences aloud using the new words.

INFORMAL ASSESSMENT

Have children turn to page 201 and find a word to which *-ing* has been added. (setting) Then ask how the base word was changed when *-ing* was added.

© McGraw-Hill School Division

Name____________________________ Date______________

Silvia's Shoes

© McGraw-Hill School Division

Name________________________ Date____________

What Carlos Sees

rat chair barn star car

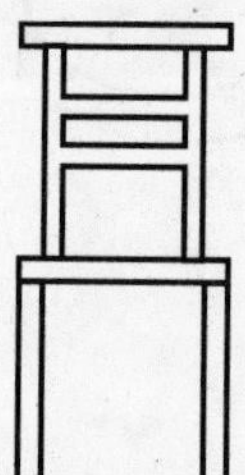

© McGraw-Hill School Division

Name______________________________ Date______________

Pick the Best One

<table>
<tr>
<td>

Sam carries water in a ________.

tail **pail**

</td>
<td>

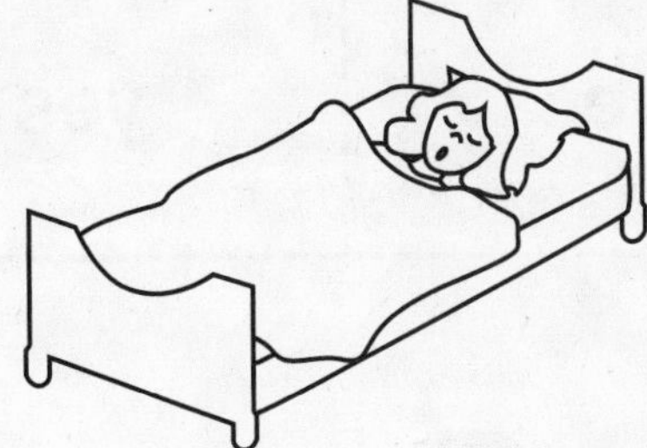

Susan went to bed at ________.

night **right**

</td>
</tr>
<tr>
<td>

This girl's coat is ________ big.

too **moon**

</td>
<td>

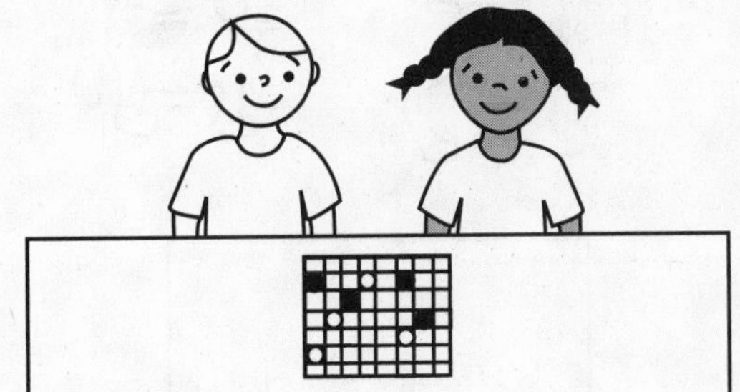

The children ________ a game each evening.

day **play**

</td>
</tr>
<tr>
<td>

The dog rides in a ________.

cart **jar**

</td>
<td>

I ride ________ bike fast.

try **my**

</td>
</tr>
</table>

© McGraw-Hill School Division

Name________________________________ Date______________

Is it Real?

yes	yes	yes	no

© McGraw-Hill School Division

Name______________________ Date______________

Fill in the Blanks

riding	running	writing	setting

The man is [ ] a horse.

The sun is [ ] in the red sky.

Mama is [ ] a letter.

A dog is [ ] with the children.

© McGraw-Hill School Division

THE STORY OF A BLUE BIRD pp. 226A–257R

Written and Illustrated by Tomek Bogacki

BUILD BACKGROUND FOR LANGUAGE SUPPORT

I. FOCUS ON READING

Focus on Skills

OBJECTIVE: Listen for /ûr/ *ir, ur, er*

Develop Phonological Awareness

Read aloud "First Flight." Say the word *bird.* Prompt children to say each phoneme. (/b/ /ûr/ /d/) Invite children to name as many words as they can that rhyme with bird. (curd, heard, stirred, word) Write the words on the chalkboard. Choose another /ûr/ word from the poem (turn, first, hurt), and have children name words that rhyme with it. Encourage children to name what sound all the words on the chalkboard have in common. Read the words aloud with children.

II. READ THE LITERATURE

VOCABULARY
brother
mother
sister
from
walked

Vocabulary

Cut out a picture of a woman, a boy, and a girl from a magazine. Glue each picture onto tag board, and tape each to a ruler. Invite children to sit at their desks. Hold up the puppet of the woman, and say: *This is the mother.* Hold up the puppet of the boy, and say: *This is the brother.* Hold up the puppet of the girl, and say: *This is the sister.* Hand three children each a different puppet. Ask the child holding the mother puppet to walk to any child's desk and hand her or him the puppet. Prompt the child who receives the puppet to say: *The mother walked from* (name of child who handed over the puppet)*'s desk to my desk.* Repeat the procedure with the boy and girl puppets. Ask the three children who are now holding the puppets to start the process over again. Continue until each child has had a turn transporting the puppet.

CONCEPT
discovering something new

Evaluate Prior Knowledge

Explain to children that this story is about a bird who discovers some new things while he is learning to fly. Tell children that they are going to think about some new things they would like to discover. Hang a large sheet of butcher paper, and use a marker to divide the paper into three equal sections. In the first box, help children draw or write the name of some people, places, or things they would like to discover more about. In the second box, help children write questions they have about this person, place, or thing. In the third box, encourage volunteers to draw or write about how they could discover more about this person, place, or thing. Challenge children to use the resources they listed in the third box to discover new things about their topics. Go on a discovery walk around the school. Point out new things along the way, such as posters or artwork on walls, new bulletin board scenes, new books in the library, and so on. Encourage children to point out new things they discover. Then have them recall what they discovered when you return to the classroom.

© McGraw-Hill School Division

Develop Oral Language

Use the completed chart to prompt responses from children.

nonverbal prompt for active participation

- Preproduction: *Point to what you want to discover more about. Point to how you will learn more about* (name the person, place or thing the child indicated).

one- or two-word response prompt

- Early production: *Do you want to learn more about* (name person, place or thing on chart)*? Can you use books to learn more about* (name person, place or thing on chart)*?*

prompt for short answers to higher-level thinking skills

- Speech emergence: *What do you want to discover about* (name person, place, or thing in child's drawing)*? How will you find these answers?*

prompt for detailed answers to higher-level thinking skills

- Intermediate fluency: *Why would you like to learn more about* (name person, place, or thing from chart)*? Where could you discover more about* (name person, place, or thing from chart)*?*

Guided Reading

Preview and Predict

Explain to children that the bird in the story is afraid to fly. Say: *The little blue bird in this story is afraid to try something new. Let's take a look at the pictures to see if we think he's going to learn to be brave and try new things.* Lead children on a picture walk using the story illustrations to reinforce the concept of discovering something new. Ask questions such as: *Where do you think the little blue bird lives? Why do you think the little bird is looking in the water? What do you think the other birds are saying to him? Does the little bird learn to fly? How do you think this makes him feel?*

GRAPHIC ORGANIZER
Blackline Master 136

Objectives

- To practice distinguishing between fantasy and reality
- To support hands-on learning
- To reinforce working together cooperatively

Materials

One copy of Blackline Master 136 per child; child copy of *The Story of a Blue Bird*

Show children how to use the chart to record events from the story. Have them draw pictures of events that are real under the column title *Real* and pictures of events that are make-believe under the column titled *Fantasy.*

To provide additional practice in distinguishing fantasy and reality, encourage children to think of other things birds can and cannot do. Invite them to draw additional pictures and add them to their charts.

© McGraw-Hill School Division

III. BUILD SKILLS

Phonics and Decoding

VARIANT VOWEL /ûr/ *ir, ur, er*
Blackline Master 137

Objectives

- To identify /ûr/ *ir, ur, er*
- To blend and read words with variant vowels /ûr/ *ir, ur, er*

Materials

One copy of Blackline Master 137 per child, pencils; crayons

Have children point to the blue bird at the top of the page, and encourage them to say the word *bird*. Tell them that some of the words at the top of the page have the same /ûr/ sound as in *bird*. Help children read the words at the top of the page and identify those with an /ûr/ sound. Then point to the first picture, and prompt children to describe what they see. You may need to explain that a group of cows is called a herd. Have them write the word that matches the picture on the line. When they finish, they can color the pictures that represent words with an /ûr/ sound.

INFORMAL ASSESSMENT

Organize children into pairs. Direct them to page 248. Have them find words that have an /ûr/ sound. (bird, brother, sister, fluttering)

Phonics and Decoding

REVIEW /ûr/ *ir, ur, er; /är/ ar*
Blackline Master 138

Objectives

- Review /ûr/ *ir, ur, er; /är/ ar*
- To support hands-on learning

Materials

One copy of Blackline Master 138 per pair of children; scissors

Arrange children in pairs, and review the /ûr/ and /är/ sounds. Then have them listen carefully as you read aloud the words at the top of the page, emphasizing the /ûr/ or /är/ sound in each word. Ask children to cut out the picture of *Shirl* and *Mark* and place them face up. Then have them cut out the word cards and place them in a pile. Have one child draw a card, read aloud the word, and place it on *Shirl* if it has an /ûr/ sound or on *Mark* if it has an /är/ sound. Encourage children to continue until each card has been drawn.

INFORMAL ASSESSMENT

Direct children's attention to the illustration on page 245. Identify one of the birds as a *dark* bird. Write the words dark and bird on the board and have children tell which word has an /är/ sound and which has an /ûr/ sound.

Comprehension

INTRODUCE SUMMARIZE
Blackline Master 139

Objectives

- To review summarizing
- To support a hands-on approach to learning

Materials

One copy of Blackline Master 139 per pair of children; scissors; construction paper; glue or paste

Read aloud the sentences. Invite children to work with a partner and cut out the sentence strips. Encourage them to put the strips in order and then use their own words to retell the story. Explain that the sentence strips help them remember the important parts of the story. Have children glue the strips in the correct order onto construction paper.

© McGraw-Hill School Division

INFORMAL ASSESSMENT

Direct children's attention to pages 246–247. Ask them to summarize what has happened in the story up to this point.

Vocabulary Strategy

INTRODUCE COMPOUND WORDS
Blackline Master 140

Objectives

- To introduce compound words
- To support a hands-on approach to learning

Materials

One copy of Blackline Master 140 per child; pencils

Read aloud the words at the top of the page. Prompt children to describe each picture. Encourage them to use two words from the top of the page to make one word that describes each picture. Have them copy the two words onto their masters. Invite volunteers to read the completed words. Ask if they can think of other compound words that could be formed from the words at the top of the page.

INFORMAL ASSESSMENT

Have children turn to page 240 and find a compound word. (someone) Encourage a volunteer to use each word part in a sentence. Then ask them to use the compound word in a sentence.

© McGraw-Hill School Division

Name________________________________ Date________________

Is It Real?

Fantasy	Reality

© McGraw-Hill School Division

Name ______________________ Date ____________

What Blue Bird Sees

shirt **bug** **nurse**

herd **fire** **churn**

____

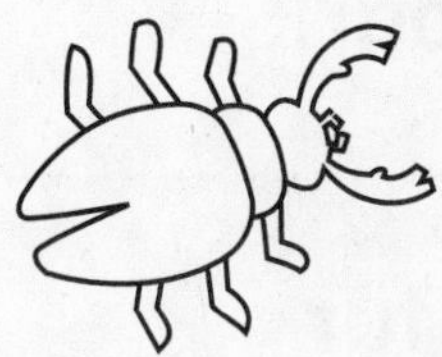

____

____

____

____

____

© McGraw-Hill School Division

Name______________________ Date__________

Match the Sound Game

hard	purr	her
dirt	scarf	burn
bark	first	large
tar	whirl	were

© McGraw-Hill School Division

Name________________________ Date______________

Retelling a Story

The blue bird sat in a nest and watched the other birds fly.

The blue bird left the nest to find out what was out there.

The blue bird joined the green bird.

The blue bird joined a flock of birds and flew everywhere.

The blue bird came back home.

The blue bird and his brother and sister flew everywhere together.

© McGraw-Hill School Division

Name____________________ Date__________

Two Words Make One

box	house	man	light
snow	flash	dog	mail

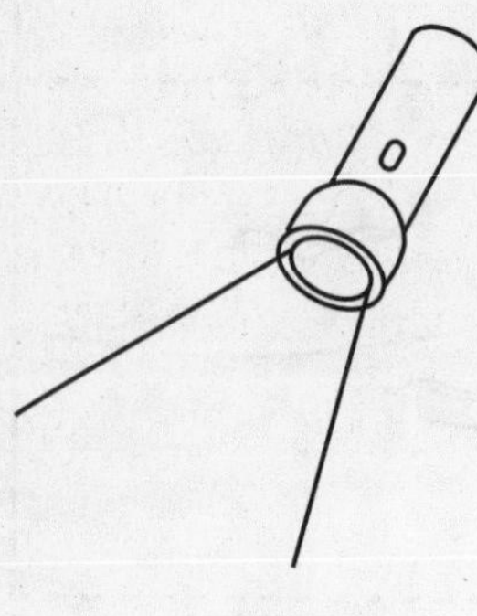

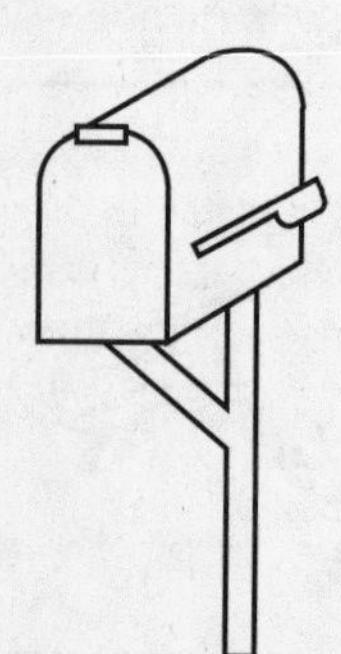

© McGraw-Hill School Division

YOUNG AMELIA EARHART: A DREAM TO FLY pp. 258A–293R

Written by Susan Alcott Illustrated by Stacey Schuett

BUILD BACKGROUND FOR LANGUAGE SUPPORT

I. FOCUS ON READING

Focus on Skills

OBJECTIVE: Listen for Diphthongs: /ou/ and /oi/

TPR

Develop Phonological Awareness

Organize the class into two teams. Ask Team 1 to show you what it looks like to jump for joy. Have Team 2 show you how they can pound their feet. Then write the words joy and pound on the board. Tell children that you are going to say some words. If a word has an /oi/ sound, members of Team 1 should jump for joy. If the word has an /ou/ sound, members of Team 2 should pound their feet on the floor. Say the following words, and guide children to respond appropriately: *down, houses, town, toys, noise, cows, brown, joy, round, boy, sound, point.* Read the poem, "Up in the Sky" and ask the teams to listen for and respond to the sounds they hear.

II. READ THE LITERATURE

VOCABULARY
horse
father
people
woman
should

Vocabulary

Show children pictures cut from magazines that show the following: a group of people, a father, a woman, and a horse. Print: ___________ *should* ___________ on the board. Tape the picture of the people onto the first line. Point to the picture and say, *people.* Point to the word *should* and say, *should.* Encourage children to complete the sentence by speaking or pantomiming an appropriate word or phrase. (be nice to each other, be honest) Repeat the process with another picture. For example, prompt children to say, *A father should spend time with his kids,* or *A horse should eat hay.* Hold up a picture of the woman. Say: *The woman feels sick. What should the woman do?* (take medicine, go to the doctor) Let children take turns taping the pictures onto the sentence and then completing it.

CONCEPT
follow a dream

Evaluate Prior Knowledge

Dramatize sleeping. Say: *Sometimes I dream when I am sleeping.* Tell children that a dream can also be something you hope to do someday. Invite children to act out a dream (e.g., to become a teacher, to fly a plane) for the rest of the class to guess.

Give each child a large sheet of paper. Have children draw a vertical line down the center. Invite them to draw on the left side of the paper a place they dream about visiting (the circus, China, the moon). Encourage children to draw on the right side of the paper the things they would take along with them if they were to go to this place.

Bring in several pictures of people doing different kinds of jobs (construction worker, doctor, librarian, astronaut, computer programmer, singer). Tape each picture along the bottom of the chalkboard. Give each child an index card and have them write their name on it. Invite children to tape their card above the job they would like to have some day. Have them draw a picture of their dream job if it is not pictured. Ask children questions about the graph, according to their levels of language proficiency.

© McGraw-Hill School Division

Develop Oral Language

nonverbal prompt for active participation	• Preproduction: *Show us* (point to class and self) *the job* (point to picture of a job) *you chose.*
one- or two-word response prompt	• Early production: *What job did you choose? What job did the most children choose?*
prompt for short answers to higher-level thinking skills	• Speech emergence: *What job did you choose? What things do you think you would do at this job?*
prompt for detailed answers to higher-level thinking skills	• Intermediate fluency: *Why did you choose this job? What do you think you will like about it? What might be difficult about it?*

Guided Reading

Preview and Predict

Explain to children that this story is about a woman who wanted to learn how to fly an airplane. Say: *Amelia Earhart had a special dream. She wanted to learn how to fly. Let's take a look at the pictures to see how she followed her dream.* Lead children on a picture walk, using the story illustrations to reinforce the concept *follow a dream.* Ask questions such as: *How many people do you think were in Amelia's family? What do you think Amelia liked to do as a child? What do you think Amelia liked to watch? What do you think Amelia is doing with all those tools? What do you think Amelia is holding? Why do you suppose the man is taking her picture? Do you think Amelia's dream came true?*

GRAPHIC ORGANIZER
Blackline Master 141

Objectives

- To practice summarizing
- To support hands-on learning
- To reinforce cooperative learning

Materials

One copy of Blackline Master 141 per child; child copy of *Young Amelia Earhart: A Dream to Fly;* pencils

Pair each English-speaking child with a child needing additional language support. As you read aloud the story, *Young Amelia Earhart: A Dream to Fly,* encourage children to point out each amazing thing Amelia does. Ask the children to summarize Amelia's accomplishments. Have one child write her or his partner's ideas on a line of the "newspaper." Continue reading aloud the story, pausing to allow children time to note important events. Encourage partners to work together to write on the last line a summary for the whole article.

© McGraw-Hill School Division

III. BUILD SKILLS

Phonics and Decoding

REVIEW /ou/ *ow, ou;* /oi/ *oi, oy*
Blackline Master 142

Objectives

- To review diphthongs /ou/ *ow, ou;* /oi/ *oi, oy*
- To blend and read */ou/* and */oi/* words

Materials

One copy of Blackline Master 142 per child; pencils

Prompt children to describe the picture in each box. Then read each sentence to children. Help children sound out the two words at the bottom of each box. Have them circle the word that completes each sentence.

INFORMAL ASSESSMENT

Direct pairs of children to pages 264–265. Instruct each pair to find an /oi/ and an /ou/ word. (boys, allowed)

Phonics and Decoding

REVIEW /ou/ *ow, ou;* /oi/ *oi, oy;* /ûr/ *ir, er, ur*
Blackline Master 143

Objectives

- To review /ou/ *ow, ou;* /oi/ *oi, oy;* /ûr/ *ir, er, ur*
- To support hands-on learning

Materials

One copy of Blackline Master 143 per child; scissors; glue or paste

Help children read and then cut out the word cards at the top of the page. If necessary, demonstrate the meanings of unfamiliar words. Prompt them to describe what they see in the first picture. Then read aloud the first sentence frame. Encourage children to find the word card that completes the sentence. Have them glue the word card to the box under the picture. Invite children to read aloud the completed sentence with you. Repeat the procedure with the remaining sentence frames.

INFORMAL ASSESSMENT

Have pairs of children look through the story for a word with the /ou/ sound. Ask each pair to share the word they find. Write their words on the chalkboard, grouping them by sound. Repeat the process with the /oi/ and /ûr/ sounds.

Comprehension

REVIEW SUMMARIZE
Blackline Master 144

Objectives

- To review summarizing
- To support hands-on learning

Materials

One copy of Blackline Master 144; pencils; scissors

Number the strips one through seven, and cut out each one. Organize the class into seven small groups, and give each group a strip. If necessary, give each group more than one strip or organize children into pairs. Invite the group with the first strip to stand and read aloud their sentence. Have the group with the second strip summarize what the first group said, and then have them read aloud their own sentence. Encourage group three to summarize the two previous sentences, and then read aloud their own sentence. Continue the procedure until the entire story has been summarized.

INFORMAL ASSESSMENT

Direct children's attention to page 277. Ask them to summarize what has happened in the story up to this point.

© McGraw-Hill School Division

Vocabulary Strategy

REVIEW COMPOUND WORDS
Blackline Master 145

Objectives

- To review compound words
- To support hands-on learning

Materials

One copy of Blackline Master 145 per child; pencils

Read aloud with children the words at the top of the page. If necessary, demonstrate the meanings of unfamiliar words. Then prompt them to name the object in each picture. Encourage children to select the two words from the top that together form the name of the object. Have children write each compound word on the line beside its picture.

INFORMAL ASSESSMENT

Ask children to find a compound word on each of the following pages: 268 (airplane), 279 (herself), 282 (something), and 284 (everything).

© McGraw-Hill School Division

Name________________________ Date______________

Extra! Extra!

The Daily Record

Amelia Sets New Record!

© McGraw-Hill School Division

Name______________________________ Date______________

Find the Right One

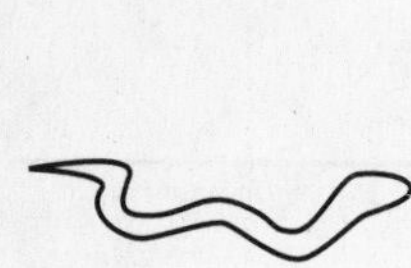  The dog began to _____ at the snake. **brown** **growl**	 Water in the pot started to _____. **boil** **join**
 A _____ of people came to the fair. **down** **crowd**	 The airplane took off with a _____ roar. **spout** **loud**
 Run when I _____ to three. **count** **south**	 The queen wears a _____. **crown** **how**

© McGraw-Hill School Division

Name______________________ Date______________

Choose the Word

hurt	snout	toy
coin	skirt	stern

One ______ was left in the basket.

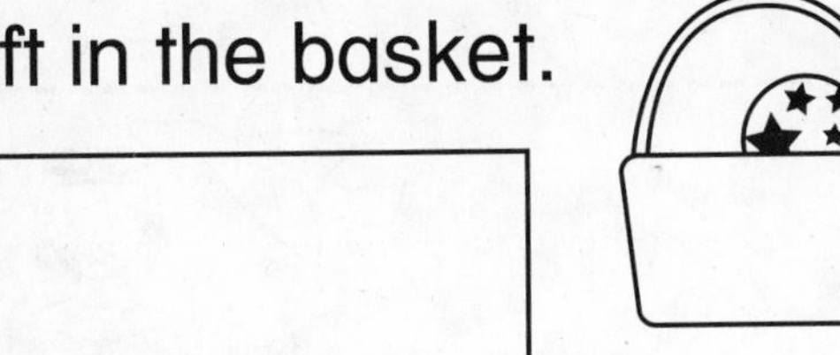

Rick fell and ______ his arm.

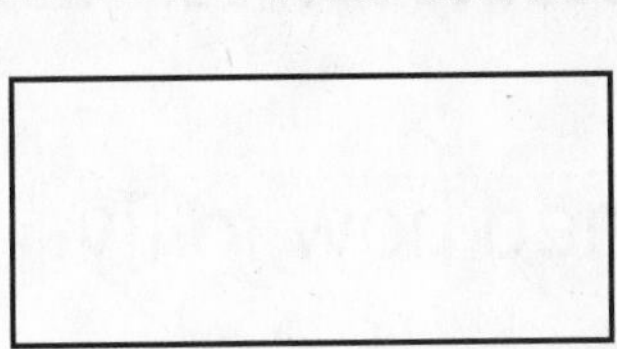

Laura put a ______ in the slot for stamps.

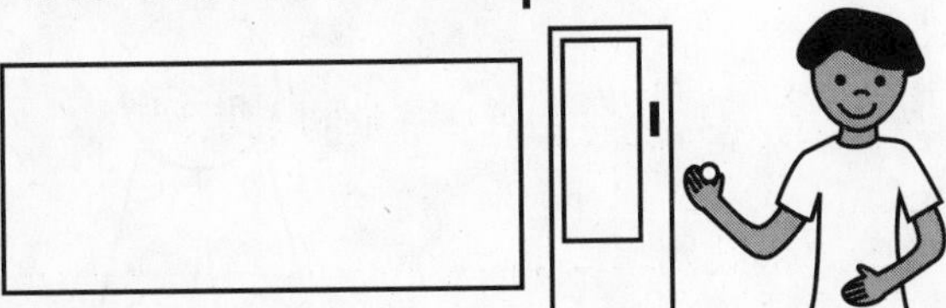

The dress had a long ______.

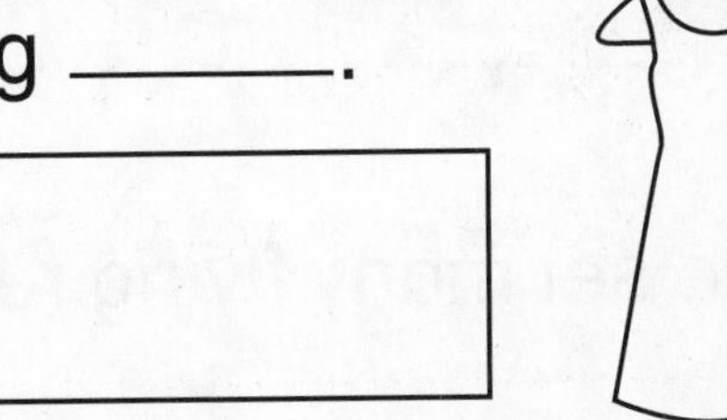

Jenny had a ______ look on her face.

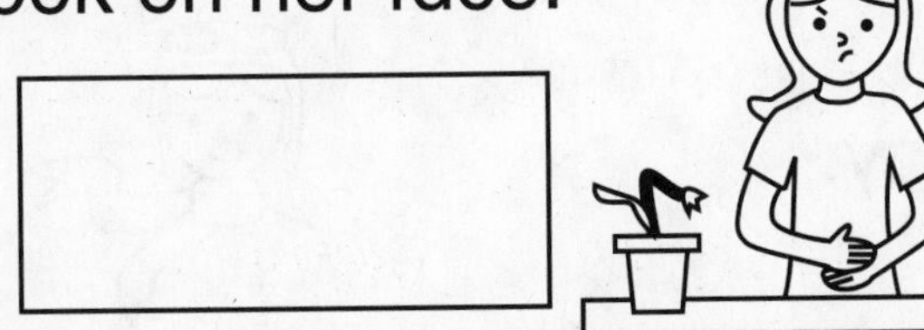

A pig's nose is called a ______.

© McGraw-Hill School Division

Name_______________________________ Date______________

Tell It Again

Amelia Earhart grew up in Kansas.

After she grew up, she worked as a nurse.

She learned how to fly.

She became the greatest woman pilot in the world.

She set many flying records.

She was lost on a trip that would have set another record.

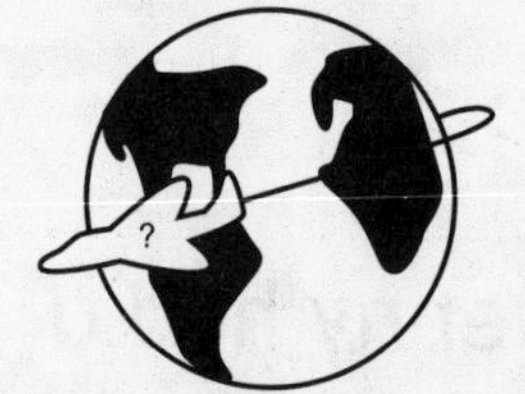

Amelia still inspires people today.

© McGraw-Hill School Division

Name______________________ Date______________

Put It Together

boat	rain	ball	brush
tooth	foot	sail	coat

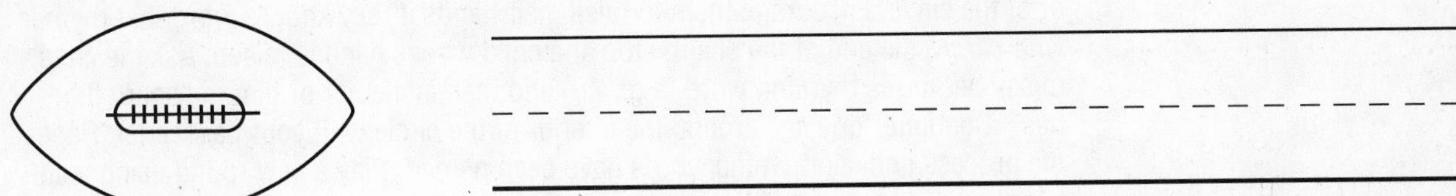

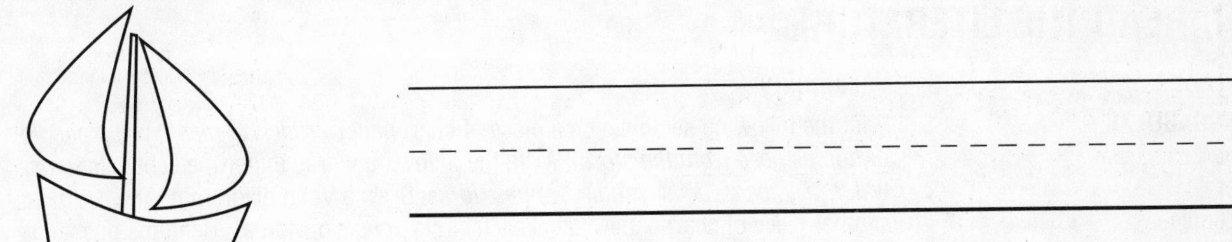

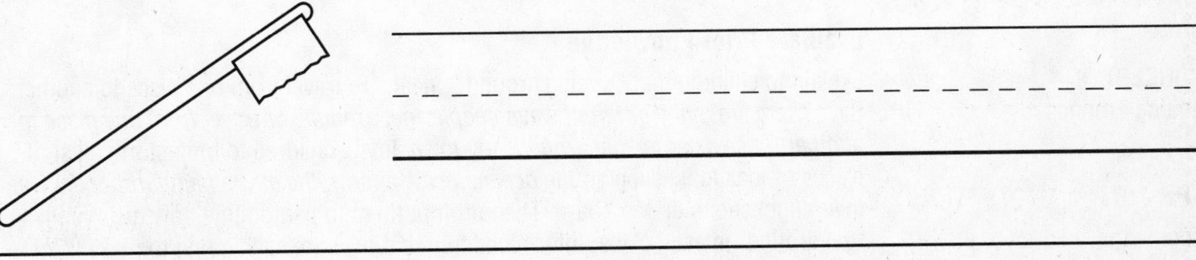

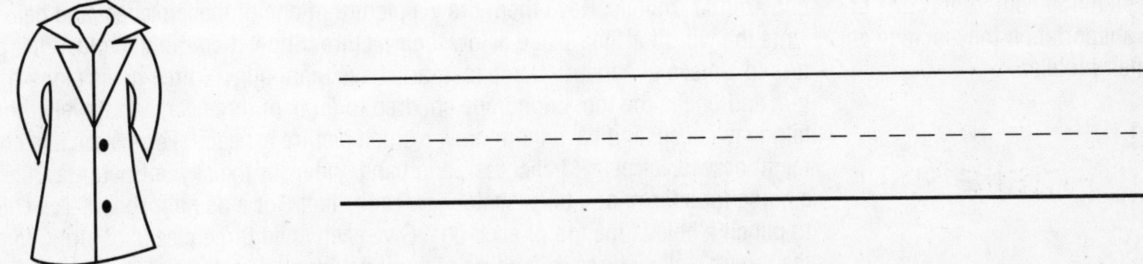

© McGraw-Hill School Division

ON THE GO! pp. 294A–303R

Time For Kids

BUILD BACKGROUND FOR LANGUAGE SUPPORT

I. FOCUS ON READING

Focus on Skills

OBJECTIVE: Listen for /är/*ar;* /ûr/ *ir, ur, er;* /ou/ *ow, ou*

TPR

Develop Phonological Awareness

Reread the poem "Going Places." Then arrange children in a circle, and have them sit down. Tell them that you are the driver of a special bus, and that they must say a word that rhymes with the word you announce if they want to ride. Teach children the following chant: *Beep, beep! Toot, toot! Ride our bus today. Beep, beep! Toot, toot! rhyming words are what you'll pay.* Stand in the middle of the circle and say: *Today's word is car.* Invite children to say the chant while you walk around the interior of the circle. Encourage them to raise their hands if they know a word that rhymes with *car.* At the end of the chant, stop at a child whose hand is raised. Ask the child to say her or his rhyming word (e.g., *far*) and then invite her or him to "board the bus." Continue "driving" around the interior of the circle with your passenger. Repeat the process until all rhyming words have been named. Play a new round using a different word (down) from the poem.

II. READ THE LITERATURE

VOCABULARY
horses
or
people
these
from

Vocabulary

Print the following sentence on a piece of chart paper: *Which of these would people or horses need from the store?* Write the following words under the sentence: *oats, water, hay, barn, beds, saddles, shoes, forks.* Draw a Venn diagram on the board or another piece of chart paper. Label each circle *people* or *horses.* Read the question and have children say whether people, horses, or both people and horses, need each of the items on the list. Prompt their responses by asking: *Would people need these (this)? Would horses need these (this)?* Write each word in the correct place on the diagram.

CONCEPT
getting around

TPR

Encourage children to pantomime the different forms of transportation they include on their mobiles.

Evaluate Prior Knowledge

Explain to children that "getting around," means to travel from one place to another. Say, *There are many different ways people "get around" or travel from one place to another. I use a car to "get around" my town.* Invite children to brainstorm a list of places or locations, such as *the ocean, a city, a farm, the sky, a neighborhood.* Write their suggestions on the board. Then prompt them to pantomime how they might "get around" in each place. Inform children that they are each going to make a "getting around" mobile. Have them draw a picture of one of these places, and help them write the word for their place below their picture. Show them how to glue their picture to a piece of construction paper, and have them punch three holes along the bottom and one at the top. Encourage children to think of three ways to travel in the setting they chose, and have them draw a small picture for each. For example, a child might draw an airplane, helicopter, and hang glider for the sky; a tractor, a truck, and a horse for a farm; or a bike, skateboard, and "feet" for a neighborhood. Tell children to punch a hole at the top of each one. Give each child three pieces of string to attach the three small pictures to the first picture they drew. Display children's work by attaching it to the ceiling with a fourth piece of string.

© McGraw-Hill School Division

Develop Oral Language

nonverbal prompt for active participation
• Preproduction: *Point to the* (name setting in child's first picture). *Point to the* (name one or all three forms of transportation the child drew).

one- or two-word response prompt
• Early production: *What is this place* (point to the setting in child's first picture)*? Have you been there before?*

prompt for short answers to higher-level thinking skills
• Speech emergence: *What different ways can you get around a* (name setting in child's first picture)?

prompt for detailed answers to higher-level thinking skills
• Intermediate fluency: *Why do people use a* (name one form of transportation child drew) *to get around* (name setting in child's first picture)? *How else might you get around a* (name setting in a child's picture)?

Guided Reading

Preview and Predict

Explain to children that this article is about how people get around. Say, *There are many ways that people get around. People use different forms of transportation to get from one place to another. Let's take a look at the pictures to see how we can travel by land, water, and air.* Lead children on a picture walk using the illustrations in the article to reinforce the concept of *getting around.* Ask questions such as: *Where do you think the boy uses his bike to get around? Which form of transportation do you think the lady with the grocery bags will choose and why? What places can trains go that cars can't? Who or what do you think travels by boat? Which do you think is faster, a car or an airplane?*

Objectives

GRAPHIC ORGANIZER
Blackline Master 146

• To reinforce summarizing
• To reinforce working together cooperatively

Materials

One copy of Blackline Master 146 per child; scissors; crayons or colored pencils; child copy of *On the Go!*

As children read the article, invite them to draw pictures of ways people travel by land, water, and air.

Review the skill of summarizing by having children use their charts to tell a partner the different ways people "get around" in the article.

© McGraw-Hill School Division

III. BUILD SKILLS

Comprehension

REVIEW FANTASY AND REALITY
Blackline Master 147

Objectives

- To reinforce distinguishing between fantasy and reality
- To practice following directions

Materials

One copy of Blackline Master 147 per child; crayons or colored pencils

Prompt children to describe what is happening in each picture. Ask them to decide if it could or could not really happen. Invite them to cut out the cards at the top of the page. Tell children to glue a card with the word *Real* below a picture of something that could really happen. Have them glue a card with the word *Fantasy* below a picture of something that could not really happen.

INFORMAL ASSESSMENT

Direct children's attention to the photograph on page 296. Have them identify the scene as *real* or *fantasy*. Ask them how they know.

Comprehension

REVIEW SUMMARIZE
Blackline Master 148

Objectives

- To review summarizing using a chart
- To practice following directions
- To support cooperative learning

Materials

One copy of Blackline Master 148 per child; crayons or colored pencils; scissors; glue or paste

Pair an English-speaking child with a child needing additional language support. Prompt children to say that there are three places people travel: *land, water,* and *air*. Read aloud each sentence to children. Have them find the part of the article that tells more about the sentence. Encourage children to draw pictures or write words on their charts that give examples of each kind of transportation. Then they can use their charts to summarize the article. Invite partners to share their answers with other pairs of children.

INFORMAL ASSESSMENT

Direct children's attention to page 298. Have them use the photograph to summarize what this page is about.

Vocabulary Strategy

REVIEW INFLECTIONAL ENDING *-ing*
Blackline Master 149

Objectives

- To review dropping *e*, doubling consonants before adding *-ing*
- To practice following directions

© McGraw-Hill School Division

Materials

One copy of Blackline Master 149 per child; pencils, crayons, or colored pencils; scissors; glue or paste

Print the words *drive, get, take,* and *move* on the chalkboard. Invite children to cut out the cards at the top of the page. Prompt children to read the first sentence and supply the missing word. Point to the word *drive* on the board and show children how to drop the letter *e* (erase it from the board) and add *-ing* to make the word *driving.* Ask children to find the card with the word *driving.* Have them glue it beside the first sentence. Repeat the procedure with the remaining three sentences. Ask the children to read the sentences with the new words.

INFORMAL ASSESSMENT

Have children find the word *decide* on page 298. Read the word with them, and ask them to copy it onto a piece of paper. Tell children to now write the word *deciding.*

Vocabulary Strategy

REVIEW COMPOUND WORDS
Blackline Master 150

Objectives

- To review compound words
- To practice following directions

Materials

One copy of Blackline Master 150 per child; pencils

Tell children that sometimes two words go together to make one word. Read aloud with children the words at the top of the page. Prompt children to name each object below. Encourage them to find two words from the top of the page to make one word that describes the object. Have them write the word beside the object. Tell children to repeat the process for the remaining three objects.

INFORMAL ASSESSMENT

Have children find the compound word *airplane* on page 299. Ask them to identify the two words from which this word is made.

© McGraw-Hill School Division

Name____________________ Date__________

Ways You Can Travel

Air	
Water	
Land	

© McGraw-Hill School Division

Name________________________________ Date______________

Real or Fantasy

Real	Real
Fantasy	Fantasy

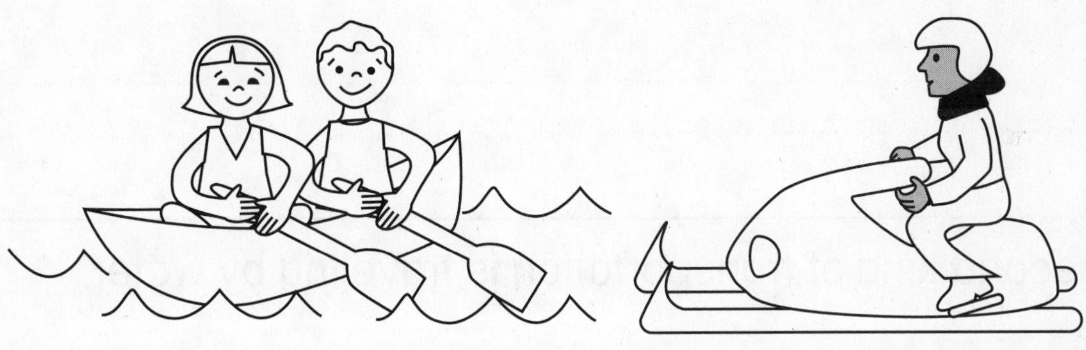

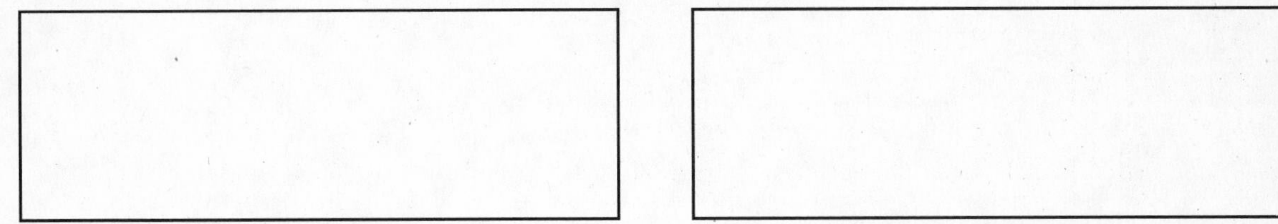

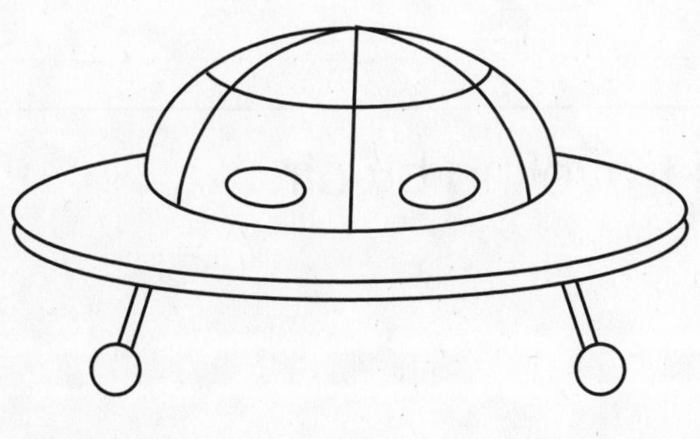

© McGraw-Hill School Division

Name________________________________ Date______________

Tell It Another Way

There are three kinds of transportation, or ways to get from place to place.

One kind of transportation is traveling by land.
A second kind of transportation is traveling by water.
A third kind of transportation is traveling by air.

© McGraw-Hill School Division

Name________________________________ Date______________

Pick the Best Word

taking	getting	moving	driving

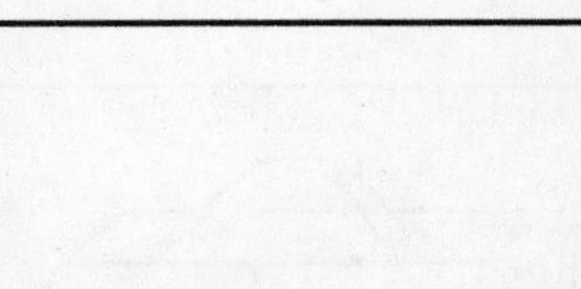

Ms. Mack is ________ the schoolbus.

Ben is ________ a train ticket.

The airplane is ________ off for Alaska.

A truck is ________ a load of tractors.

© McGraw-Hill School Division

Name______________________________ Date______________

It Takes Two

road	suit	rail	house
doll	case	lunch	book

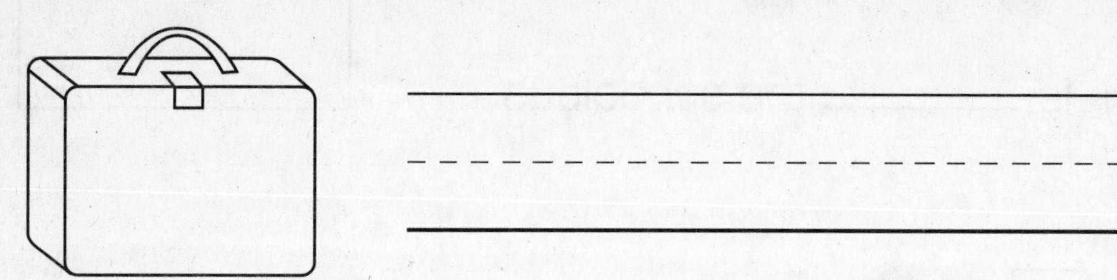

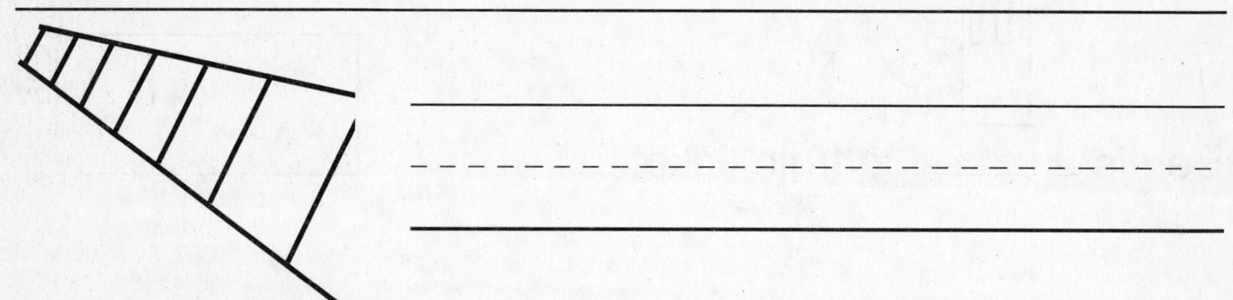

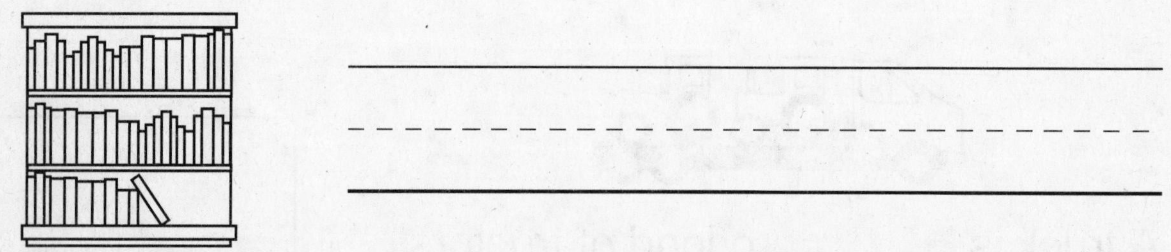

© McGraw-Hill School Division